JOURNEY
OF THE
PRIESTESS

Frontispiece: *Ivory statuette of the Minoan Goddess with details added in gold, or of a priestess impersonating her, stretching out her arms entwined with snakes as if before an altar or displaying to worshippers; probably from Knossos, now in the Boston Museum, gift of Mrs W. Scott Fitz, photo courtesy Museum of Fine Arts, Boston; c.1600–1500 BC.*

JOURNEY
OF THE
PRIESTESS

The priestess traditions of the ancient world
A journey of spiritual awakening and empowerment

ASIA SHEPSUT

Aquarian/Thorsons
An Imprint of HarperCollins*Publishers*

Dedicated to
all who, wittingly or unwittingly,
showed me the way,
but most especially,
before they leave their traditional home,
to the book staff of the British Library.

The Aquarian Press
An Imprint of HarperCollins*Publishers*
77-85 Fulham Palace Road,
Hammersmith, London W6 8JB
1160 Battery Street,
San Francisco, California 94111-1213

Published by The Aquarian Press 1993
1   3   5   7   9   10   8   6   4   2

© Asia Shepsut 1993

Asia Shepsut asserts the moral right to
be identified as the author of this work

A catalogue record for this book
is available from the British Library

ISBN 1 85538 282 2

Typeset by Harper Phototypesetters Limited,
Northampton, England
Printed in Great Britain by
Scotprint Limited, Musselburgh

A Note on the Rivers: Not all rivers that symbolize the life and death of Tammuz and Ishtar for different lands have been plotted on the maps. The Nile, Tigris and Euphrates are the longest and widest gift of the Goddess to the ancient world, and even in present drought conditions they have not dried up. It is interesting to think that the Mediterranean basin in an earlier geological age was all dry land, and only filled up with water late in Gaia's history.

The rivers were just as important for the running of the nomadic civilizations of the Steppes, whether European Celtic or Asiatic Scythian. The Dniester, Don and Oxus are but three of them. The Pactolus in Anatolia washed down gold to the smelters of Lydian Sardis, which were dedicated to Kybele as they processed the gift of the river: it is too tiny to plot on the map on this scale. The same is true of the Ilissos, Athens' own river, which, running down from the Hymettus mountains, has now gone underground, like the invisible London tributaries which feed the Thames.

For the Late Antique world, it was the ribbons of the Nile running into the Mediterranean, forming the Delta, that supported the cities prominent in trade and religion round the entire basin - such as Naucratis, Sais and Alexandria.

The Jordan takes us to the Holiest of Holy Lands, in which Christ, the last Tammuz, was baptized. It symbolizes the sad division in the Land of Canaan which only the cohorts of the Goddess can heal.

Thames and Potomac stand for Britain and the USA, where so many people with Mediterranean roots now find themselves, who have a certain influence on events there still, as well as the machinery to communicate its messages to the world at large.

△ Chertomlyk

Don

Sea of Azov

Kul Oba △ Karagodeuashkh

Black Sea (Euxine)

Colchis

Athens

LYDIA

SCYTH

CRETE

LYCIA

CILICIA

Lake Van

● Harran

Hierapolis ●
● Ebla

Tell Brak

Tigris

Nineveh ●
● Tepe Gawra
● Hasanlu

Lake Urmiah

Ugarit ●
Arwad ●
Amrith ●

Euphrates

MESOPOTAMIA

Tell Bill ●
Assur ●
● Arbela

ASSYRIA

Mediterranean Sea

SYRIA

● Nuzi

Byblos ●
Sidon ●
Tyre ●

Mari ●

E

● Tell Asmar

Megiddo ●
● Samaria

Jordan

● Khafajeh

Ascalon ●
● Amman

Sippar ●
?Akkad ●

● Kish
● Babylon

JORDAN

Nippur ●
● Adab

Gizeh ● Heliopolis
Memphis ●

?DUMAT

● Isin
Umma ●
Uruk ●
● Lagash
● Larsa

SUMER

EGYPT

● Petra

Nile

SINAI

Ur ●
● Eridu

● Hermopolis
● Amarna

● Taima

Ik

Abydos ● Dendereh
VALLEY OF KINGS ●
Deir el-Bahari ● Thebes (Karnak)

Hieraconpolis ●

Nile

?Dilmun (Bah

NUBIA

● Mecca

Aral Sea

SCYTHIA

Caspian Sea

Oxus

To Zanskar

BACTRIA

PERSIA

•lis ●

Indus

To Britain

FRANCE

Antibes

SPAIN

Aliseda

Cerro de los Santos ●

Elche ●

Baza

Gades

Almeria

Tarquinia

SARDINIA

Cagliari

Mediterranean Sea

Cartha

AFRICA

CELTS

Taman
Peninsula

Dniester

Danube

Black Sea

● Singoe

*Bosphorus
Sea*

THRACE

Alaça Hüyük ●
● Hattusas

*Sea of
Marmora*

PHRYGIA

○ THASOS
Dardanelles ● Cyzicus
● Troy

● Gordium

Dodona
●

GREECE

LEMNOS

Aegean Sea

Pergamum
●

Thetis ●

EUBOEA

LESBOS
CHIOS

LYDIA

ANATOLIA

Phocis
Sardis ●

Delphi ● Thebes
● Chalcis
Aulis

Clazomenae
Claros

● Hierapolis

Eleusis
Marathon

Colophon ●
● Magnesia

Mycenae
Brauron

SAMOS

Ephesos
●

Orchomenos ●
Corinth SALAMIS

Miletus ●
● Didyma (Branchidae)

Argos ●
Athens DELOS

Halicarnassus ●
CARIA LYCIA

Hermione
●

Pylos ●
● Sparta

NAXOS

Cnidos ●
Xanthos ●

● THERA

Patara ●

CYPRUS

CYTHERA ○

RHODES ● Lindos

Paphos ●
● Kition

Gozo

MALTA

Knossos Mallia
● Palaikastro

CRETE
● Zakro

Haghia ● Phaestos
Triadha

Mediterranean Sea

Cyrene ●

Sais ●
Delta

Naucratis ●

● Macadi

LIBYA

Siwa Oasis

EGYPT
Memphis ●

Nile

Cumae

LY

CONTENTS

LIST OF ILLUSTRATIONS

Note: The table follows conventionally accepted date-bands, despite the fact that most chronology for dates pre-600 BC is based, after the close scrutiny of experts, on shifting foundations. The margin of shift that could be indicated on the table is as wide as 1,000 years in the prehistoric (pre-3200) dates, to a 200/300-year gap that needs somehow to be closed up during the beginning of the first millennium BC.

Dating controversies in recent literature that challenged the standard framework of Egyptian chronology were first broached by Velikovsky in the 1950s. He knew that something was awry in dating calculations when it came to cross-referencing events of the great civilizations of the ancient world: however he lacked sufficient archaeological training to handle the data with accuracy. Most recently, Peter James and his archaeologist colleagues, each specializing in different areas, have pooled their expertise in *Centuries of Darkness* (London, 1991), to pinpoint accurately the areas of slippage in a veritable Rift Valley of ancient chronology. Each contribution points to the need to redate artefactual markers within the period *c.*1200–600 BC, and this could include our priestess material.

Their theories are highly plausible, but being so recent, they still need to be digested, and I have therefore not felt able to start tinkering with the chronologies adopted by *The Cambridge Ancient History* on the one hand, or *Chronologies in Old World Archaeology* (ed. R. Ehrich, Chicago, 1965, new edition due 1993) on the other.

The main purpose of this table is to locate notable priestesses very roughly into a time-frame, and it adequately conveys the sequence of their office within an overall historical perspective.

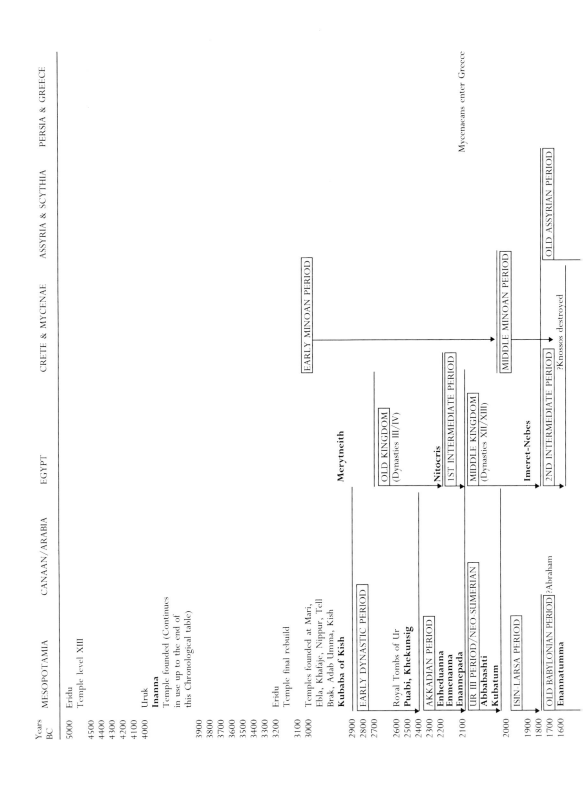

Years BC	MESOPOTAMIA	CANAAN/ARABIA	EGYPT	CRETE & MYCENAE	ASSYRIA & SCYTHIA	PERSIA & GREECE
5000	Eridu Temple level XIII					
4500						
4400						
4300						
4200						
4100						
4000	Uruk **Inanna** Temple founded (Continues in use up to the end of this Chronological table)					
3900						
3800						
3700						
3600						
3500						
3400						
3300						
3200	Eridu Temple final rebuild			EARLY MINOAN PERIOD		
3100						
3000	Temples founded at Mari, Ebla, Khafaje, Nippur, Tell Brak, Adab Umma, Kish **Kubaba of Kish**					
2900	EARLY DYNASTIC PERIOD		**Merytneith**			
2800						
2700			OLD KINGDOM (Dynasties III/IV)			
2600	Royal Tombs of Ur					
2500	**Puabi, Khekunsig**					
2400	AKKADIAN PERIOD					
2300	**Enheduanna**		**Nitocris**			
2200	**Emmenanna** **Enannepada**		1ST INTERMEDIATE PERIOD			
2100	UR III PERIOD/NEO-SUMERIAN **Abbabashti** **Kubatum**		MIDDLE KINGDOM (Dynasties XII/XIII)			Mycenaeans enter Greece
2000	ISIN-LARSA PERIOD					
1900			**Imeret-Nebes**			
1800	OLD BABYLONIAN PERIOD	?Abraham	2ND INTERMEDIATE PERIOD			
1700				MIDDLE MINOAN PERIOD		
1600	**Enannatumma**		?Knossos destroyed		OLD ASSYRIAN PERIOD	

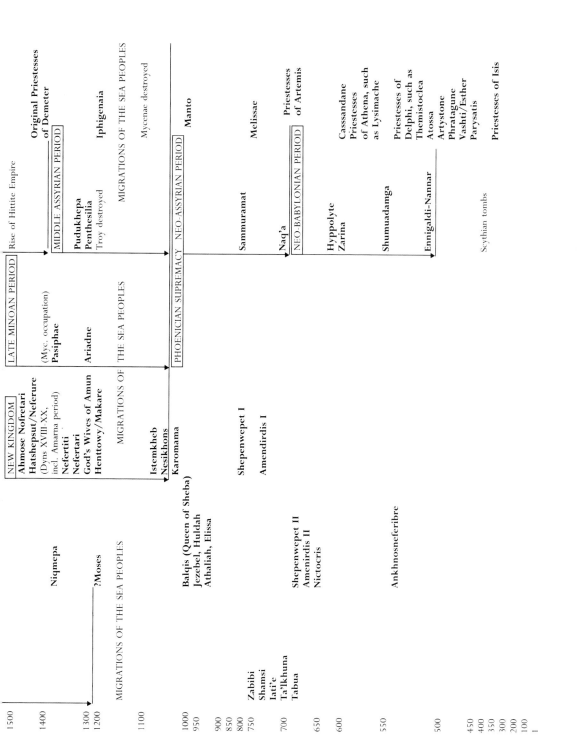

THAMES

———

INTRODUCTION

Thames

About a year ago as I was lying on my sofa one evening and looking up at a Persian metalwork light globe, illuminated into a fretwork of dark against light, I felt the presence of a circle of women in the room around me. All I could discern was their comfortable bulk, and that they wore white scarves round their heads. They felt Middle Eastern. I had never had an experience like this before. As they dissolved, I was sure of two things: they were trying to communicate with me, and they were ordinary, but holy, people. What religion they belonged to was irrelevant.

In the year that followed that vision, the entire Middle East was whipped into a Gulf War, caused by raw, unchecked male energy of the worst sort. Surely the God Mars held sway in his most cruel aspect - or was it the Goddess in her vengeful form, crying for attention after so many centuries of neglect? It caused me to consider the day-to-day wastage of martial energy in the world overall, in pointless violence, rape and hate, now encountered by ordinary people almost as a matter of course. Yet the eruption of war, all round the Mediterranean, has usually occurred without the assent of the female.

The return of the priestesshood of Venus, Daughter of the Moon, known by many different names, is sorely needed to bring men back to themselves, as Isis resurrected Osiris. Its tradition stretches back into the mists of time, and we women need first to graft ourselves back to it if this task is to be undertaken. This book traces the remains of what turns out to be a submerged mainline tradition for priestesses whose main characteristics have over the centuries remained constant. These are summarized in Chapter II. General background is often dwelt on at length, to give the context against which priestesses worked. Each chapter is presided over by the relevant regional Goddess who is a role type for the priestess, and each main section of the book has the corresponding river(s) of the area as life-giver, since they were usually presided over by goddesses, and often named after them (perhaps the Ister is the most striking). This introduction begins with an English river with the nature of the Goddess's lover, Tammuz.

As well as the main text of the book giving factual information, there are additional personal reflections, which the reader may agree with or not. As everyone is at different starting points, I have tried not to preach or labour parallels in too great detail, certain that readers can draw conclusions for themselves from the evidence, given a start in the method of making comparisons.

The main sources of information used for this book are the artefactual and documentary records of the ancient past, most of it unearthed by archaeologists from Middle Eastern sites only within the last 100 years. These sources hold precious information about women who then held great power, and whose influence gradually spread to Western practice from the third millennium onwards, until it finally took root in Greece and Rome. Interesting information about particular historical priestesses is still emerging. It tends to be distributed in time-clusters, rather than as a uniform spread (see Chronological Table). Thus a few spectacular individuals stand out, around whom it is possible to assemble some general conclusions about the role of priestesses of all ranks.

For some cosmic reason the West has always adopted the codes of far away Middle Eastern prophets and sages: Judaism, Christianity and Islam all derive from that region. Previous to these, priestesshood under the ancient religions (priesthood too) gradually filtered westward over the centuries from those very lands. We could say the peoples of the countries encircling the Mediterranean, coastal or inland, have from the beginning of history constantly reacted with each other like one vast family, originally around one root Tradition which has gradually diversified into many facets. This is the network out of which, in the ancient Near East, the role of the priestess evolved, known to us in records from the late fourth millennium onwards, though female spiritual leadership probably existed much earlier, before there were temples. Today in that very same area where priestesshood began, its memory is built into female genes, but has been rendered inoperable by succeeding monotheistic religions. Yet the long atrophied gifts of the priestess are on the brink of painful re-emergence. Western women have only a comparative head-start; perhaps their initial role is to open the pathways for their Eastern counterparts.

More attention is given here to the very ancient world in the third and second millennia (abbreviated 3M and 2M) than to later eras, because this epoch is not so widely known. Information about Roman priestesses is abundant, and would fill a book in itself. Thus it was decided to end in the Classical period still dominated by the Greek world, with only a few pointers to Roman developments. All dates given are BC. As a very rough guide, 'Bronze Age' refers to the second millennium, and 'Iron Age' to the first millennium. The third millennium is understood by archaeologists as mainly 'chalcolithic', meaning that it welded together the benefits of a vast Stone Age past with new

experiments in metallurgy, with consequent trading/travelling activities. (The silver found in the Royal Tombs of Ur, for instance, has been proved to derive from mineral-rich Almeria, in Spain.)

The reason we know such a lot about the early history of the Middle Eastern priestesshood is that writing and artefacts were executed in durable materials, at the rise of urbanism. In Europe, whose prehistory shows no sign of urban agglomerations, if records and artefacts of leather, wood and bone did exist from rural contexts, they have perished. What we do have left to go by are the remnants of an oral tradition (which we can call 'The Hyperborean Tradition'), of which Wicca is probably a pale shadow. This book concentrates mostly on the hard information supplied by the 'Mediterranean Tradition'.

At the rise of Greek civilization in Mycenaean times the Mediterranean Tradition began to blend more intensely with the Hyperborean Tradition, which the Mycenaeans were linked to from the north. From then on interchange worked both ways, and priestess practice from the 8C BC benefited from both founts. In fact the sparser evidence from earlier millennia points to the constant injection of inspiration from nomadic, 'barbaric' tribes on the fringes of 'civilization' who practised shamanism, still a need for urban centres today.

Looking at the fine faces of the nomadic Kurdish women of northern Iraq who came into the news as I began to write, I was struck by similarities with ancient sculpture from the same lands (Figure 1). Other physical types whose modern counterparts can be seen alive in the Middle East today will be recognized throughout the book. Many of the priestesses illustrated often look surprisingly European. The interplay of peoples from round the Mediterranean encompasses many facial types.

After what to spiritual women can only be called 'The Dark Age of Monotheism', a scattered handful of females have made progress in regaining self-esteem and the right of women to use all the faculties they hold in common with men – yet publicly acknowledged spiritual authority eludes them. They still have much to learn about using their powers without loss of femininity, or causing serious damage to men in the process. With physical, economic and psychological issues still far away from being resolved harmoniously, the issue of female priesthood is now at the forefront of public debate, but only in the context of the Christian Church, and one branch of it at that. On the other hand, many influential women working outside orthodox bodies are in fact operating as priestesses, often at a very high level, caring for souls. I believe the example of ancient history can contribute towards enlarging what is at the moment a small canvas that leaves most potential priestesses out of the picture altogether.

That is why the scope of this book covers the Mediterranean Tradition as a whole, and takes into account the present situation in the Middle East, where women's voices have so far rarely been heard at the forefront of spiritual matters, despite notable exceptions. *They are the very people whose direct heritage this book describes.* I therefore hope

1 A marble head found in a rubbish dump at the temple site of Uruk, probably part of a cult statue; now in the Iraq Museum, c.3200 BC.

the readership will come from all round the Mediterranean and beyond, and that present-day women, whether from countries of peace or of war, perhaps refugees now living in the West, will think what they can do to redress the gender balance in their territory's spiritual affairs, even if from a distance.

Although men alone cannot be blamed for the backwardness of women's spiritual status as it now stands, whether in the East or West, there is no escaping its consideration as a major factor in the spiritual damage done to women, which has deeply scarred them over generations. This does not mean I have an anti-male axe to grind, for the other half of the story seems to be that women themselves called this treatment upon themselves for betraying their high office.

In fact much of this book shows how in ancient times attempts were made to reconcile the two energies in a temple context, particularly exemplified in the sacred marriage rite. It is therefore necessary for men to read this book as closely as women, both helping each other to come to grips with the nature of spiritual balancing. The need for male and female to work together in the world of religion has begun at a more mundane level by working together on physical and mental tasks. On this foundation, spiritual work can start. As a token of this I asked Michael Duigan, who knows more about Egypt and Crete than I do, to contribute the chapters on priesthood in those two great civilizations, from his point of view.

The broad historical backdrop sketched out above would not have come to life if I myself had not started from school days to try to find an answer to the puzzling question of why women were not allowed spiritual authority. By the beginning of the 1980s, I had encountered at varying depths four main world religions in theory and/or practice: Christianity (school days); Hinduism (like the Beatles, in the Sixties I meditated and sat at the feet of Indian gurus); Islam (I belonged to a Sufi group for 10 years), and an impression of Judaism (from Jewish friends). Apart from the Vedantic School, with its doctrine of the *shakti*, for all these traditions spiritual precedence rested on being male! There are no Muslim women religious leaders, and the situation for Christians is beggarly. Even though in liberal Jewish circles female rabbis have started to appear, whose intellectual knowledge and spiritual authority are impressive,

The Jewish Chronicle of 6 March 1992 described the increasing anger of Jewish women who feel prevented, despite their qualifications, from playing as full a part in synagogue life as men. Yet Sumerian (proto-Hebrew) women used to be priestesses at Ur and Harran. The main clue to their original matriarchal power is that 'Jewishness' to this day is passed on through the female line alone.

The significance of the Jewish faith for the Mediterranean Tradition as a whole is that it is the most ancient of the religions surviving there, its lunar dating system equating their year 5752 with the youthful solar Christian 1992, and a junior lunar Muslim 1412! It thus has embedded in it ancient attitudes which can be traced back to Sumerian roots in Mesopotamia, whose records have a great deal to offer us about a priestess practice which was deliberately suppressed as Judaism opted for overt monotheism from the middle of the second millennium. This is the point at which Jews looking back to their roots come to a stop. Such a short-sighted historical perspective is equally true of the other traditions.

Mentally struggling with the forbidding judgmentalism of the three Semitic faiths, at a time when I had started to travel frequently to the Middle East, I came across Merlin Stone's *Paradise Papers* (first published in America as *When God was a Woman*), which first introduced me to the idea that men had not always dictated spiritual matters. It brought home to me with a crunch that the teachings of the monotheistic religions of Islam, Christianity and Judaism had between them brought about the social and spiritual suppression of women. Why? I turned to courses in Near Eastern archaeology and history (having originally trained as an art historian), not aware at the time what information I would turn up. With hindsight it proved to be a long journey, which revealed startling factual information which archaeologists and linguists have known for years, but have not presented in a form palatable to non-specialist readers. We have to thank these researchers for establishing the facts upon which we can take further steps to build conclusions and make syntheses, as here. Much of this book depends on their individual studies, which are referred to by main author name, and usually listed in the bibliography. However, as this is a general book I have avoided distracting footnotes. The interpretations are my own responsibility, unless mentioned otherwise.

Strengthened by the discoveries I was making about priestesses, by the new perspective given by *The Paradise Papers*, and chanting daily sections of the 'Thousand Names of the Goddess' in Sanskrit,[1] I then took the decision to walk back, psychologically, over the Bridge of Monotheism, which spans what turns out to be only a narrow divide between our modern world and the old. On its further bank I reached the far-flung Asiatic continent stretching back to ancient beginnings.

I returned further and further on into the past, into the history, art and religion of Egypt, Mesopotamia, Iran, Syria, Jordan, Palestine, Turkey, Crete and Greece. I visited those countries, often several times, to see monuments and museums and tune in to the atmosphere of land and mountain, which sang in the ears at a high frequency, electrifying the soul as it reconnected with far memory. I was continually taken aback to find how much of the ancient traditions had been absorbed into the rituals and imagery of monotheism, their origins conveniently forgotten. Men and women's spiritual parity was in fact made explicit in the earliest writings of Christianity and Islam, but not carried out.

Was it women's collective unsuitability that meant priestesses were relegated to a subordinate position (or indeed had no existence at all) under patriarchal religion, or was it certain individual women whose behaviour had brought the profession down to its lowest level, gaining the mere label of harlotry? Or did men become tired of being run by women, so that under cosmic dispensation it was *allowed* that their end of the see-saw should go up – just as we have tired of male dominance today?

Men were never, in fact, from the outset of history, correspondingly suppressed by women on a grand scale, and were throughout ancient history more numerous in temple life than women. In the ancient Near East the average woman was regarded much as today, as her father or husband's property, castigated if not properly veiled. Usually only priestesses and women in the élite earned independence and high esteem. It was not that much rosier in 3000 BC than it is now, perhaps because, if Hindu doctrine is correct in its calculations, the beginning of the Age of Destruction (the Kali Yuga) began after the Flood (*c.*3000 BC), not in the twentieth century. Our idealization of ancient history is only a matter of degree, for it was in the primordial Golden Age that the *natural* parity between male and female occurred, and of that we have no record.

Was there a deliberate male conspiracy during the second millennium to overthrow a priestesshood which had run down and needed to be protected against its own worst self (to which period the myth of Adam protesting he was tempted by Eve refers)? Men's awe and fear of female power still underlies present ecclesiastical attitudes, which are based on the distant past. Breaking free from male control, spiritual domination included, evokes an unreasoned male backlash. Its primitive nature is encapsulated in the story of the brilliant woman mathematician, Hypatia, who in Roman times was sliced to death in Alexandria by monks from the nearby monastery wielding oyster shells because she dared to discuss mathematical problems with her peers, who happened to be males in high places. [2]

Of course, women do not qualify as priestesses *because* they are female, but then men should not qualify as priests *because* they are male. Spiritual worthiness - the substitution of the seven vices by the practice of the seven virtues - is still the first criterion. However, countless women have the highest spiritual qualifications

and it is clear the world needs that added female flavour now so lacking.

I feel the circle of white-scarved women who 'visited' me was the present-day collective soul of those who wish again to wield true spiritual power in a world that needs it more than ever before. Their homeliness implied to me that every 'ordinary' woman has a priestess in her. So I hope this book will open up possibilities not only for those with special gifts for high priestesshood, but also for the 'average housewife'. There are places to fill in all ranks of priestesshood, as ancient history shows - and all are needed.

Because we are still at the experimental stage, I do not feel entitled to instruct would-be priestesses so much as to share the information I have gathered, with personal thoughts about using it for oneself. Nor is this a definitive history of priestesshood, which has still to be written, for I am only too aware of how much more information could have been included. It tries simply to give an overall view of the main outlines, with close-up studies of outstanding individuals to give it flesh.

I take it for granted that the people who read the following pages, male or female, will come from various religious backgrounds, or a mixture of several, both orthodox and unorthodox. Although I take my material from a variety of specific religions, I do so with the aim both of restoring interest in the roots of one particular tradition for one person, as much as of trying to ascertain universal principles which are beyond any particular religious form. Bound in with this is the leading problem of whether a priestess should operate from within an orthodox religious tradition, or can do so outside the given forms if she has a true understanding of the Eternal Law (*sanātana dharma*, in Sanskrit). We have to bear in mind too that women are of different types and that this means priestesshood is likely to manifest in a variety of ways, as priesthood should. It is unreal to impose a Virgoan ideal on a Sagittarian, or a Cancerian on a Capricornian!

My arguments, then, rely on drawing lessons from history, ancient stories and images, the vast untapped store that leads straight to the submerged female tradition, with the aim of working at female self-reorientation in our present so modern, and yet never before so linked to ancient, times. As regards the unorthodox aspects of spiritual practice which were gradually excluded from the body of monotheistic theology, to an extent I also take for granted that the reader will have already encountered work on, among other things, crystals, chakras, dreamwork, female spirituality and astrology, which in the ancient religions were still part of orthodox practice, and no doubt will in time again find their way back to mainstream religion, or *vice versa*. If it is felt I have not explained any of these fields fully enough and they remain unfamiliar, the answer is to try to find a relevant specialist book, or gain more background in ancient Near Eastern archaeology or mythology. Our journey traverses an entire universe of subjects which can only be touched upon in pressing ahead with the main theme.

Taken overall, as this is a first attempt to work with ancient history in this way, I hope others will pick up suggestions and pursue them further, since there is much detail to be completed. I certainly hope the nature of the factual information in this book, alongside discussion of the practicalities of becoming active in our present global tradition, whether Mediterranean or Hyperborean, will encourage readers to enter the arena, even if at a very tentative and exploratory level at first. I hope it will bring the silent majority into both hidden and open operation, like yeast in bread. This would, I believe, bring a smile to that dim circle of white-scarved women I saw, whose inarticulate presence seemed to say, 'The Time has Come.' To a great extent I feel it is they who invisibly dictated this book and who stand behind us all, waiting for us to increase in knowledge, and take action.

1. The first 83 names are discussed by me under my Sufi name in the Epilogue of *In All Her Names*, ed. Joseph Campbell, Charles Musès and others (HarperCollins, 1991).
2. A fuller account of the incident is given on p.53 of *The Year of the Goddess*, an anthology by Lawrence Durdin-Robertson, picture researched and edited with further insertions by myself (HarperCollins, 1990).

SUMER

EUPHRATES

1

ESTABLISHING THE SACRED MEASURES

Role type: Inanna

The first temple of ancient Sumer (southern Mesopotamia, present-day southern Iraq) consisted of a small reed hut (*giguna*) with an altar and small platform inside. (Marsh Arabs in southern Iraq still know how to build elaborate houses from bunches of plaited reeds.) Written on clay, a cuneiform source says of the sanctuary at Uruk, where gender balancing first began, that the Goddess Inanna and the God Anu 'abide together in the *giguna* that is the seat of joy'. This image is the keynote to the workings of any temple, ancient or modern.

The remains of such a primordial shrine have been found at the lowest of 18 layers at Eridu. It was built on virgin soil *c.*5000 BC and was run by a priesthood. Possibly the numbers of reeds used and their criss-crossing spelt out, in a three-dimensional abacus, cosmic numerical interplays. We shall never know. As generations passed, and life became more complex, so the hut accrued other rooms round it, and was replaced by walls of longer-lasting mud-brick. Such a process was charted by the archaeologists Lloyd and Safar as they disinterred the later layers of the temple site at Eridu. By 3000 BC the mature temple plan had fully evolved. Altogether 18 distinct levels, or rebuildings, had accrued on top of each other over almost 2,000 years of use.

When the centre of ecclesiastical power moved to Uruk in around 4000 BC and the first priesthood on record came into being, Eridu still went on for several hundred years more. At Uruk, too, 18 layers of the Eanna temple rebuildings were dug out by German archaeologists, the last layer extending into the Persian and Hellenistic periods (5C-2C BC). One cuneiform source says that Anu gave the temple of Eanna as a wedding gift to his consort Inanna. The temples of Anu the God of the Heavens, and of Inanna, Queen of Heaven, therefore continued in use for over four millennia up to the time of Christ, with priestesses officiating there from generation to generation (this is clearly borne out by numerous mentions on clay tablets, as well as by the remains of priestess possessions).

From the archaeological record alone Uruk was, therefore, the first urban community run with the full participation of female spiritual authority in parallel with a male priesthood. Each had their own temple to their respective God or Goddess of the opposite sex, in a system of gender balancing.

It is not often that one can splice together the facts of archaeology with a literary text, but this is one of the rare instances. An entire myth has survived in cuneiform writing on clay tablets (Figure 2) from the third millennium, which tells how the Goddess Inanna of Uruk procured all the measures of life, including the female specialities which only women can give, from the God of Wisdom and the

Deep Waters, Enki of Eridu. The story that follows from ancient Iraq of 5,000 years ago rings strangely to Western ears, due not only to the tablet sometimes having pieces broken off, and to translation problems, but also to its archaic, repetitive style. The God of Eridu and the Goddess of Uruk come over as distinct

2 The story of Inanna and Enki, the charter of priestesshood, written in columns of cuneiform on a large clay tablet; found at Nippur in Iraq, photo courtesy The University Museum, University of Philadelphia, c.2000 BC.

personalities and the story is a vivid one, with an underlying meaning of central interest to us now, as its subtitle could read: 'How priestess power was taken [back] from the priests'. It bears retelling at this juncture (with some of the repetitions left out), as translated by S. N. Kramer in Diane Wolkstein's book, *Inanna*, since it shows in mythological form how the first priestesshood was founded in Sumer through female persistence. (Passages in curved brackets are reconstructed lines based on repetitions elsewhere in the poem, where there is a break in the tablet; passages in square brackets summarize the repetitions of the full story.)

INNANA AND THE GOD OF WISDOM
Inanna placed the *shugurra*, the crown of the steppe, on her head.
She went to the sheepfold, to the shepherd.
She leaned back against the apple tree.
When she leaned against the apple tree, her vulva was wondrous to behold.
Rejoicing at her wondrous vulva, the young woman Inanna applauded herself.
She said:
  'I, the Queen of Heaven, shall visit the God of Wisdom.
  I shall go to the Abzu, the sacred place in Eridu.
  I shall honour Enki, the God of Wisdom, in Eridu.

  I shall utter a prayer to Enki at the deep sweet waters.'

Inanna set out by herself.
When she was within a short distance of the Abzu,
He whose ears are wide open,
He who knows the *Me*, the holy laws of heaven and earth,
He who knows the heart of the gods,
Enki, the God of Wisdom, who knows all things,
Called to his servant, Isimud:
  'Come, my *sukkal*,
  The young woman is about to enter the Abzu.
  When Inanna enters the holy shrine,
  Give her butter cake to eat.
  Pour cold water to refresh her heart.
  Offer her beer before the statue of the lion.
  Treat her like an equal.
  Greet Inanna at the holy table, the table of heaven.'

Isimud heeded Enki's words.
When Inanna entered the Abzu,
He gave her butter cake to eat.
He poured cold water for her to drink.
He offered her beer before the statue of the lion.
He treated her respectfully.
He greeted Inanna at the holy table, the table of heaven.
Enki and Inanna drank beer together.
They drank more beer together.
They drank more and more beer together.
With their copper vessels filled to overflowing,
With the vessels of Urash, Mother of the Earth,

They toasted each other; they
  challenged each other.
Enki, swaying with drink, toasted
  Inanna:
  'In the name of my power!
  In the name of my holy shrine!
  To my daughter Inanna I shall
    give
  The high priesthood!
  Godship!
  The noble, enduring crown!
  The throne of rulership!'
Inanna replied:
  'I take them!'
Enki raised his cup and toasted
  Inanna a second time:
  'In the name of my power!
  In the name of my holy shrine!
  To my daughter Inanna I shall
    give
  Truth!
  Descent into the underworld!
  Ascent from the underworld!
  The art of lovemaking!
  The kissing of the phallus!'
Inanna replied:
  'I take them!'
Enki raised his cup and toasted
  Inanna a third time:
  'In the name of my power!
  In the name of my holy shrine!
  To my daughter Inanna I shall
    give
  The holy priestess of heaven!
  The setting up of lamentations!
  The rejoicing of the heart!
  The giving of judgements!
  The making of decisions!'
Inanna replied:
  'I take them!'
[Fourteen times Enki raised his cup
  to Inanna.
Fourteen times he offered his
  daughter five *Me*, six *Me*, seven
  Me.
Fourteen times Inanna accepted
  the holy *Me*.]

Then Inanna, standing before her
  father,
Acknowledged the *Me* Enki had
  given to her:

  'My father has given me the *Me*:

  He gave me the high priesthood.
  He gave me the godship.
  He gave me the noble, enduring
  crown.
  He gave me the throne of
  rulership.

  He gave me the noble sceptre.
  He gave me the staff.
  He gave me the holy measuring
  rod and line.
  He gave me the high throne.
  He gave me shepherdship.
  He gave me rulership.

  He gave me the princess
  priestess.
  He gave me the divine queen
  priestess.
  He gave me the [duties of]
  incantation priest.
  He gave me the noble priest.
  He gave me the libations priest.

  He gave me truth.
  He gave me descent into the
  underworld.
  He gave me ascent from the
  underworld.
  He gave me the *kurgarra*.

  He gave me the dagger and
  sword.
  He gave me the black garment.
  He gave me the colourful
  garment.
  He gave me the loosening of the
  hair.
  He gave me the binding of the
  hair.

He gave me the standard.
He gave me the quiver.
He gave me the art of
lovemaking.
He gave me the kissing of the
phallus.
He gave me the art of
prostitution.
He gave me the art of speeding.

He gave me the art of forthright
speech.
He gave me the art of slanderous
speech.
He gave me the art of adorning
speech.
He gave me the [duties of] cult
hierodule.
He gave me the holy tavern.

He gave me the holy shrine.
He gave me the [duties of] holy
priestess of heaven.
He gave me the resounding
musical instrument.
He gave me the art of song.
He gave me the art of the elder.

He gave me the art of the hero.
He gave me the art of power.
He gave me the art of treachery.
He gave me the art of
straightforwardness.
He gave me the plundering of
cities.
He gave me the setting up of
lamentations.
He gave me the rejoicing of the
heart.

He gave me deceit.
He gave me the rebellious land.
He gave me the art of kindness.
He gave me travel.
He gave me the secure dwelling
place.

He gave me the craft of the
woodworker.
He gave me the craft of the
copper worker.
He gave me the craft of the
scribe.
He gave me the craft of the
smith.
He gave me the craft of the
leather maker.
He gave me the craft of the
fuller.
He gave me the craft of the
builder.
He gave me the craft of the reed
worker.

He gave me the perceptive ear.
He gave me the power of
attention.
He gave me the holy purification
rites.
He gave me the feeding pen.
He gave me the heaping up of
hot embers.
He gave me the sheepfold.
He gave me fear.
He gave me consternation.
He gave me dismay.

He gave me the bitter-toothed
lion.
He gave me the kindling of fire.
He gave me the putting out of
fire.
He gave me the weary arm.
He gave me the assembled family.
He gave me procreation.

He gave me the kindling of strife.
He gave me counselling.
He gave me heart-soothing.
He gave me the giving of
judgements.
He gave me the making of
decisions.'

(Still reeling with drink) Enki spoke
  to his servant, Isimud:
    'My *sukkal*, Isimud –
    The young woman – is about to
      leave – for Uruk.
    It is my wish that she reach her
      city – safely.'

Inanna gathered all the *Me*.
The *Me* were placed on the Boat of
  Heaven.
The Boat of Heaven, with the holy
  Me, was pushed off from the
  quay.

When the beer had gone out from
  the one who had drunk beer,
When the beer had gone out from
  Father Enki,
When the beer had gone out from
  the great God of Wisdom,
Enki looked about the Abzu.
The eyes of the King of the Abzu
  searched Eridu.
King Enki looked about Eridu and
  called to his servant Isimud,
  saying:
    'My *sukkal*, Isimud – '
    'My king, Enki, I stand to serve
      you.'
    'The high priesthood? Godship?
    The noble, enduring crown?
    Where are they?'

    'My king has given them to his
      daughter.'

    'The art of the hero? The art of
      power?
    Treachery? Deceit?
    Where are they?'

    'My king has given them to his
      daughter.'

[Fourteen times Enki questioned
  his servant Isimud;

Fourteen times Isimud answered,
  saying:
    'My king has given them to his
      daughter.
    My king has given all the *Me* to
      his daughter, Inanna.']

Then Enki spoke, saying:
    'Isimud, the Boat of Heaven,
      with the holy *Me* –
    Where is it now?'
    'The Boat of Heaven is (one quay
      away from Eridu).'

    'Go! Take the *enkum*-creatures.
    Let them bring the Boat of
      Heaven back to Eridu!'

Isimud spoke to Inanna:
    'My queen, your father has sent
      me to you.
    Your father's words are words of
      state.
    They may not be disobeyed.'

Inanna answered:
    'What has my father said?
    What has Enki added?
    What are his words of state that
      may not be disobeyed?'

Isimud spoke:
    'My king has said:
    "Let Inanna proceed to Uruk;
      Bring the Boat of Heaven with
        the holy *Me* back
        to Eridu." '

Innana cried:
    'My father has changed his word
      to me!
    He has violated his pledge –
      broken his promise!
    Deceitfully my father spoke to
      me!
    Deceitfully he cried:
      "In the name of my power! In
        the name of my holy shrine!"

Deceitfully he sent you to me!'
Scarcely had Inanna spoken these
  words
Than the wild-haired *enkum*-
  creatures seized the Boat of
  Heaven.

Inanna called to her servant
  Ninshubur, saying:
    'Come, Ninshubur, once you
      were Queen of the East;
    Now you are the faithful servant
      of the holy shrine of Uruk.
    Water has not touched your
      hand,
    Water has not touched your foot.
    My *sukkal* who gives me wise
      advice,
    My warrioress who fights by my
      side,
    Save the Boat of Heaven with the
      holy *Me*!'

(Ninshubur sliced the air with her
  hand.
She uttered an earth-shattering cry.)
The *enkum*-creatures were sent
  hurtling back to Eridu.
Then Enki called to his servant
  Isimud a second time, saying:
    'My *sukkal*, Isimud – '
    'My king, Enki, I stand to serve
      you.'
    'Where is the Boat of Heaven
      now?'
    'It is (two quays away from
      Eridu).'

    'Go! Take the fifty *uru*-giants,
    Let them carry off the Boat of
      Heaven!'

The fifty flying *uru*-giants seized
  the Boat of Heaven.
But Ninshubur rescued the boat
  for Inanna.

Enki called to his servant Isimud a
  third time, saying:
    'My *sukkal*, Isimud – '
    'My king, Enki, I stand to serve
      you.'
    'Where is the Boat of Heaven
      now?'
    'It has just arrived at Dilmun.'

  'Quickly! Take the fifty *lahama*-
    monsters,
    Let them carry off the Boat of
      Heaven!.'

But Ninshubur rescued the boat
  for Inanna.

A fourth time, Enki sent the sound-
  piercing *kugalgal*.
A fifth time, Enki sent the *enunun*.

But each time Ninshubur rescued
  the boat for Inanna.

Enki called to his servant Isimud a
  sixth time, saying:
    'My *sukkal*, Isimud – '
    'My king, Enki, I stand to serve
      you.'
    'Where is the Boat of Heaven
      now?'
    'It is about to enter Uruk.'

    'Quickly! Take the watchmen of
      the Iturungal Canal,
    Let them carry off the Boat of
      Heaven!'

Isimud and the watchmen of the
  Iturungal Canal seized the Boat
  of Heaven.

But Ninshubur rescued the boat
  for Inanna.

Then Ninshubur spoke to Inanna:
    'My queen, when the Boat of
      Heaven

Enters the Nigulla Gate of Uruk,
Let high water flow in our city;
Let the deep-going boats sail
  swiftly through our canals.'

Inanna answered Ninshubur:
  'On the day the Boat of Heaven
  Enters the Nigulla Gate of Uruk,
  Let high water flow over the
    paths.
  Let the old men give counsel;
  Let the old women offer heart-
    soothing.
  Let the young men show the
    might of their weapons;
  Let the little children laugh and
    sing.
  Let all of Uruk be festive!
  Let the high priest greet the Boat
    of Heaven with song.
  Let him utter great prayers.
  Let the king slaughter oxen and
    sheep.
  Let him pour beer out of the
    cup.
  Let the drum and tambourine
    resound.
  Let the sweet *tigi*-music be
    played.
  Let all the lands proclaim my
    noble name.
  Let my people sing my praises.'

And so it was:
On the day the Boat of Heaven
  entered the Nigulla Gate of
  Uruk,
High water swept over the streets;
High water flowed over the paths.
The Boat of Heaven docked at the
  holy shrine of Uruk;
The Boat of Heaven docked at the
  holy house of Inanna.

Then Enki called to his servant
  Isimud a seventh time, saying:
  'My *sukkal*, Isimud – '

'My king, Enki, I stand to serve
  you.'
'Where is the Boat of Heaven
  now?'
The Boat of Heaven is at the
  White Quay.'

'Go! She has aroused wonder
  there.
The queen has aroused wonder
  at the White Quay.
Inanna has aroused wonder at
  the White Quay for the Boat of
  Heaven!'

The holy *Me* were being unloaded.
As the *Me* which Inanna had
  received from Enki were
  unloaded,
They were announced and
  presented to the people of Sumer.

Then more *Me* appeared – more *Me*
  than Enki had given Inanna.
And these, too, were announced,
And these, too, were presented to
  the people of Uruk:
  'Inanna brought the *Me*:
  She brought the placing of the
    garment on the ground.
  She brought allure.
  She brought the art of women.
  She brought the perfect
    execution of the *Me*.
  She brought the *tigi*- and
    lilis-drums.
  She brought the *ub*-, the *meze*-
    and the *ala*-tambourines . . .'

Inanna spoke, saying:
  'Where the Boat of Heaven has
    docked,
  That place shall be called The
    White Quay.
  Where the holy *Me* have been
    presented,
  That place I shall name The Lapis
    Lazuli Quay.'

Then Enki spoke to Inanna, saying:
  'In the name of my power!
  In the name of my holy shrine!
  Let the *Me* you have taken with
    you remain in the holy shrine
    of your city.
  Let the high priest spend his days
    at the holy shrine in song.
  Let the citizens of your city
    prosper,
  Let the children of Uruk rejoice.
  The people of Uruk are allies of
    the people of Eridu.
  Let the city of Uruk be restored
    to its great place!'

The myth illustrates several points which could quite feasibly have a basis in historical fact. Taking Inanna as a divine prototype of the priestess, the story shows from the human analogy of a drinking session how women gained their power over dispensation of the *Me* (both the general measures and the female measures which are peculiarly their own in any case) only when male attention was taken off guard.

It shows also that once the male side realized what it had relinquished, no persuasion - or force - would convince women the *Me* should be returned, despite harassing tactics. This means that any ground gained must not be given back.

Finally, once established as a *fait accompli*, the male side acceded to Inanna's possession of the *Me* graciously and to her authority over them. How often have we seen that happen too? But the process of taking or stealing power first causes anguish. Sometimes, though, it may be the only way to break the deadlock. If permission is asked, in this situation it is rarely given - nor will males give away what *they* have gained.

This principle, most often played out in domestic situations, lies at the heart of the debate in the Protestant Church regarding the ordination of women, and is well borne out in the life of Florence Tim Oi Li of Hong Kong, who was the first Anglican woman priest. Her original calling to take orders was rejected by two Archbishops of Canterbury, and by the 1948 Lambeth Conference. But her exceptional example as a deaconess when the Japanese captured Hong Kong moved R. O. Hall, Bishop of Hong Kong, to ordain her. Quoting from her obituary which appeared in *The Independent* on 29 February 1992:

After the war, Bishop Hall was censured and Li was told that, if she continued to work as a priest, the bishop would be compelled to resign. She wrote to Bishop Hall, 'I am a very tiny person, a mere worm', but she did not resign her orders, which she considered to be permanent, a gift from God which could not be erased.

This is an exact repeat of the Inanna/Enki story with just a change of names!

It is valuable to read the list of measures gained by Inanna slowly and carefully, and consider what they mean. Each demands close attention, for each is specific, covering positive as well as negative powers relevant to both high spiritual, and everyday local, life in Sumer. (The precise meaning of some of the words has not yet been fully determined by the experts, but we get the general sense.) They are not only measures, like rules, but overall powers ranging from the sublime to the humdrum, which contribute to the ordered running of physical life within the web of cosmic life. I like to think of all the things I enjoy in life, both physical and metaphysical, ordinary and divine, and write down at the back of my diary my equivalent list of *Me* for life today. You might make such a list too.

The striking feature of the list is that there is no split between spiritual, mental and physical, as has happened in monotheistic theologies. Women's great gift is to release the spiritual in the physical and the physical in the spiritual. The male attitude, whether in women or men, creates separate zones between realms, in itself useful, but then often fails to reconnect them.

By analogy with the myth, if today people of the West, and of the Near East, are living almost wholly under the patriarchal measure of a monotheism whose male attitudes have ossified (further compounded by its side-effect, secularism), it must be time to think once again of sharing the *Me* equally, and opening out the natural connections.

Thinking of the list of measures in the story, and of your own ideal personal list, are there any which are not in your life-style today, which you would like to have instated, or *re*instated? To bring them about, will you have to discuss your way through, or do a bit of stealing, by soft or harder means? Discussion with friends, as well as hard thinking and visualization, is needed here, and it is worth setting aside half an hour each day for a whole month to draw up your List of Measures and your strategy for securing them.

The matriarchal measure is more understanding of organic subtleties - not inclined to accept man-made, often machine-like or robotic rhythms which jar against cosmic intervals. As women take on priesthood again, they will have to implement the natural measures, not only instinctively, but by studying them consciously. In trying to put them into practice, they will strike against feelings of guilt within themselves, caused by those events in their lives where they have been persuaded to go against their natural sense of measure. In everyday incidents they will meet the male force in its hostile form (in both men and women) which does not want – and fears – natural measures such as gradualness, quietness, softness, proportion and the curve, as well as the astounding strength and power women have to offer. These qualities are easily withered by opposition, but if sensitivity is killed, so the gateway is closed for everyone connected to that sensitive person.

This is not to say that Inanna does not come over as one of the most assertive prototypes in Western literature! Boldness has its part too, but it need not be at the expense of gentleness. At our point in history, though, the time has come, after two grand swings of the pendulum to both female and male dominance, to think not so much of stealing authority from men, as finding a way to come to grips with each other by discussion and being together, exploring and sensitively analysing situations, so as to blend the two approaches *without loss of polarity*! (By this I mean

that the aim of the process is not for women to lose their femaleness, or men their maleness, which has been a sad result so far of Western experimentation on gender identity.) Let the myth of Inanna and Enki be your starting-point!

You may be surprised just how much those around you desire the *Me* you have to offer, whether administered undercover or accompanied by a major policy speech. You will find people looking to you for measure, especially men. In February 1992 Timothy Leary, famous as the Professor of Psychology of the Hippie Era (now in his seventies) ended an interview on a World Service radio broadcast by saying, 'To all you women out there, please take over – we men need you!'

The words *mete* (measure) and *mater* (mother/measurer) are the same word. The Goddess Demeter was Divine Measurer. Don't underestimate just how much you can demand if it is reasonable, but demands need to be presented in a palatable way! Do not betray your trust seeking your own personal advantage on small everyday matters. If women set the measures, men will follow them in the end if they are reasonable and rely on natural cosmic law.

If we go back to the archaeological record to find out more about individuals who served the Goddess Inanna, it is from Uruk alone that we first gain precious, concrete information about women in cultic life. Many women are depicted on early seal impressions, which seem to be the earliest record of their activities, though it is difficult to be completely certain who they are, since we have no written captions to fully explain them.

The impressions were made by carved cylinder seals rolled across mud clods which capped commodity jars or were slapped over knots on parcels or doors to prevent tampering, as we use sealing wax today. The seals belonged to temple officials, both male and female, whose main function was to oversee the measurement of time by observation of stars and planets for agricultural reasons, but who then in consequence monitored the collection and distribution of produce. Their stamp on a mud sealing conveyed the personal authority of that individual. Most ingenious was the temple administration, for a network of distribution extended between Sumer and the Gulf to the south, all the way up the Euphrates into Syria to the north, to Mari and Ebla to the west (see later in this chapter), and as far to the east as the Indus river. Economics and temple life were indivisible, and could be again today.

The scenes on the seals of the late fourth millennium, both from Uruk and from related temples further afield, appear to record ceremonies marking high points of the yearly round, in which the owner of the seal took part. One of the earliest known prints, when rolled out (these days, inside museums, onto plasticine),

3 Worshippers approach a female, possibly a primitive type of priestess, who holds a goblet and sits on a low bull-foot stool. Depiction on a cylinder seal now in a private collection, c.3100 BC.

shows a woman seated on a low platform with bull feet (Figure 3). She holds a ceremonial cup and is flanked by male worshippers, one holding up his arms in obeisance. The man behind him brings pots of liquid and three churns are stacked behind him. Asher-Grève interprets the female figure as a primitive high priestess of Inanna since she is seated on a bull-footed stool, symbol of Anu the Bull Sky God, and therefore of divine presence. If so, the female figure would represent the Goddess who brings life and plenty, a portion of which is being returned to her in grateful acknowledgement. Why else would she be treated so reverentially?

A similar sealing in the Louvre shows a senior woman seated in the same manner (men are never shown in this crouched position in Sumerian art) in front of the sacred reed hut or *giguna*, being approached in thanksgiving by a male and a female surrounded by small jars. Although her pose may seem too natural for the representative of a goddess, and could simply be a venerable wise woman, Asher-Grève points out that in Mesopotamian art only gods and goddesses are seated on thrones; worshippers stand or bow and make gestures with their arms, which usually have specific meanings.

Why should this woman be associated with dairy and agricultural produce? Simply because woman is a more obvious symbol of the fruitfulness of the universe which enfolds the Earth than a man. Inside her womb grows a replica human being, or little Earth, to which she gives birth and which she nurtures with food made by her own body. Thus any woman stands for the ultimate Life-Giver, the Universe itself, which in turn

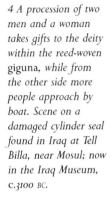

4 A procession of two men and a woman takes gifts to the deity within the reed-woven giguna, *while from the other side more people approach by boat. Scene on a damaged cylinder seal found in Iraq at Tell Billa, near Mosul; now in the Iraq Museum, c.3100 BC.*

is understood as the Celestial Woman. This lies behind the thinking that women should be the ones to make meals - and should perhaps be given the appropriate gratitude.

Because of the subject of these two cylinder seals, Asher-Grève believes they belonged to high priestesses - but this cannot be proved. On slightly later seals, carved much more skilfully by now, no figure before the shrine receives worshippers, but it is interesting to consider an important variation (Figure 4). It appears to show Inanna's divine lover, Tammuz (a different being from her husband Anu, since he is lower on the hierarchy, simply embodying the year), coming by boat down one of the many irrigation canals drawn off the river in southern Mesopotamia, to visit his beloved Inanna for the sacred marriage ritual. He is being rowed to his own reed shrine (a male temple this time), indicated by the flanking scrolled pillars which are his emblem. His *giguna* is approached by two naked male worshippers with girdles as gifts, and a female in a short gauze skirt greets the God with raised hands, perhaps singing. Perhaps she is the human bride who represents Inanna, coming to the God's house to unite with Him and lay the foundation of another year of plenty (see Chapter 3).

A detail on the best-known artefact of early Mesopotamian art, the limestone 'Uruk Vase' (Figure 5), shows a more developed counterpart to this seal. Inanna stands before the doorway of her female temple (indicated by the standards knotted into looped tops, the earliest sacred knots), to receive the fruits of a plentiful harvest from naked worshippers led by a man in robes belted with a tasselled girdle, arriving for the sacred marriage. A chip out of the vase means that all we have of the bridegroom is the end of his tasselled girdle! Interesting for us is the figure of Inanna herself, for again we must consider that this

5 A priestess in horned hat representing Inanna stands outside her shrine to receive offerings, the most of important of which is her bridegroom (off picture). Detail of the Uruk Vase now in the Iraq Museum, c.3100 BC.

is actually a priestess dressed up as Inanna, with just enough of a cow-horned head-dress to help us read later, fuller versions of such attire. Like the female figure in the seal of Figure 4, the lady clenches her fist and lifts her thumb to her nose in greeting.

⁘

All these pictures bring home to me the unchanging basics of an aspiring priestess's daily life: firstly, the reed hut represents sacred space, standing at the Centre of the World, of the Universe. Woman has always been associated with the 'space and place' for others to work in. You need your own *giguna*, your own sacred space. This you can understand as the Womb of the Goddess, which in reality is the vast, containing Universe. It stands at the same time for the Source of Life of which your own womb is a symbol.

This sacred space can be any chamber at all – a spare room in your home, the garden shed cleared out, a tent, your bedroom. Possibly you can only manage a corner of a room, but that is fine. Wherever it is, however you do it, create some spot which ritualizes The Centre of the World, via which all your symbolic actions and prayers can be addressed to the higher, invisible realms. A dressing table or mantelpiece makes a good altar. A stool or table in front of it is needed for you to stand behind, or sit on (or a rug if you prefer to sit on the floor). If you have a mantelpiece, it may stand over a fireplace, another ancient symbol of The Centre. You will notice that creating this sacred space will have an immediate, regulating effect on activities of a more practical nature that go on outside it.

You may already carry out elaborate rituals in your private space. I personally feel little need for complicated apparatus and actions, but people vary in what they need to do in order to reconnect (Latin *re-ligare*) with the higher worlds, depending on background and human type. Hence I am not suggesting anything specific – there is a wealth of example to draw on from many traditions which the reader can seek out depending on where they 'are at'. A wealth of ancient hymns and scriptures have been translated from all the traditions of the world, ancient and modern, thanks to the publishing explosion of the twentieth century. The Fellowship of Isis in Ireland has long carried out the simple procedure of using these prayers in their own rites, more often than trying to invent their own. They use ancient Sumerian, Egyptian or Greek hymns, or rituals given in ancient records, quite as much as the currently practised rites of orthodox religion.

Personally, I feel in the end a sacred space should be as empty as possible to have the Power of the Great Void: the Chinese and Japanese understand this best. But some things may yet be necessary in the *giguna*, because abstract truths are easier to contact through physical analogues, and the Sumerians made their religion work this way, at every level. At the top of the scale, *a* woman stands for the benevolent Universe, and you are therefore the most important · item in the *giguna*. The woman who takes on such a role at the level of religion is the priestess who, through the female mode of being, transmits universal truths in a form understandable to the times in which she lives.

The balance of femaleness to maleness in a woman varies from individual to individual, but she is still on balance predominantly female. That is why this book is primarily addressed to women. That is why, also, it concentrates on the problem area of gender difference, rather than the areas of development men and women have in common. At the present juncture the sex tangle needs teasing out into its separate strands before anything else can be done.

The exalted responsibility of full priesthood as described in detail later is only for a few, but there are simple ways in which all women may, whatever their walk in life, reflect the Universal Feminine at a modest level, most obviously as givers of life in the form of babies and food. It feels good to fulfil such a role, as a water drop can reflect the Ocean, if others could only be more mindful that this is the principle at work; otherwise women are merely treated as reproductive cows tied to the kitchen, and this debilitates them spiritually. In theory Islam regards each couple as priest and priestess of their own home, and does not recognize a hierarchy of priesthood outside the domestic domain. Men and women could both kindle this symbolism between each other. Feminists have over-reacted by despising domestic roles and could reconsider their position in this light.

Even women who have no difficulty in fulfilling traditional roles probably still need to reimbue their tasks with the Goddess dimension. The simplest way is for men and children to show gratitude for the life-giving nourishment imparted to them daily, and to see the women in their life as channels of the Goddess. This is one way in which they then find the Goddess Herself, which in turn enables a man to remain faithful to the central woman in his life instead of moving from one partner to another, for the lasting marriage is that with the Goddess, through a human. And there is no reason why men should not be food-givers and nurturers (even if they cannot try parturition), since it makes them more whole to reverse roles on a complementary basis. Whichever sex you are, experiment in the domestic domain to affirm the presence of the Goddess in the produce you grow, buy, prepare or eat, and the way it is channelled to others, for priesthood develops out of this.

❧

Often the most physical turns out to be the most close to the divine: extremes meet. The Sumerians understood this so well, for they were the first to perfect the art of farming, and to understand its dependence in turn upon the behaviour of the planets (the Gods and Goddesses), and the signs of the zodiac they stood in. The live-giver, Venus, their Inanna, was by reason of that power also the life-taker, and to be respected, acknowledged, propitiated.

So the full-time job of a priestess is to maintain the connection with the Gods and Goddesses, taking appropriate action to inspire others to apply the divine measures too. Thus, as the story of Inanna shows, women physically embody the mysteries of the Creation, not only as breast-nourishers, but also as measurers, and this is why as priestesses they are different in nature from priests, and should not be called priests as the Christian Church does.

Two further prime biological factors set women apart from men: the first is the 27/30-day menstruation cycle, a simple, regular and repeated measure that has a practical everyday use if no mechanical measuring devices exist. (It is so basic to female spirituality that it is discussed separately in Chapter 4 in connection with the Moon Priestesses.)

The second is the nine-month gestation period of pregnancy during which by a miraculous process of biological geometry the foetus is formed into a perfect miniature human being. Spring in the ancient world was greeted as the mating time not only for animals, but also for humans, occurring in the astrological sign of Taurus the Progenitor. Human babies conceived in this month would be born nine months later under the sign of Capricorn, the Goat-God Tammuz, whose place later was taken, through precession, by Aquarius, symbolized by the perfect man emptying the waters of the womb. These two signs fall either side of the winter solstice, the time for celebrating the birth of the Divine Child.

The priestesses so far illustrated in this chapter seem to have behind them an equation of the abundance of produce with the person of a woman who represents the life powers. These powers need to be thanked - and renewed by rituals. At the time those seals were carved, the actual temples of Uruk had developed from the primal reed hut still commemorated on the seals into magnificent structures of mud-brick, by now resting so high on their primitive levels that they had become natural ziggurats. Archaeological evidence shows that offerings were now brought to the interior of the temple complex and, if meat, often burned/cooked on a mud-brick altar in the centre of the *giguna* or holy of holies, sometimes before a statue of the deity. Probably the marble face of the Lady of Uruk (Figure 2) came from such a cult statue, which would have had its hair, eyes, clothes and limbs added in different, costly materials such as gold, lapis lazuli and alabaster.

Cult statues dispensed with the need for a human priestess to be there to receive offerings for the Goddess on ordinary occasions. Worshippers would also place statues of themselves, eternally fixed in an attitude of prayer, in the holy of holies, so they would not need to be there in person either every time they offered to the Goddess. Most were self-portraits of local people, some of the more august being clearly of high rank and riches; among them are the priests and priestesses who could afford to have such images made, and whose rank allowed such a privilege. This is precious evidence for us, since they amount to portraits of actual people.

One such is the enthroned lady from Mari dating to the mid third millennium (Figure 6), who is considered to be almost certainly a high priestess. She is completely enveloped in skirt and cloak of goat- or long-hair sheepskins whose fleeces fall into carefully combed tassels. Her stature is heightened by the domed hat which is an indication of her exalted office - headgear that Popes eventually adopted (indeed, thinking of the Tarot cards, we could think of her without distortion as one of many Papesses who really existed). The very fact that she is seated on a throne indicates she is entitled to represent the Goddess. There must be a ritual meaning for the choice of her dress, for which we have no written clues. Possibly wearing sheepskins (sheep in the Middle East do not have curly fleece as in Europe) refers to her people's primordial mountain or northern origins, since Mesopotamia itself does not offer naturally occurring sheep-grazing land. The dress is remarkably like the sheepskin clothing worn by Kirghiz nomads on the Russian steppes today, who constantly move with their yurts and flocks across the plains. If, however, what she is wearing is goat fleeces, then they could refer symbolically to Inanna's consort, Tammuz, whose animal was the goat, more at home nibbling bushes on sparse, rocky mountain terrain than brought down to the mud-flats of Sumer.

A mother-of-pearl inlay processional scene, also found at Mari, depicts three ladies in plain robes pinned at the shoulder with enormous metal pins (usually gold when found in excavations) (Figure 7), at the end of which would often hang their cylinder seals attached at the end of a string, and onto which were also threaded large beads of valuable

6 Alabaster statue of a high priestess wearing a polos head-dress and draped in goat- or sheepskin skirt and cape. Found in Syria in the Temple of Ishtar at Mari; now in the Damascus Museum, c.2600–2400 BC.

7 Detail of principal figure from a white shell inlay in slate showing high priestesses in polos, and sheepskin robes. Found in Syria in the Temple of Dagan, Mari; now in the Damascus Museum, line drawing after Ilse Seibert, c.2600–2400 BC.

material. The lady illustrated wears the same round polos on her head as the priestess statue just described. The full scene shows a procession (if the scene has been correctly reconstructed by its archaeologist, Parrot) towards what seems yet another fleece, surrounded by people who have placed it on a bull-footed bed! Sadly, the fragment showing what was to be found on the bed has been lost in the dissolving mud of Mari (Figure 8).

Such processions must have taken place at Uruk as well as Mari, and at other temples all down the Euphrates and Tigris rivers. Their role was to link the measures and methods of economic production to the worship of the Gods, as initiated in Sumer. To the West, the tradition reached as far as Ebla in Syria, and from there come the charred wooden remains of another female figure enveloped, like the priestess of Mari, in the goat skins of Tammuz, lover of Inanna. The view is emerging that this was standard dress for priestesses of high rank at the beginning of the third millennium.

❧

A robe can serve as something enveloping in which one's everyday personality is engulfed and lost as in meditation or prayer one's thoughts turn inwards, away from the endless pressures of daily existence. Perhaps this is the deepest idea behind women remaining cocooned as they do in the modern-day Middle East when they go out into the street - that they remain anonymous and inwardly rooted.

8 All that remains of the walls of the Temple of Dagan, where the shell inlay was found, and other juxtaposed sanctuaries in the lee of the ziggurat, since their excavation at the site of Mari near the Euphrates river in north-east Syria. Photo taken by the author in 1990.

If you are from such a background, then you will already have an *abaya* or *chador* in which to wrap yourself for prayer and contemplation. Western women are less likely to have such a garment and will need deliberately to choose or make a mantle that seems right for them according to their locality. Only to use it when going into your inner depths can often work like a switch, taking you instantly out of the outside world as you swing it round yourself.

༺ⱺⱻⱺ༻

9 Squat limestone statuette of a lady in the worshipping position. Purchased from Iraq; now in the British Museum, c.2500 BC.

One would not guess from the mud stumps that remain of the Mari temple walls that the sanctuaries were magnificently decorated with such cladding as the slate slab inlaid with priestesses (Figure 7). At Tell Brak, north of Mari, also in northern Syria, Max Mallowan found the remains of what he named as the Eye Temple, which again had been rebuilt one layer over another in the centuries from *c.*3000 BC onwards. The infill of the walls contained thousands of beads of semi-precious stones, puddled in with the mud and, in the main sanctuary, the altar of the earliest temple was bordered with strips of gold, a frieze of solid blocks of lapis lazuli and a row of stone rosettes. Before it, tiny worshipper tablet statues an

inch or two high appeared in hundreds, in the form of sketchy bodies topped by a large pair of eyes, giving the name to the temple. Some of them are polos-headed, which, when compared to the official sculpture (Figure 6), seem to be what a priestess of lower rank could afford.

Women officiating at Uruk perhaps looked like the little statuette in the British Museum, whose face is matched by so many modern Iraqi female faces (Figure 9). In the White Temple of Anu, Inanna's Sky God husband, priestesses would have inhaled the earthy smell of mud-

brick, whitewashed every year, and the aroma of freshly-cut grain and other agricultural produce brought in from surrounding fields, irrigated by an intricate network of canals stretching as far as the eye could see. If they took part in processions through the courtyard leading to the main temple of Inanna near the E-Anna ziggurat, they would have passed great columns of mud-brick studded with glazed red, white and black cones embedded in their surface (Figure 10), a truly imposing setting.

The earliest temple at Khafaje, dedicated to the Moon God, is one of the most interesting for the evidence it gives of temple life at this early period. The hoof-prints of a herd of cows have been preserved in the hardened mud of the inner enclosure of the temple courtyard. Around it were chambers filled with the debris of workshops for leatherwork, metalwork, pottery, and a bakery. This evidence helps to interpret a whole series of small cylinder seals from Uruk and other temples which show rows of seated women engaged in making pots, weaving on looms, making cheeses, and working at a full range of other crafts. Asher-Grève believes such seals may have belonged to the supervisors, or even individual craftswomen, for stamping their goods. Whether they were the workforce of a high priestess, or under male or female supervisors of a more secular sort may in time be revealed when more texts are

10 A fragment of a decorated mud wall from one of the temples at Uruk; now in the Vorderasiatische Museum, Berlin, c.3200 BC.

translated. We have already read in the myth of Inanna and Enki that the *Me* included the crafts; part of a text on another clay tablet, translated by S. N. Kramer in his *From the Poetry of Sumer*, runs:

For Inanna - the fuller cleansed her
    garments,
Inanna - the carpenter made her
    hold the weaving-spindle in her
    hand,
Inanna - the potter kneaded cups
    and pitchers.
The potter gave her holy drinking
    bowls.
The shepherd brought her his
    sheep, guards them for her,
Brought her all kinds of luxurious
    plants as her harvest.

Certainly in the realm of textiles the main workforce was female, and the workshops were part and parcel of the temple administration in providing for its daily needs. Spinning and weaving have always been associated with the priestesshood of the Goddess (see also Chapter 9) and the wearing of woollen garments with priesthood - but wearing an untreated fleece suggests an even more ancient symbolism.

The lady who presided over the housekeeping aspects of the temple had high status and was known as a *shazu*. One such lady dedicated a stone vase to Inanna in her temple at Nippur which indicates her high standing. Other

women personnel, some of whom were owned by the temple because they were so poor (such as widows or orphans), included hairdressers, milleresses, breweresses of beer, shepherdesses, buyers, musicians, dancers and singers.

Specific texts from Ur, southern Iraq, show that at the temple of Nanna, as well as the more male-dominated workshops of the workers in wood and ivory, the gold- and silver-smiths, stoneworkers, carpenters, leatherworkers, rope makers and reed weavers, there was a dress factory where 98 women and 63 children were employed.

Seeing how practical were the material needs of the temple, indispensable as a basis for bringing down from the Unmanifest the more invisible cosmic measures of life, the conclusion can be drawn for our own situation that there is no reason why practical activities should not be part of a priestess's exalted spiritual life. Anyone reading this book has a daily round of physical tasks which can be locked back to the cosmos if we only think of them in that way.

As you knit and sew, think how in ancient days these occupations were linked to the running of the temple. The practical is sacred, every stitch a prayer. Convents emphasized this in medieval times - but there is no need to join one to make physical work holy!

Many books have been written on why physical work leads literally to enlightenment. Ouspensky in his *Tertium Organum* gives perhaps the best explanation: if the surfaces of the three-dimensional world are rubbed, stroked, combed or otherwise tended, the invisible dimensions will manifest. The radiance of a newly cleaned and polished house is more than physical - notice for yourself - and the more love and attention you put into the rubbing, the more this uncanny effect, which can be called 'holiness' or 'spiritual sheen', is brought about. That is why everyone in the house should take part in cleaning the house, otherwise only the woman reaps this kind of benefit. Young children love it because their spirit is fed by the process, as well as their active muscles used.

Given that few of us will have the opportunity in our lifetime to work in an official temple or church to our fullest spiritual capacity, our home has to be our temple, just as the first mosque at Medina was built around the dwelling of Ayeshah, Muhammad's favourite wife

(indeed, traditionally, the Prophet had no home of his own: he visited the abodes of each of his wives, which were their own domain).

Once the sacred space of the *giguna* has been created, the other activities around it will fall into place and are not inimical to it. Avoid making the split that causes disregard for the material world, yet keep the *giguna* apart from the rest of the house or flat, or keep one corner of your room apart if you just have one room. Religion that is alive sparks from the pull between spirit and matter, so polarity must be retained, but connected at certain openings.

❧

This is borne out by the excavation of the Moon Temple of Khafaje, where evidently the practicalities of combining agricultural life with petitions to the Gods for continuing prosperity led to a temple plan with three zones: outer and inner precincts, and a holy of holies (the *giguna*) - exactly the layout used in the great temple of Jerusalem two millennia later, and the basis of all cathedral ground plans.

People with herds of cows would be allowed as far as the outer court, craftspeople to the inner court, and only priests and priestesses to the *giguna*. At Khafaje the hoof-prints of the cows are preserved – and the workshops. The high priestess would be unlikely to be a craftswoman as well, but would enact the high rituals in the holy of holies. All the same, earlier training in a craft would be an important part of her spiritual development, as in modern Masonry. Every knitter knows that one dropped stitch undoes the whole fabric, every potter what changes of pressure are needed to mould a clay pot, and so on. Later this knowledge becomes applicable to the guiding and moulding of souls.

We have visual and written information about the kinds of ritual the high priestess took part in. One of them, the ritual banquet, seems to have developed as a climax to the processions of offering-bearers bringing their produce to the *giguna*. It seems clear the senior man and senior woman of the community – whatever they may have been entitled – conducted a stately drinking ceremony accompanied by music and dancing to celebrate the gathering and display of agricultural produce and stock at spring or harvest time.

Perhaps, among other things, it also commemorated that drinking party Inanna had with Enki that resulted in obtaining the measures from Eridu, celebrated because of the final note of co-operation between the sexes on which the story ended! This scene is commonly shown on early third-millennium artefacts from Mesopotamia, and sometimes in Sumer the ritual entailed imbibing a final drink that led to a journey to the Netherworld, a journey without return, leaving the body behind in 'death' while the spirit moved on. This is the subject of the next chapter.

2

JOURNEY TO THE NETHERWORLD

Role type: Inanna

DRESS AND ACCOUTREMENTS

There is a comparatively large amount of information about Sumerian queens in the third millennium. They occupied high administrative positions of state, including that of high priestess. The difficulty is distinguishing between the two roles. As regards secular functions, Barnamtara of Lagash, for instance, was named *Ama urua*, 'Mother of the State', but was not a priestess. Royal ladies from Umma, Adab, Nippur, Uruk and Mari are named in various texts written in cuneiform on clay tablets (the names have conveniently been collected by Julia Asher-Grève), and often the nature of their households can be reconstructed from inventories.

The only queen who is known to have reigned in her own right, as opposed to being consort of a ruler, was the owner of a brewery, Kubaba of Kish, who established the economic strength of Kish and features in the Sumerian king list as ruling a fabled 100 years. Her name resembles the Iron Age Kybebe, Lydian version of the Goddess Kybele of Anatolia. Barnett believes this means Kubaba was an Anatolian matriarch who developed Kish by establishing the important trade links between Sumer and Anatolia making Kish the first capital of that land after the Flood.

But of all the ladies we could list, the most is known about Puabi of Ur, since the remains of her actual person have been discovered. It is perhaps the most dramatic female burial of all time. Her tomb, Royal Grave no. 800, was disinterred in 1928 by Leonard Woolley and his team of Arabs at Ur and identified for certain as that of 'the Lady Puabi' (the cuneiform was transliterated at the time as 'Shub'ad'). The funeral had taken place around 2500 BC in a tomb built alongside that of a king (Royal Grave no. 789), possibly her consort who had predeceased her. With her was buried a female retinue of 12 women and 14 men, the latter comprising a group of soldiers guarding the entrance, and grooms tending two asses harnessed to a sledge. The funerary rite resembles first-second dynasty Egyptian royal burials of the same period or earlier when, for instance, the first woman Pharaoh, Merytneith, had 118 retainers buried with her at Abydos, as well as her valuable possessions. However, the fact that equids and chariot (possibly a wheat-threshing sledge in Puabi's case) were also buried with her calls to mind exactly similar Scythian burials on the steppes of Asia many centuries later, in the 6C BC.

It is not known whether Puabi was a queen who reigned in her own right, like Kubaba, or whether she was simply a queen because she was the consort of a king. From the nature of her burial, she could also have been a 'divine royal priestess' of the kind listed in Inanna's *Me* in the last chapter. She could have been both if, as in Egypt, being a queen was automatically to qualify as high priestess. Many clues from the objects buried with her suggest she was indeed both, hence it is worth looking more closely at the details.

Turning first to the inscriptional evidence, Puabi is one of the few women named as 'lady' (*nin*) on one of her own cylinder seals (described below). At first glance *nin* may refer only to royal executive status, yet we need not rule out that such high-born ladies were also automatically priestesses. The only other named woman with the prefix 'lady', also on a cylinder seal from Ur, was 'Ninbanda *nin*', described on her seal as the wife (*dam*) of a king of Ur, Mesannepada. We know of five named queens from Ur, of whom four – Ashusikildingir, wife of Akalamdug; Nugig, wife of Mesannepada; Ninbanda, younger wife of Mesannepada; and Gansamannu, wife of Meskiagnun – are presented as wives of kings. The inscription of the fifth, Puabi herself, does not explain her importance as deriving from the male she is attached to.

A further cylinder seal from another grave at Ur, but found loose, so unassociated with a particular body, is inscribed with the name of 'Khekunsig, *nin-dingir* of Pabilsag', Pabilsag being the name of the God she served. Here the word *dingir*, 'divine/holy', has been coupled with *nin*, suggesting this person was without question a priestess, but the addition of *dingir* could mean she was a *high* priestess, able to represent the Goddess in ritual. Scholars are still discussing the full implications of the word *nin*, so minds are not yet made up.

To qualify having an entire retinue buried with her, clad in such riches, signifies in itself that Puabi was of the highest rank, but the ritual overtones of the mass burial go a long way to convincing me that only a high priestess would wish consciously to leave the world in this way, quite apart from having the status to command it. Some male burials had also taken place in this fashion during the same period at Ur, and two other women were buried as sumptuously as Queen Puabi: a woman from Royal Grave 1130, and a 'young princess' in Royal Grave 1068. As we cannot deal with all of them, we may stay with that of Puabi as being the most revealing and complete in the information it gives us of an élite group of women in Sumer at this time. Many other women of lower rank were accorded this special treatment in death at this period: in the vast 'Death Pit' (Royal Grave 1327) which lacked its central burial chamber due to

damage, most of the people buried (68 out of 74 people) were women. Those interested in the full account should read Woolley's excavation report, which demonstrates that archaeological fact is often more extraordinary than imaginative fiction.

When found by Woolley, Puabi lay in a separate chamber. Her low wooden bed had servants crouched around it. Later her skeleton was brought back to the Royal College of Surgeons in London, where many other Ur skeletons were stored – until unfortunately they were destroyed by bombing in World War II. The forensic scientist Arthur Keith studied them, and amongst his notes still at the college is his pronouncement that Puabi had a delicate frame, was about 1.5m tall, with small hands and feet, and that she had died around the age of 40. (Other studies compared the bones of women from burials of the same era at Kish, who were pronounced to be of Semitic type, related to people from East Anatolia/Syria and Palestine, whereas the skeletons of Ur were quite definitely to be classified as 'Sumerian'.)

Laid on the bier of the burial chamber, it was hard to reach Puabi for the stunning wealth of precious objects surrounding her, she herself being gorgeously attired for her last journey. At her shoulder were pinned no less than three lapis lazuli cylinder seals, all depicting the sacred drinking ceremony mentioned at the end of the last chapter. The most important, already referred to, has her name on it, simply reading 'Puabi *nin*', 'Lady Puabi' (Figure 10a). The dumpy lady with a rolled hairdo seated at the top appears to be a portrait of Puabi taking part in a ceremony which includes three seated men, who could be priests, kings, or a combination of both. Her second seal shows three priestesses ministered to by servants while lyre music, singing and feasting proceed around them. The third shows couples drinking through straws from pots and being served with food. It is interesting to note that the cylinder seals of most ladies at Ur at this period would nearly always show such a banqueting scene, often juxtaposed with lions attacking prey, the symbol of Inanna, Goddess of Time, whom they as women mirrored.

We can even more vividly imagine the feasting and dancing that went on at these occasions from a cylinder seal belonging to someone from yet another tomb at Ur, a *dumu-kisal*, which translates as 'child of the court', or 'temple ward'. This person may have been a female lyre player since the owner of the seal was found next to such an instrument, and the scene on the seal itself (Figure 11) shows women like Puabi on one side, and men like the priests on her seal on the other, dancing and singing to a bull-harp being

10a The sealing made by a cylinder seal of Queen Puabi, which includes her name on it in cuneiform; c.2500 BC.

played by a lady, perhaps a portrait of the owner of the seal. Accompanied by two children who greet or hold the harp, the ladies sway to the music, sing and clap their hands.

Inside the main body of Puabi's tomb, all the ladies of her retinue, like Puabi herself, had gold wreaths and combs stuck in their thick wigs, and wore elaborate jewellery. Alongside some of them were found scallop shells still containing the remains of dried greenish eye make-up, which was probably originally deep blue. Some items of the hair decoration stuck into their wigs might have had feathers inserted, and gold toiletry sets for plucking eyebrows, cleaning nails and so on, were attached to their belts like bunches of keys.

From Puabi's figure alone we can gain some idea of the opulence of a third-millennium lady's ritual dress. Her appearance was a lot more complicated than that of the original priestess sitting outside her *giguna* at Uruk.

It was probably deemed appropriate that Puabi be buried in her high priestess garments, kept for high days only. She wore a variety of headbands (Figure 12) fitted over her lumpy hair-do, which possibly included a wig, wrapped with an under-turban onto which the main head-dresses were fixed for comfort. These included a wide gold hair band, a wreath of lapis lazuli beads and carnelian rings with gold ring pendants, and a similar circlet of beads with gold beech leaves and

11 The sealing rolled from a cylinder seal belonging to a 'temple child' found in another Royal Grave (no. 1237) at Ur. Below the ritual drinking ceremony a procession centres on the bull harp; now in the Philadelphia Museum, c.2500 BC.

gold flowers, all topped by a hair comb of gold with three gold flowers inset with lapis lazuli which would have nodded with the movement of her head. At her ears were enormous lunate gold ear-rings, and twisted round her hair were further hair-rings of spirally twisted gold wire (not shown in Figure 12, the reconstruction done by Kate Woolley). Round her neck was a necklace of small gold and lapis lazuli beads with the eight-petalled rosette of Inanna in the middle. Puabi's female retainers had slightly more modest versions of the same parure. Taken off their bodies, and now out of context, the parures

of the Ur ladies can be seen in a newly designed gallery in the British Museum and in the Philadelphia Museum, and most of that of Puabi herself is in the Baghdad Museum in Iraq.

Over her underdress (mostly perished) the whole of Puabi's torso was covered in a cloak made of strings of beads made of gold, silver, lapis lazuli, carnelian and agate (Figure 13), though when excavated the threads had rotted. Around her waist was a belt of beads of tubes of gold, carnelian and lapis in 10 rows of alternating colours, from which

12 Queen Puabi's elaborate parure fastened over a bouffant wig, as reconstructed by C. L. Woolley's wife, Katharine; taken from the excavation report.

13 Queen Puabi's bead cloak and belt as reconstructed after the excavation; taken from the excavation report.

were suspended rings of gold wire, which had probably been sewn onto an undergarment of cloth, since decayed. Against her right upper arm, three huge gold pins, which probably fixed the fabric of her cloak or robe, were still in place. Attached to them were the three lapis lazuli cylinder seals described above, as well as tiny animal amulets.

On her hands were no less than 10 finger rings, all of gold, two inset with lapis. Slung over her hips was yet a further loose belt of clumsy, egg-sized beads of gold, lapis and carnelian, of the ceremonial type brought to the shrine at festivals by offering bearers, as illustrated in the last chapter. Round her knee was a further circlet of beads, possibly a garter!

Of the fabric of her undergarment nothing remains. The only clue we have for its appearance are tiny fragments of bright, ochrous red woollen cloth found on her female retainers. If Puabi, too, wore a bright red undergarment, the blue, gold and orange of her beads would have stood out in startling splendour against it.

The richness of Puabi's appearance corresponds to descriptions given in cuneiform texts of the bride at the sacred marriage, laden with semi-precious stones cascading over a bright *pala* robe, 'the garment of ladyship', fastened by a bead belt. This girdle not only signified royalty, but was also called a 'birth girdle', as it lay over the womb. Looking again at the seals illustrated in the last chapter, possibly it was such a girdle that was offered to the priestess/goddess at the time of the sacred marriage. When not in use, seven little stones, said to be used by the Goddess to predict the fate of mankind, were attached to it. (The later meaning of the girdle to the ancient Greeks is discussed in Chapter 9.)

The shoes worn by the priestess-bride were also symbolic of her stepping into the shoes of the Goddess, and might be left behind on a footstool in the temple (there was no trace of Puabi's shoes, however). On key occasions the priestess would wear a horned head-dress to signify that she had taken on the role of the Goddess, whether in respect of her representing the all-nourishing cow, or referring to the horns of the moon or of Venus. (Puabi's head-dresses, however, have more of a decorative, seasonal flavour.)

Next to Puabi herself, on what had been a side-table or shelf, a spare headband was placed, thought by one writer to have belonged to her male partner in the sacred marriage rite (see

Chapter 3), since plain gold versions of the same type were worn by males in other graves. It was a band of tiny lapis beads with little animals and fruits in gold affixed with gold wire, perhaps representing the four seasons, and certainly appropriate for someone playing the part of the divine lover, Tammuz, embodiment of the year. If her male partner did wear it at their union, it surely referred to the coming and going of the year: it hardly seems to have been made for mere personal adornment, but to convey a meaning about life on Earth.

Lying behind Puabi's bier was a golden bowl and silver drinking-tube – equipment used in the sacred drinking ceremony as depicted on the cylinder seals. More metal straws and bowls, and strainers to keep out the floating pieces of fermenting grain in the primitive brew, were found in the outside chamber, along with stacked jars of clay, silver, copper, gold, lapis lazuli, obsidian, shell and green calcite. It is therefore quite credible that Puabi's cylinder seals give a faithful rendition of Puabi and her retinue taking part in the New Year celebrations (see Chapter 3).

Puabi's second seal (not illustrated) shows a harp of the kind found in her tomb with the skeleton of a lady of her retinue under it, fingers at the place where the strings would have been (Chapters 7 and 8 discusses the connection between priestesses and music).

Of course there is difficulty in deciding how many other of the women with Puabi would rank as priestesses, since we know that high-born ladies in Sumerian towns did have large personal households which involved many different posts of a practical nature, filled by both sexes. Many ladies with complex personal households in turn held an important role in the temple, not always as priestess, but as grand housekeeper, running it along the lines of a house writ large. This administrative post often made them more important than their husbands, but it was evidently not the same as being a priestess, for most of them did not appear to be involved in rituals connected with Gods and Goddesses, other than supervising the collection of offerings at important feasts. Their occupation involved the handling of local produce, as well as exchange goods traded from surrounding countries. Barnamtara, 'Mother of the State', traded not only with neighbouring Sumerian cities, but also with merchants from Elam and Dilmun, and other queens of Lagash dealt with merchants from as far away as India and Yemen. When some of the goods came in the form of tribute, somewhat like status gifts exchanged at Christmas in big business nowadays, the 'grand housekeeper' was the one to whom they were presented. The process of bringing gifts to the lady, seen in its primitive form on the seals of the last chapter, was now inflated to a grand scale. Asher-Grève believes that the borderline between such a woman's personal and state possessions would have become blurred, and we may ponder whether Puabi's riches are her own, or those of her office.

Whoever they were, almost certainly the ladies buried with Puabi died to the strains of harp music, as apparently did others in neighbouring tombs of the period. From a nearby burial, called 'The Great Death Pit', in which no less than 74 people were buried together with three harps and the famous pair of rearing goat statues, we know that each held a cup, either of limestone, shell or silver, from which they must have drunk a potion enabling them to sink into death peacefully, for none showed signs of struggle as they lay in orderly rows.

We do not, though, really know whether Puabi herself chose the moment at which to go down with her court to the Netherworld, the 'Land of No Return'. Nor do we know the reason why this great death ritual, a mass euthanasia, took place. Of course Puabi could have died naturally, upon which her retinue would then have had to die as well, as happened in Early Dynastic Egypt in the same era. In her tomb, only she held a large fluted gold beaker. Was it a purely religious event, or did an impending crisis, seen ahead of time through a combination of psychic foresight and astrological divination, dictate the lesser evil of pre-emption by abandoning earthly existence?

The reason why such wealth was taken underground with these ladies is also unclear. Maybe they were returning to the Earth the minerals taken from it, so that no unworthy usurper could have them. I believe there is a fuller explanation.

Overwhelmingly, the tableau of Puabi's tomb as uncovered by Woolley seems to have been an acting out of the myth of Inanna who visits the Underworld and is trapped there for three days until she is freed by the Gods in exchange for her lover, Tammuz, who has to be sent there as her substitute - we could say as her hostage. The first part of the story bears retelling in full, since at each of the seven stages of her descent Inanna relinquishes an item of her dress, jewellery or make-up, each representing a *Me*. They are so similar to Puabi's own accoutrements that one could make a serious case for Puabi having deliberately dressed herself as Inanna for her own journey to The Other Side. Here is the story as translated by William Sladek of Johns Hopkins University. (The scholarly diacritical marks to indicate breaks and restorations have on the whole been omitted for ease of reading; some reconstructions are indicated by square brackets.)

INANNA'S DESCENT

From the Great Heaven She has set
  her mind on the Great Below.
From the Great Heaven the
  Goddess has set her mind on the
  Great Below.
From the Great Heaven Inanna has
  set her mind on the Great Below.
My mistress has abandoned heaven,
  abandoned earth, and is
  descending to the netherworld.
Inanna has abandoned heaven,
  abandoned earth, and is
  descending to the netherworld.
She abandoned *en*-ship, abandoned
  lagar-ship, and is descending to
  the netherworld.
She abandoned her temple in
  Uruk, the House of Heaven (E-
  Anna), and is descending to the
  netherworld.
She abandoned her temple in Bad-
  Tibira, the E-Mushkalamma, and
  is descending to the netherworld.
She abandoned her temple in
  Zabalam, the Giguna, and is
descending to the netherworld.
She abandoned her temple in Adab,
  the E-Sharra, and is descending
  to the netherworld.
She abandoned her temple in
  Nippur, the Baradurgarra, and is
  descending to the netherworld.
She abandoned her temple in
  Kish, the Hursagkalamma, and
  is descending to the
  netherworld.
She abandoned her temple in
  Akkad, the E-Ulmash, and is
  descending to the netherworld.
She took the Seven *Me*.
She collected the *Me* and grasped
  them in her hand.
With all her *Me* in her possession,
  she went on her way.

She put a turban, the pure head-
  dress, on her head.
She took a wig for her forehead.
She hung small lapis lazuli beads
  from her neck.
She placed twin egg-shaped beads
  on her breast.
She covered her body with a *pala*
  dress, the garment of ladyship.
She put mascara, which is called
  'Let a man come, let him come',
  on her eyes.
She pulled the pectoral, which is
  called 'Come man, come' over
  her breast [see Figure 14].
She placed a golden ring on her
  hand.
She held the lapis lazuli
  measuring rod and measuring
  line in her hand.

Inanna travelled towards the
  netherworld,
Her vizier, Ninshubur, travelling
  behind her.
Inanna the pure said to Ninshubur:
  'Come my faithful vizier, of my
    temple E-Anna:

'My vizier who speaks consoling
words,
'My hero [sic] who speaks
trustworthy words:
I am going to give you
instructions, my instructions
that must be followed.
I am going to say something to
you, which must be observed:
When I have descended to the
netherworld,
And when I have arrived in the
netherworld,
Make a lament for me in my
ruined temples.
Beat the drum for me in the
sanctuary.
Make the rounds of the temples
of the gods for me.
Scratch at your buttocks, the
private place.
Like a pauper, clothe yourself in
a single garment,
And all alone set your foot in the
E-Kur, the temple of Enlil.
When you have entered the E-
Kur, the temple of Enlil,
Lament before Enlil, God of the
Atmosphere:
  "Father Enlil, don't let anyone
  subjugate your daughter in
  the netherworld.
  Don't let your precious metal
  be alloyed there with the dirt
  of the netherworld.
  Don't let your precious lapis
  lazuli be split there with the
  mason's stone.
  Don't let your boxwood be
  chopped up there with the
  carpenter's lumber.
  Don't let young lady Inanna be
  subjugated in the
  netherworld!"

When Enlil does not help you in
this matter, go to Ur.

In Ur, when you have entered the
temple called the House of the
Well Being of the Land, the E-
Kishnugal, temple of Nanna,
Lament before Nanna,
Moon-God:
  "Father Nanna, don't let
  anyone subjugate your
  daughter in the netherworld.
  Don't let your precious metal
  be alloyed there with the dirt
  of the netherworld.
  Don't let your precious lapis
  lazuli be split there with the
  mason's stone.
  Don't let your boxwood be
  chopped up there with the
  carpenter's lumber.
  Don't let young lady Inanna be
  subjugated in the
  netherworld!"

And if Nanna does not help you
in this matter, go to Eridu.
In Eridu, when you have entered
the temple of Enki,
Lament before Enki, God of the
Sweet Waters:
  "Father Enki, don't let anyone
  subjugate your daughter in
  the netherworld.

*14 A priestess's gold
pectoral - in the fullest
sense of the word -
found at Susa, Iran;
now in the Louvre,
c.1500 BC.*

Don't let your precious metal
be alloyed there with the dirt
of the netherworld.
Don't let your precious lapis
lazuli be split there with the
mason's stone.
Don't let your boxwood be
chopped up there with the
carpenter's lumber.
Don't let young lady Inanna be
subjugated in the
netherworld!"
Father Enki, the Lord of great
Wisdom
Knows about the life-giving plant
and the life-giving water.
He is the one who will restore
me to life.'

When Inanna travelled on towards
the netherworld,
Her vizier Ninshubur travelled on
behind her,
So she said to her vizier,
Ninshubur,
'Go now, my Ninshubur, and obey
orders.
Don't neglect the orders that I gave
you.'

When Inanna arrived at the palace
Ganzir,
She pushed aggressively on the
door of the netherworld.
She shouted aggressively at the gate
of the netherworld.
'Open up, doorman, open up!
Open up, Neti, open up: I am all
alone and I want to come in!'
Neti, the chief doorman of the
netherworld,
Answered Inanna the pure:
'Who are you?'
'I am Inanna, and I am going to
the east.'
'If you are Inanna and you are
going to the east,

Why have you travelled to the
Land of No Return?
What inclination has led you to
take the road from which no
traveller returns?'
Inanna the pure answered him:
'Gugalanna, the husband of my
elder sister,
Ereshkigal, has died . . . [I have
come]
To see his funeral rites,
And to take part in his lavish
wake . . .that is why.'
Neti, the chief doorman of the
netherworld,
Answered Inanna the pure:
'Stay here, Inanna: I will speak to
my mistress.
I will speak to my mistress
Ereshkigal, and I will tell her
what you said.'

Neti, the chief doorman of the
netherworld,
Entered the house of his mistress
Ereshkigal and said to her:
'My lady, there is a lone girl
[outside].
It is Inanna, your sister, and she
has arrived at the palace
Ganzir.
She pushed aggressively on the
door of the netherworld.
She shouted aggressively at the
gate of the netherworld.
She has abandoned her temple
E-Anna and has descended to
the netherworld.
She has taken the seven *Me*.
She has collected the *Me* and
grasped them in her hand.
She has come with all her *Me* in
her possession.

She has put a turban, the pure
head-dress, on her head.
She has taken a wig for her
forehead.

She has hung small lapis lazuli
beads from her neck.
She has placed twin egg-shaped
beads on her breast.
She has covered her body with a
pala dress, the garment of
ladyship.
She has placed mascara which is
called "Let a man come" on
her eyes.
She has pulled the pectoral which
is called "Come man, come"
over her breast.
She has placed a golden ring on
her hand.
She is holding the lapis lazuli
measuring rod and measuring
line in her hand.'

When she heard this, Ereshkigal
slapped the side of her thigh.
She bit her lip, she . . .
She said to Neti, her chief
doorman:
'Come, Neti, my chief doorman
of the netherworld.
Don't fail to do what I am going
to tell you.
Let all the seven gates of the
netherworld be bolted.
Then let each door of the palace
Ganzir be opened separately.
And as for her: after she enters,
When she has been subjugated
and her clothes stripped off,
they will be [carried away].'

Neti, the chief doorman of the
netherworld,
Was attentive to the instructions of
his mistress.
He bolted the seven gates of the
netherworld.
And then he opened each of the
doors of the palace Ganzir
separately.
He said to Inanna the pure:
'Come on, Inanna, and enter.'

And when Inanna entered,
The turban, the pure head-
dress, was removed from her
head.
'What's going on here?'
'Be satisfied Inanna! The *Me* of
the netherworld are being
fulfilled.
Inanna, you must not open your
mouth against the sacred
customs of the netherworld.'

When she entered the second gate,
The small lapis lazuli beads
were removed from her neck.
'What's going on here?'
'Be satisfied Inanna! The *Me* of
the netherworld are being
fulfilled.
Inanna, you must not open your
mouth against the sacred
customs of the netherworld.'

When she entered the third gate,
The twin egg-shaped beads
were removed from her
breast.
'What's going on here?'
'Be satisfied Inanna! The *Me* of
the netherworld are being
fulfilled.
Inanna, you must not open your
mouth against the sacred
customs of the netherworld.'

When she entered the fourth gate,
The pectoral which was called
'Come man, come' was
removed from her breast.
'What's going on here?'
'Be satisfied Inanna! The *Me* of
the netherworld are being
fulfilled.
Inanna, you must not open your
mouth against the sacred
customs of the netherworld.'

When she entered the fifth gate,
The gold ring was removed
from her hand.
'What's going on here?'
'Be satisfied Inanna! The *Me* of
the netherworld are being
fulfilled.
Inanna, you must not open your
mouth against the sacred
customs of the netherworld.'

When she entered the sixth gate,
The lapis lazuli measuring rod
and measuring line were
removed from her hand.
'What's going on here?'
'Be satisfied Inanna! The *Me* of
the netherworld are being
fulfilled.
Inanna, you must not open your
mouth against the sacred
customs of the netherworld.'

When she entered the seventh gate,
The *pala* dress, the garment of
ladyship, was removed from
her body.
'What's going on here?'
'Be satisfied Inanna! The *Me* of
the netherworld are being
fulfilled.
Inanna, you must not open your
mouth against the sacred
customs of the netherworld.'

When Inanna had been subjugated,
the garments that had been
removed were carried away.
Then her sister, Ereshkigal
(Goddess of the Netherworld)
rose from her throne.
And Inanna took her seat on her
sister's throne.
The Anunnaki, the seven judges of
the netherworld, gave their
judgement against her:
They looked at her with the look
of death.

They spoke to her with the speech
of anger.
They shouted at her with the shout
of guilt.

The afflicted woman was turned
into a corpse.
And the corpse was hung on a
hook.

After three days and three nights
had passed,
Her vizier, Ninshubur,
Carried out the instructions of her
mistress.
She made a lament for her in her
abandoned temples.
She beat the drum for her in the
sanctuaries.
She made the rounds of the
temples of the Gods.

We leave Inanna stranded in the
Underworld, the world of the
psyche, and will make the return
journey with her, via a later,
Babylonian version of the story, in
Chapter 5. For already there is
enough food for thought in the
descent alone, both in
considering Inanna/Puabi's
adornment, and the symbolism of
the descent of Inanna in its
application to priesthood.

There is no doubt that Inanna
and Puabi wore precious
materials because their true
power is their reflection of
spiritual states, though others of
lower discernment would merely
regard them as material wealth.
We should not underestimate the
Sumerians' metaphysical sense:

they had a unique ability to discern physical materials as spirit in concrete form. In the story above Inanna is described as 'precious metal', a 'block of lapis lazuli', and the rarest of woods, 'boxwood'. That is why those substances were used in a religious context.

A late text from Uruk translated by Ronald Sack of North Carolina State University describes the problems of repairing the jewellery which festooned the divine image of Inanna in the temple: 'two golden breast ornaments', 'two golden wires removed from cylinder seals', seven lapis lazuli rings . . . fastened with two golden wires', '86 golden flowers and golden *tenshu* ornaments belonging to the *kusitu* garment of Nana . . . 1176 golden stars, golden rosettes and golden ornaments for the *kusitu* garment belonging to Nana . . .' Her high priestess is therefore likely to have dressed in the same mode.

A further text exists in which the Sumerians explicitly equate gold with the sun and silver with the moon, a symbolism retained by civilizations thereafter, even in the earliest coinage of Archaic Greece in the 6C BC. In Sumerian mythology, the God Ninurta ascribes to metals and stones magical properties. Lapis lazuli especially was understood as an

entirely sacred substance, representing divine power, whatever shape it was carved in, whether necklace beads or the curling beard of the Bull of Heaven attached to a harp. The myth of the descent clearly equates the substance, appearance and position of the separate items of Inanna's dress with the most important of the *Me* over which she had charge.

❧

Similarly for today, the aspiring priestess's dress, jewellery and make-up should act as doors to and from the realms beyond physical existence. What in fact is conveyed through your own dress, make-up and jewellery at the moment? Do they radiate higher realities, or do they simply serve to glorify yourself? As you dress for everyday or special events, carefully consider what you are trying to say about your place in the universe to others who inevitably look at you. Losing the cosmic connection results in mere dressing up.

In trying to make that slight shift where you make each area of the body once more open up to a cosmic realm at the place where it manifests in the human microcosm, it helps to make a list of the seven main zones as related to yourself, and reassess what you are doing with each of them. Often their importance is only understood if it is extricated from an unhelpful entanglement with another centre, or is temporarily stopped. One of the easiest ways of analysing them could be to equate each of the gates Inanna passed through with the relevant chakra in your own body. As there are many books on the subject, I will only sketch their separate functions, as a reminder:

1. The root chakra lies at the base of the spine, which connects with Universal Existence itself. Women are gifted at using it by simply Being There; they do not have to prove their existence by Doing. Obviously this is a difficult chakra to actually mark and I would choose the garment as a whole, 'the *pala* garment of ladyship' to indicate the root chakra.

2. The sex chakra, behind the pubic region, is the physical manifestation of the first split in the *meta*physical universe between maleness and femaleness. In earthly existence it provides a fast, but brief, means of cosmic connection, unless linked with the other chakras all in working order. Many people exploring the chakras tend, erroneously, to colour the other chakras with sex chakra characteristics. This indicates the need to re-establish the integral territory of each zone. The sex chakra is not a one to blatantly emphasize unless you want to draw attention to it in its sole right. For women breasts are really part of the pubic chakra if sexuality is emphasized. ('Let a man come, let him come!')

3. The navel chakra just beneath the rib cage is at a major nerve bunch of the body that services the transformation of breath. It was beautifully decorated in Elizabethan dress and Hindu sculpture, which could give some ideas. Breath is life, and enables the bearer to be centred, co-ordinated, in the service of the entire chakra tree. It is the golden mean between the upper four and lower two chakras and is therefore of crucial importance in binding together the Heaven and Earth halves of the body, through breath.

4. The heart chakra, at the level of the breasts, when properly used radiates love and the idea of nutrition, not only personally given, but on behalf of the Goddess's Universal Love and Inner Connectedness. It is meant to give, not take: watch yourself in the way you use it, and monitor the direction of the current. A brooch or pendant are good markers for it, though some versions of the Goddess figure mark the chest area with two red straps making a saltire cross.

5. The throat chakra is an organic lyre, potent vehicle of the speech and sacred song of the Universe. What do you use your voice for at the moment? Does your neck chain or throat jewel reflect the way you use your

voice, or the way you would like to start using it?

6. The forehead chakra, often marked in Renaissance portraits by a drop pearl and by Hindus with a red spot, refers to intelligence and the brain that transmits it. How well does your mind link to the laws of life and co-operate with the throat and heart chakras in passing them on? Does it spend its time thinking of trivialities and passing fancies? Interestingly, in the myth of the descent, it is the eyes made up with mascara which are to mark the forehead chakra, which is traditionally two-petalled.

7. The crown chakra, the top area of the head, is the area through which multi-connection is made with the Spirit, God and Goddess, Cosmic Principles. Only those who have truly earned a crown should wear one; meanwhile a lesser form of headgear, such as a headband, will indicate how far this chakra has opened.

An enormous amount of preliminary work on yourself can be done by analysing what you are doing with your chakras – how they are being misused, or disconnected from co-operation with the others. I am sure each person can work this out for themselves, given the above main guidelines; the thing is that it can be made fun through the principle of marking them appropriately for your particular case, and laughing at yourself for the way they have sometimes become wrongly wired to each other!

Ask yourself which chakras are running you, and how you would ideally like them to run. If chakra two features too strongly, give up using it for a year; if chakra seven is living in a world of its own, give that one up for a while and give attention to the others – then you can come back to seven and link it up with the rest of the tree. There are endless combinations of affirmation and renunciation you can undertake to get the whole system recircuited. In fact the analogy of the wiring of a house or a circuit board can give some helpful clues about interconnection and reconnection – as well as insulation.

Overall, for a priestess to work effectively, these chakras have first to be freed from operating only in the service of the ego, and reactivated at a higher frequency in the service of cosmic law. Dress, jewellery and make-up are used simply to remind us and others of these gateways to the invisible realms, marking the position of the chakras on the outer surface of the body, and quietly radiating their inner qualities for those able to understand, to the world outside.

Whether Puabi intended personally to enact the myth of Inanna's descent we will never know for certain, but the symbolic nature of her dress overpowers any sense that she was simply a plutocrat showing off her wealth. We, too, can make the journey inwards into the depths of the psyche, inspecting and rehabilitating each chakra as regards its former service to the ego. We learn, on completing the descent, that our identity is that of a mere hunk of meat when bereft of our link with these centres. The myth shows the divine powers (Ereshkigal and her strange retinue of psychic entities in the Netherworld) ensure no-one is able to operate with full powers until the descent has been completed and a thorough inspection of the psyche made. And if you do not undertake it willingly, the events of life itself will force you to do so, changing the order of prominence of the chakras, forcing you, perhaps, to use your mind more, or your heart more, and so on. Everyone has their own unique story, and I am sure many books will be written in the next decade, describing the wonders of personal descents and reascents!

Every chakra rightly used is a virtue at work - wrongly used,

each turns to vice. The Journey to the Netherworld is summarized on a third-millennium drawing found on a piece of shell from Mari, where a female figure is swinging on, or off, her goatskin cloak (Figure 15). Because of the horned head-dress it is pretty certainly a cipher for Inanna's descent to the Underworld, summarized by the Tammuzian goatskin robe of the high priestess. The shedding of layers is what strip-tease is really about, and this image so well summarizes the journey of the priestess that it could be adopted as the logo for the emerging Aquarian priesthood, along with Inanna's flower.

Another intriguing fact of the spiritual and yet so physical alchemy that has to be wrought is that the solitary inner journey is in itself not enough. In the myth Tammuz, Inanna's partner, provides the balance to the whole turn of events. The process of transformation is only fixed by the union of the male and female who both make the journey alternately for each other's sake. Such a counter-balance can be accomplished by several means: its Greek version (see Chapter 10), as celebrated at spring and autumn at the Mysteries of Eleusis, commemorated Kore/Persephone's descent to Hades whence her mother,

15 Drawing scratched on a small shell plaque which summarizes the stripping and reclothing of Ishtar/Inanna during her descent to the Netherworld, found at Mari in the temple of Ishtar; now in the Louvre, c.2500 BC.

Demeter, balanced Persephone's Underworld husband, Pluto, by requesting Kore's return to upper Earth every half year. This return was secured by other means in ancient Mesopotamia, described in the next chapter.

AKKAD TO LAGASH

TIGRIS

3

UNION WITH THE COSMOS

Role type: Athtar

THE SACRED MARRIAGE

In the British newspaper *The Independent* in February 1991 a story appeared about the dedication of a young Hindu girl as shaktic priestess (*devadāsī*) – though sadly in a corrupt form. Irawa was sold by her parents to a priest, was bathed in a pool, dressed in leaves and led in procession to the temple of the Goddess. How reminiscent of the description of Ishtar, the Babylonian Inanna, as bride of Tammuz in the form of a cedar tree! In Mesopotamian ritual the priestess representing her would be entwined with cedar sprays, her royal bridegroom offering her further greenery. He himself is described in a cuneiform text as wearing a green tiara and a garment studded with ears of corn.

People lining the streets to the temple threw clouds of turmeric at the Hindu maiden, while devotees of the Goddess dragged themselves along the street behind her in self-abasement. Once inside the temple, Irawa had to swear an oath to have sex (one could not call it by any more exalted name) with any man chosen by the priest – who usually turns out to be the priest himself – and any rich men in the village who would give donations to the temple. Her role as a *devadāsī*, servant of the Goddess, was clearly a bastardized version of that formerly exalted role, and luckily in this case she was extricated from this situation by the civil authorities. Yet even in third-millennium Mesopotamia priests betrayed their trust in their treatment of priestesses, for two people I know who have past-life recall of temple life know they were used by senior priests for their own gratification rather than in the service of the

Gods. There is a difference between detached, ritual sex and personal sex, and in the temple context the latter has no place.

A more heartening account of present practice was told to me by a man who was in India during World War II. A young colleague of his decided to visit the *devadāsīs* of the local village temple. Great care was taken by the leading old lady in charge of them to match him to someone appropriate. The experience throughout was dignified, and he came away filled with holy exaltation. The use of the ultimate female energy (the *shakti*), channelled through the sexual act, was properly done. Marglin's book (see Bibliography) gives a full account of the lives of the few remaining *devadāsīs* of Pūri in modern times, giving many insights into how *naditu* priestesses must have lived in the ancient world. Temple prostitution (which is what it has usually become) is now banned by law in India, but continues illegally, as in the case of Irawa. Despite its abuse, priests and farmers genuinely retain the age-old belief that the Goddess must be appeased if rain is to fall, crops to grow, and sons be born.

This was the underlying idea behind the rite in the third millennium, according to the cuneiform records from Mesopotamia, which provide plentiful references to the sacred marriage throughout its history. We therefore have to be more wary about calling it 'temple prostitution' in that era, unless it really was just that. Probably by the end of the first millennium in the ancient Near East, it may sometimes have deserved that description. The present-day case of Irawa shows that if it did become prostitution it was far from being the fault of the woman involved, but rather of those who had power over her life.

Sexual union as a religious rite is quite opposite to the role of the priestess who is worshipped as the incarnation of the Goddess Power or *Shakti* within the inner sanctum. She remains forever identified with the Absolute Shakti and is therefore virginal. This type of shaktic priestess, then, was a naked girl of perfect form and health to whom offerings were made. Jennings wrote that:

It is a singular fact that upon this adoration of the *Shakti* seen throughout nature hinges the whole strength of the Hindu faith . . . all the principal ceremonies culminate in the worship of *Shakti*, or Power, and require for that purpose the presence of a young and beautiful girl as the living representative of the Goddess. The woman thus worshipped is ever after treated as a nun and subsequently supported by alms.

Similarly in Katmandu, Powell this century described a temple of the Living Goddess:

... wherein resides a young and virginal girl of Brahmin caste, enshrined for a set time so that she can be worshipped in the flesh through offerings of flowers, butter and money. At a certain festival she is brought forth again to the door of the temple where flower petals drop from her open hands ... After this ceremony she is replaced by a new maiden and steps out into the world again to lead an ordinary life.

An article in the British newspaper *The Independent* of 22 March 1992 describes some of the young girls who in recent years have continued to fulfil this role.

In Tibet, travellers have described the incarnation of the Dorje Phagmo, or Thunderbolt Sow, as incarnated by successive young girls, much as the Dalai Lama is incarnated by successive young boys, recognized by monks at an early age by tell-tale signs. The Dorje Phagmo embodies the Goddess for life.

During the third millennium Sumer and western India were in close trading contact by land and sea, as was mentioned briefly in the last chapter, and it is fascinating that, as with so much else in India, an ancient practice such as shaktic priestesshood should survive to this day. (In fact any priest or priestess entering the holy of holies took off all clothes as a token of their returning symbolically to the Unmanifest.) Such practices can be traced in some measure even in Judaism: the Tora mentions once the marriage between Jahweh and the Shekinah (the Holy, Silent Peace), and in another rare mention from a papyrus found at Elephantine, Jehovah is understood as the moon uniting with his consort, the sun, at the time of the neomenia, or new moon. As Judaism grew away from its Sumerian roots, however, all aspects of Goddess worship were gradually intellectualized as it focused on the One God.

The act of sexual union, or its opposite, the contemplation of its potentiality in virgin embodiment, are highly life-enhancing rituals which contain in them the seeds of spiritual downfall: promiscuity and child pornography being their respective betrayals. Sexual rites are now taboo in our contemporary mainstream religions because they are so open to abuse – whether by the men involved, or by the women, if they lose, or are made to lose, their connection with the Great Shakti, the Goddess Power. If the sex trigger becomes disconnected from the rest of the chakra tree described at the end of the last chapter (the interconnection signified by a snake, Figure 16), the fall from Eden inevitably occurs. This is one inner meaning behind the image of the temptation of Adam and Eve standing on either side of the Tree entwined by the snake, and why ever since its disconnection sex has been the object of so much mutual distrust and abuse within religious doctrine and practice, quite apart from everyday life.

This fact explains why the rite of sexual union had to disappear as human history wore on into the monotheistic era and the Last Days of the Piscean era, to which doom-filled prophecies refer as 'the End of the World'. Hopefully in the transition to a new era, the time has come round for it to be put back in its rightful place in the ladder of heavenly connections, since its removal from religion, as well as misunderstandings about maleness and femaleness at all levels of life, have led to endless complications and contortions in theology, whichever monotheism or philosophy is concerned.

These have created a split between matters of the spirit and matters of the flesh, or confused them with each other, which is just as bad, and have increased conflict as the needs of either sex (physically, mentally and metaphysically) are ignored, disrespected or caricatured. Before monotheism these disjunctions seem not to have occurred quite so seriously.

As far as monotheism is concerned, the sacred marriage is understood as a marriage of abstract qualities, of Jesus to Mary in Heaven, or of human soul to soul or mind to mind. These are valid modes of union too, but are themselves operating as self-sufficient worlds detached from the whole chakra tree. Why is the physical act itself so important and so holy for the proper activity of the other centres, and *vice versa*? The attitudes of ancient Mesopotamia have much to tell us.

Every New Year, throughout ancient Mesopotamia's history, the eleven-day interval, or intercalary period, between the lunar and solar cycles at the conclusion of the year, was marked by a great festival. Only fragmentary accounts survive of the events that happened to mark it. Many priestly purification rituals took place at midnight or

16 Prehistoric clay sealing of the sacred marriage; found in the temple precinct of Tepe Gawra, Kurdistan, now in the Philadelphia Museum, c.3300 BC.

dawn, with prayers directed to the stars or rising sun. Libations, songs and food offerings reached a crescendo, and the temple was cleansed ready for the following year. The king himself had to undergo a strange ceremony of self-abasement before the statues of the Gods in the temple, supervised by the priests. The priests would make a full recitation of the epic poem describing the Creation of the World at the beginning of Time (the Book of Genesis is a related version of that account). There were athletic games which included wrestling matches. Statues of Gods were brought from outlying temples in processions to visit those of Goddesses in central temples where they were placed side by side for a numinous sacred

marriage. A procession of the leading men and women of the main cities, of Assur, Babylon or Uruk depending on the period, walked along the main street from the main temple to a festival temple outside the main city gate. Here the horoscope of the whole country for the following year was made known by the astronomer priests (known as the Tablets of Destiny). To seal the efficacy of the entire festival, the king in the neo-Babylonian period 'shook the hand of the God', thus receiving blessing on behalf of the kingdom for the coming year.

From fragmentary sources it has been pieced together that at some point during all these solemn events not only were the statues of a God and a Goddess brought together, but also for reasons of sympathetic magic an

17 From Babylon in the time of Nebuchadnezzar, glazed tiles show the Lions of the Great Goddess Ishtar padding along the processional way to the Ishtar Gate, through which the New Year procession would have passed; now in the Berlin Museum, 605-562 BC.

earthly enactment of their union took place between the king as the God and the queen/priestess as the Goddess, in the inner sanctum of the main temple, expressly for the good of the kingdom. Feasting was the order of the day before and after this climactic ritual, as a result of whose consummation a propitiously wealthy New Year would be ensured.

Many scholars have written about the sacred marriage rite in learned articles, and most describe it as 'of the utmost importance, if not the essential and pivotal element of Babylonian religion' (E. D. van Buren). The male incarnated the divine maleness, and the divine femaleness was embodied in the high priestess, who was often also the queen. If the ritual was repeated simultaneously in temples throughout the country, priests and priestesses of lower rank would take the place of king and queen, playing the part of God and Goddess worshipped in those particular temples. Thus the marriage was represented, to take but a few examples, of Nanna and Ningal (the Moon God and his consort) at Ur, of Enlil and Ninlil (the Atmosphere God and his consort) at Nippur, of Inanna and Tammuz (Queen of Heaven and Shepherd of the Earth) at Uruk, and so on.

Through their act of union – which was not first and foremost a matter of personal passion – by analogy the whole land and its flocks, herds and tribes of people would be set into union, to bring forth fruit. As van Buren says, 'The perfect accomplishment of the ritual was so important for the welfare of the whole people that everything was done . . . to bring about the desired results.'

Since the human act itself was performed in private in the inner sanctum of the temple, it constituted a sacred mystery, and that is what it really still is, personally or ritually. It was understood as presided over by the Scorpion Goddess of Nuptial Consummation, Ishkhara, more commonly known as Shara, and hence on some cylinder seals referring to the sacred marriage, a scorpion is shown near, or under, the bed. Probably the name 'Shara' is a variant of the name 'Ishtar', as in Semitic words 'I' at the beginning, plus a 'ta' syllable, can be inserted into the main root consonants to reinforce the key meaning. 'Ishtar' itself is thought to be related to words meaning 'tree' (*gish*) and 'Decider of Fate' (*namtar*). 'Ishkhara' is probably a variant on the name 'Ishtara', or 'Ishtar' with the feminine ending pronounced.

An interesting occurrence of

the scorpion under the bed comes on a Mesopotamian seal showing the bride awaiting the ceremony before her partner appears (Figure 18). Looking closely, it is unusual to see a bull head at the end of the bed as well as the bull legs we already know indicate a sacred action in the presence of the Sky God. The moon and his daughter Innana/Ishtar (the eight-pointed star of Venus) are shown in the sky above.

The upper register of the seal shows lions attacking prey, symbolic of the Great Goddess, held apart by a hero, provisionally identified by experts as Gilgamesh, an oriental forerunner of Hercules and/or Apollo. Because the lady who owned the seal has a scene on the lower register referring to the sacred marriage, it could be inferred that it belonged to a person who took part in the ceremony herself, in honour of the Great Goddess.

The preliminaries to the full marriage ceremony can be pieced together from different sources, both written and pictorial, albeit into a patchwork from very different periods and places in Mesopotamia. The consort might make a ceremonial journey to his bride by boat decorated with branches in leaf if it was a riverine and canal district, as illustrated in the scene in Chapter 1, or by cart decorated with lapis lazuli and gold if he were coming by land (the sledge in Puabi's tomb has sometimes been interpreted as such a vehicle). These ceremonial vehicles were often kept in the temples when not in use.

18 On a cylinder seal the bride is shown preparing for the sacred marriage (indicated by the scorpion underneath the bull-headed and footed bed), attended by her retinue; photo courtesy of The Oriental Institute of the University of Chicago, c.2400 BC.

The bridegroom would bring gifts with him, such as a girdle of strung stones, or an animal. It is said a lion cub and a panther cub were placed over the temple door at Lagash to celebrate the marriage of the God Ningirsu (God of Thunder, similar to Jupiter), with the Goddess Baba. Sometimes in Mesopotamian art the couple are shown sitting opposite each other at the drinking ceremony, with the gifts draped on a stand between them.

Other sources describe the bride's preparations. She would bathe in the river, immersing herself completely to purify herself and restore her virginity if already given. She would massage her skin with cedar oil and dress in her *pala* robe, liberally adorned with precious metals and stones, like Puabi's attire. It was kept in place by a girdle, and the ritual of unfastening the girdle is sometimes mentioned. (It is interesting to compare the similar preparation of brides in the Middle East or India who are as a matter of tradition laden with ornamentation, even if poor.) Such jewellery probably replaced a simpler dress from earlier days that consisted simply of vegetation: there is an account of a bride of Ishtar, successor of Inanna, looking like a cedar tree with sprays of cedar woven into her hair and dress. Ishtar was also

represented by the date-palm. There are mentions of the bridegroom wearing a green tiara, and on one occasion of wearing a garment of ears of corn - Ishtar's consort, Tammuz, being particularly associated with the harvested wheat. A hymn describing one of the earliest unions of a God and Goddess describes them as the Holy Corn and the Holy Palm.

The feast connected with the sacred marriage ceremony was a wedding feast, and intended to re-enact the gathering of all the Gods to witness the sealing of the fate of the entire country - in other words, as the zodiac as a whole is contemplated and the horoscope cast for the year ahead, so human representatives of the main departments of earthly life gather once a year for an overall review. Taking the analogy to a conclusion, the marriage of Heaven and Earth is furthered by the sacred marriage ceremony, by earthing the stellar and planetary powers onto the human plane.

As regards the detail of the actual sacred marriage ritual, it is known that after the feast the couple would be led in procession to the doorway of the *giguna* ('the holy abode of joy and gladness') guarded by a priest, who monitored the ritual (Figure 19). If the ritual took place at a

19 The sacred marriage, with Scorpion Goddess Shara under the bed, takes place after eating and drinking, while an officiating priest monitors the ritual; traced from a cylinder seal found in the houses surrounding the temple of Shara at Tell Asmar in Iraq, now in the Iraq Museum, c.2900–2850 BC.

ziggurat, then the ceremony took place in its top-most chamber. It is said the *giguna* was usually built of cedar and adorned with choice stones and metals, and was described as 'awe-inspiring' and a 'pure and dark, secret place upon which none might look'. At other times it appears the *giguna* may have been a chamber inside the ziggurat at its very base, as at Ur, when it would, according to Mesopotamian cosmology, have been likened to a cave inside a mountain. This cave was understood as the doorway to the Netherworld, as is any tomb.

I need not labour the connections so often made between love and death as the supreme moments of consummation that meet at extremes. The Goddess Ninhursag presided both over the Holy Mountain/Ziggurat/Tomb, and over the products of the womb, being the Goddess of Childbirth. A famous cylinder seal in the Royal Ontario Museum shows her seated on the Mountain that contains her Cave, receiving the homage of a row of priestesses. In Sumerian mythology the God Enlil in the form of a bull is described as inserting his penis into the Mountain in order to bring about the gushing and sprouting of all water sources and vegetation. I therefore like to

think of this seal as particularly appropriate for priestesses, as it celebrates the Goddess of the Holy Womb, the Sacred Inner Space which the world needs to contain it. In Roman Catholic art the Virgin Mary is sometimes shown with a bleeding heart, which I think is a euphemism for her Womb.

References are also made to another chamber, the *guenna*, which was said to be near the king's throne room, and which would also have been next to the nuptial chamber. This seems to have been an ante-room where music was played, or it could have been the throne room itself. In a later period the God Marduk at Babylon had both throne and bed in the same chamber. Descriptions vary, but there is a general picture that the priest-king was received by his divine bride (Figure 20 shows an ordinary couple at the moment of meeting), taken into the *guenna* and seated upon the throne, facing the priestess as Goddess seated on her throne, since some texts refer to two thrones with two footstools. Ishtar's most famous human lover in sacred marriage was the hero Gilgamesh, and when he presented himself to her he is described as having first to receive from her a favourable oracle regarding his future rulership before being allowed to take his place on his throne and proceed with the ceremony.

Perhaps it was as they sat facing each other that the couple took a drink that had a psychotropic effect. The tiny pictures on cylinder seals often show the pair raising their goblets while servants and musicians minister to them (see previous chapter). They may have eaten, since texts mention that the food and drink were a foretaste of the abundance that would result from their happy union; a pot with straws and a row or two of cakes are often depicted next to the marriage bed on the cylinder seals.

The marriage bed itself is described as made of 'choice wood, palm-wood, or gold, silver and costly stones' and was placed in the nuptial chamber, or *giguna*. This was originally conceived as a bower of plaited sprays of greenery, deriving from the primitive reed hut in which the original divine couple first joined. The *giguna* has already been dwelt on in Chapter 1, and clearly the fact that the holy of holies is the same as the nuptial chamber is charged with significance. The earthly act of consummation is simply a symbol of the entry of Heaven (all that Spirit holds in itself as seeds) into the physical world, symbolized by the cave

inside the mountain. Seen in cosmic terms, the marriage of Heaven and Earth is perhaps best known from Egyptian art (Figure 21), where Heaven is represented by Nut, the Sky Goddess arching over Geb the Earth God. But cruder versions of this idea appeared in Mesopotamian art long before, as for example on a stamp seal from the Gulf, where Sumerians traded (Figure 22). The Mesopotamian rendition survives in Hindu icons of Kali squatting

20 Perhaps an ordinary couple, or the priestess and royal consort meeting at the beginning of the sacred marriage ceremony outside the nuptial chamber; found at Lagash, Iraq, now in the Louvre, c.2000 BC.

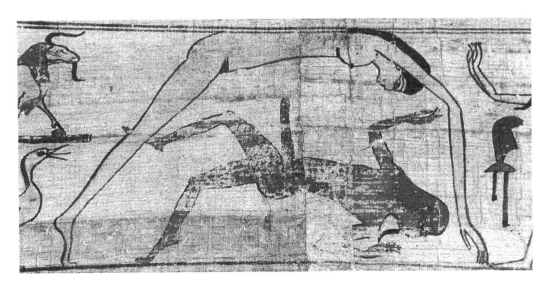

21 Nut, the Sky
Goddess, arches over
Geb, God of the Earth,
a cosmic marriage
scene repeated on
many Egyptian
papyri; this is one of
several in the British
Museum.

22 On a stamp sealing, the sacred
marriage is shown with the drinking
ceremony as a cosmic event with a star to
mark the beginning of the year; found on
the island of Bahrein, now in the Bahrein
Museum, c.2000 BC.

over a male corpse, implying that
the alternation between death
and life, as in the entire Ishtar-
Tammuz story cycle, is the crux
of the matter.

There are many texts which
describe the joy of the sacred
marriage and Kramer's book on
the subject is perhaps the best
anthology of contemporary
poems and hymns. These include
some by kings of Ur later than
the time of Puabi and her
consort, at the end of the third
millennium. They refer constantly
to their role as divine consort of
Inanna/Ishtar, daughter of Nanna,
the Moon God, to the
sumptuously decorated chamber,
bed and throne they had made
for the occasion, and their
gratitude for the kingship, and
indeed deification, bestowed on

them through their union with the Goddess. These neo-Sumerian kings most often saw themselves as playing the part of Tammuz in relation to the Goddess, and had the title of 'royal shepherd'. (Christ was not the first to call himself shepherd, by two millennia at least, for it was a general ancient Near Eastern sacral title for leaders of human flocks and Jesus was but the last to take on the role of the dying and resurrected Tammuz.) One such hymn, by King Iddin-Dagan runs:

At the New Year, time of the rites,
A bed was raised for my Queen.
It was purified with reeds and
    perfumed cedar,
And once ready for my Queen,
A cover was thrown upon it,
A pleasant cover to increase the
    pleasure of lying there.
My Queen then bathed side by side
Bathed side by side with
    Iddin-Dagan!
And once the holy Inanna had
    washed,
Then was she sprinkled with
    aromatic cedar oil.
The King then proudly approached
    her sacred lap,
He joined proudly with the
    glorious triangle of Inanna,
And Tammuz, the Bridegroom, lay
    with her,
Tenderly pressing her beautiful
    breast!
When the Queen had long lain at
    the groins of the King,
She murmured, 'Iddin-Dagan, truly
    will I prolong your life!'

Many of these kings dedicated costly stone vases in temples to the Goddess in their role as 'beloved consort' or 'beloved shepherd' of Inanna (as they were neo-Sumerians they had returned to the old name of Inanna). Women also dedicated vases to Inanna, the vase obviously symbolic of the sacred containment of her uterus. It could be such women had themselves participated in the rite.

Two necklaces of this period, of gold, agate and carnelian beads set in silver, have been excavated from the priestess quarter of Uruk, each inscribed on their centre bead. The larger necklace had the inscription: 'Abbabashti, beloved *naditu*-priestess of the King of Ur, Shu-Sin', the smaller: 'Kubatum, beloved *naditu*-priestess of the King of Ur, Shu-Sin'. Surely these are touching mementos of sublime ceremonies. They were probably wedding gifts from the king on two separate occasions when the sacred marriage ceremony was celebrated. Such kings' hymns of adoration to the Goddess make inspiring reading; their human affection for her human counterparts is just as moving.

Many little clay models of a marriage bed on low legs have been found in temple sites, made as if viewed from above, with a loving couple embracing on it (Figure 23). At times there seems to be little difference between a bed and an altar. The whole subject is beautifully summed up for me by a sculpture in a private collection, illustrated in Seibert's book, of a priestess whose parted robes show the divine couple on a pendant bed hanging round her neck and resting against her stomach, indicating that she must have been a *naditu*-priestess.

23 A terracotta bed, made as a votive offering, shows the loving couple expressing their wish for marital harmony to the God or Goddess to whom it was dedicated; Mesopotamian (picture from Ilse Seibert's book), private collection, c.2000 BC.

Ilse Seibert says the *naditu*-priestesses were drawn from the noblest of women and were addressed as 'priestess' (*entu*), or 'lady' (*nin*). Such women would be called '*nin-dingir*', or 'lady of the God', implying that they were the priestess appointed to take the part of the divine bride. Texts show that the choice and induction of such a priestess was crucial and if anything happened to her it was considered a bad omen. She was to dedicate herself to the service of the God: 'If she sin against her husband (the God) the sanctuaries of the sublime Eridu will crumble, the walls of the city will be destroyed.'

From Uruk, the famous festival stone vase (detail, Figure 5) shows two characters, interpreted in Chapter 1 as the priestess representing Inanna and the king with long tasselled girdle representing Tammuz as they meet at the gate of the sanctuary. Texts of Gudea, ruler of Lagash after the neo-Sumerian period, also describe his role as consort of the Goddess Bau, whereby he was nominated 'shepherd of the people' and thus worthy to be her bridegroom. As he approached her sleeping chamber he poured out libations and made a sacrifice of various foods. When musicians started to play, he himself took up the flute. After the Goddess had foretold his fate, he was permitted to sit on the throne and was given the crown and sceptre of authority, obtainable only through the Goddess. There is a statue of him holding a palm-branch, which may signify his participation in the sacred marriage, since he refers to Bau as the date palm. The inscriptions on this and other statues follow the wording, 'The Goddess Bau has given Gudea life', which is what the Goddess promises Iddin-Dagan after their successful consummation.

After the ceremony, the priest would emerge to announce that the rites had been fulfilled properly, to the gladness of the assembly (such monitoring and announcements for ordinary marriages goes on in villages of the Middle East today, as it did for important marriages in Elizabethan times in England). There may have been more feasting and music, and then the divine consort would be escorted back to his own domain.

❧

Can this rite be revived today? I am sure it can, but only with extreme care. It may be difficult to find a partner who has such an exalted view of the sexual act, and who is willing to enact ritual sex, rather than personal sex, at key festivals of the year. There are many traps, and I believe the best test of a partner, on both sides, is to first secure the marriages of mind, through mutual mental activity, and of the spirit, through shared spiritual activity. If the flowing together of the subtle bodies is first achieved, like two amoebas flowing into each other, making one, the translation of that mix into the physical sphere is a genuinely meaningful act, linking to the universe, and not self-dependent. The profound difference will be felt, and it is worth going to some lengths to establish it. Whether it will ever come back into institutional religion seems unlikely, and possibly unnecessary, but it can return in full potency within the privacy of domestic shrines.

Keep a diagram of the seven chakras to the forefront of your mind and try to be aware of which ones are operating as you work with your partner. This is of course the theoretical ideal - actual events have a way of doing things in a different order! Nonetheless, one cannot avoid the truth that a well-laid foundation of work on the full chain of centres, its actual form depending on the tradition you are drawing upon, pays off in both permanence and usefulness in the long term - and permanence is needed for the unfolding of cosmic measures. Be prepared to build things up slowly and carefully – as well as giving in judiciously to grand sweeps of intuition! After laying down the main lines, you are then ready to switch on the whole network and make full use of its illumination.

The following is an adaptation of a document which was handed to me by someone who had belonged to a secret society. It gives instructions for the conduct of the marriage ritual itself. I am struck by its insistence on the particular position to be adopted, since it coincides with most depictions of the sacred marriage in Mesopotamian art (Figure 24) and is repeated as late in time as on Greek signet seals. I therefore consider these instructions to have somehow been handed down from the area that included ancient Mesopotamia, where the ritual was practised and given a standard depiction, from at least five millennia ago. They derive from a secret inner teaching known to initiates in the ancient Near Eastern civilizations, and must have been retained after the Classical Greek era by certain Gnostic Christian groups, then finally transmitted to Europe via the Templars, Cathars and Rosicrucians. As it is shown on excavated objects, which are no secret, I no longer feel a reservation about revealing the written document, whose wording I have adapted to fit our present idiom:

Man and woman see each other and want to be one, since the Universal Human (the entire Universe) is half male, half female. Yet even after a man and a woman have come together, there is often a great sense of disappointment, as if true union has eluded them, as if in fact physical union has brought about a separation.

The reason for this lies in the wrong use of energies, given that male and female energies are opposite. As in the wiring of an electric plug to produce an

24 Clay plaque showing the act of sacred marriage as most commonly depicted in Mesopotamia. The lady bends forward and ritually takes the sacred drink from a pot through a reed; found in the Scribal Quarter at Nippur, Iraq; photo courtesy of The Oriental Institute of the University of Chicago, c.2000 BC.

effective current of electricity, so the two humans must be rightly connected. A description now follows of an effective ritual.

Let the room be twilit, perhaps illumined by fire or candlelight. Let the man and woman stand side by side naked before an altar flame and consciously bring before them the love that moves the life of the universe. Let them thus come together at heart, then mind and then sex roses. For the latter, the man stands behind his beloved and takes her hands. She bends forward, perhaps leaning her arms on chair back or mantelpiece for stability [note how in the Mesopotamian examples illustrated, the lady leans forward to a pot into which she inserts a baton, on which she could lean]. The man enters her from behind and remains inside without movement. The ordinary man will move back and forward in a frenzy and waste the transmission of passive power emanating from the woman. He must rest in her energy which, although passive, is also powerfully active and needs time to connect to the male force.

This takes time to learn and at first the man will be unable to restrain his usual automatic reaction. Each time intend to withstand for a little longer: the more movement back and forth there is, the more quickly his semen will pass, and the circuit will end. The man in all his active power must listen to the passive contained in it, and the woman in all her seeming passivity must be allowed to pass on the waves of her energy to the man. She may from time to time contract her vagina to maintain the penis erect, though it is unlikely much of this will be necessary. Couples attuned to each other can spend all night like this (in this case lying down), or one hour, and even ten minutes rejuvenates.

The most effective circuit is created in this particular position; it follows the same position as that of all other animals. It allows a full circuit to be set up, between a negative and a positive side of each body. Face to face will criss-cross the currents and cause, comparatively speaking, a short-circuit!

When one uses this simple technique, knowing that the Great God and Goddess, the ultimate powers for ever united in each other, desire the union of all creatures in them, it is possible to unite very briefly during the day without undressing - to revive the current - by remaining joined for a minute. Ejaculation or orgasm are not the aim - the connection of positive and negative poles is what counts.

For those new to this approach it may seem impossible, especially as people in the twentieth century feel they know all there is to know about sex.

This ancient teaching was used as a means to higher illumination if the semen was retained and the energy released was transmuted, causing the blossoming of the crown chakra, but this approach should only be used under proper guidance. At an intermediate level it can be used by people in the normal ejaculative way. By coming into phase with each other the heart and mind centres also have a chance to blossom in synchronization, so that the lovers feel they are one soul, one mind and one body.

Since man became afraid of the power of woman he has tried to ignore her *shakti* (passive power). Yet his only salvation is to listen to it. This will give true satisfaction to both. Frantic body motion, and gymnastic contortions are eliminated. Nor are 'performances' required. As sound is heard in silence, so lasting energy is generated from stillness. In this state of connection, listen to the space of the room, your street, your town, your country, in stages bringing to mind the universe itself. You are connected for the sake of the universe, to bring Heaven and Earth together in harmony.

The power aroused not only energizes the man and woman for several days or even weeks: through the phenomenon of resonance the result of the act is to bring harmony to the surrounding environment - to a village, town, or even a country, bringing them back to cosmic synchronization. Do it for the world!

This is an inner teaching and should be practised only by those who intend to use this knowledge responsibly. Those who take it for themselves will receive nothing.

This is clearly a ritual where the woman will lead the man in educating them in the new approach, since they will need to be endlessly patient with trial and error. Of course, as ritual sex, it has a serious, but also a profoundly joyful flavour, to be kept for special occasions. It does not rule out making spontaneous, personal love on other occasions in other positions.

❦

The reason why the matter of female authority in religion is so vital is that, although spiritual knowledge in itself is for the most part sex*less*, at the very core of any religious tradition is the inescapable gender ingredient. This is ultimately metaphysical, and derives from the fact the World has been Created (hence the recitation of the Creation Myth at the New Year Festival) from the Divine Androgyne. Hindu doctrine describes how the Divine Androgyne consists of two halves, Purusha and Prakriti (the Divine Male and the Divine Female): the Ultimate Pair of Opposites. This first exists in the realm of Spirit, and only then unfolds into psychological and physical manifestation. The desire for union between men and women is simply the longing for a return to the androgynous state, which Plato in *The Republic* describes as the search for one's other half. We are deluded into thinking that the nature of the desire is purely physical, but when all the chakras are working together it is quite clear that the originating urge is to connect with and access the higher worlds.

The original name of Ishtar, successor to Inanna, came from Arabia as 'Athtar'. Athtar was an androgyne deity, sometimes depicted as a bearded female. In time Athtar came to be known as a Goddess who was sometimes male, sometimes female, the Warrior Goddess who was also the Goddess of Love. At Mari amongst many deities worshipped were Eshtar-Ush (male) and Eshtar*at* (female), in other words the male and female foci of the one deity, Eshtar, also understood as an androgyne. No wonder, then, that Ishtar presides over the sacred marriage, when male and female return to androgyny, and hence the role type for this chapter is the ultimate Androgyne, Athtar, who is Wholeness.

In the Bible Adam and Eve represent the Androgyne as manifested in the physical world (hence they come to wear clothes, and leave Eden once they realize they have manifested and have lost direct touch with the Centre). In the same way, Heaven (The Great Above) and Earth (The Great Below) make the World, and the sacred marriage also symbolizes the marriage between Heaven and Earth, as described

earlier in this chapter. Because 11 days marked the difference between the lunar and solar years and was the interval that allowed one cycle to catch up with the other, the marriage also supremely enacted what in astronomy is called the *syzygy*, the coming together of sun and moon, not forgetting that in Middle Eastern mythology overall the sun is often female and the moon male! (Goodison's book explores the subject extensively.) The important thing is the reconciliation of their seemingly irreconcilable cycles, whichever way round their energy is understood.

Spiritual progress just cannot be made without understanding, and coming to terms with, the matter of gender in religious practices. For those with an understanding of astrology, we could say Pluto passing through Scorpio during the decade of the Nineties is forcing us to get to the very root of the connection between sex, death, self-transformation and their role in religion, to find a total, not a partial, solution. All those with a strong Pluto influence in their lives know that this not only means a deep involvement with these ultimate journeys of life which mysteriously relate to the practice of sex, but as much with *giving it up* in order to gain mastery over its hold on the gates leading to spiritual ascent!

The shaktic process lies at the heart of religion, and can easily be put into operation once more, as appropriate! Temples were invented in the third millennium, and religious blueprints can be readjusted at this time of world decay and renewal. It is, however, crucial to understand that the shaktic process does not *have* to be channelled through the sexual centre: for example, in the age of chivalry it was cultivated through avoidance of sexual union, an alchemy learned from the Arabs. The male and female energies can be exchanged with others at every chakra level, and distance is no barrier. At times it becomes even a necessity to dispense with physical sex for a long period to develop transmission at other levels, and in convents, monasteries, and some priesthoods the closing down of the sex chakra was made permanent because of the higher benefits entailed.

However, the usefulness of sexual power, a fuel readily available for transmutation to the higher centres, cannot be achieved by its suppression, only by tantrism, or techniques of transformation, on which there are many books and teachers, though very few genuine (because they are only really interested in

sex on its own!) As sexuality is the lowest step of the Serpent Power on its journey up the spine to the top of the skull, a Beloved Other is vital for its further progress. Even though one can argue that the Partner can be encountered and engaged with in different ways at other levels (to become a Bride of Christ as do nuns, or to search for the Beloved-as-Spirit as do the Sufis), because the physical body is divinity incarnate, leaving it out makes the journey a great deal more difficult to cope with and often leads to its abortion. In actual fact the Kundalini's serpent journey can as well start from the crown chakra and move downwards, or from any of the other centres moving both ways, just as one can turn on the lights of a stairwell from a switch on any landing. But actually to leave out an entire connecting centre is asking for trouble, and has led to unreal views of women by the male priesthood, with the by-products of cold-heartedness and/or warped sexuality. A deaconess speaking on a television programme recently calculated that as many as 30 per cent of priests in the Church of England had homosexual tendencies.

For nearly 3,000 years up to the time of Christ, the trigger set off by making love in the flesh in the holy of holies was used both practically and symbolically in the effective execution of linking the invisible principles of Heaven Above, to the realm of nature and economics in the World Below. In our present materially based way of life, this could be a means whereby the present abuses of sexuality can be redeemed: by reconnecting them to religion as the ancients knew so well and so lovingly how to do.

I end this chapter with an epilogue that conveys the sublime mood of the true marriage rite. It is a poem written by a very ancient friend whom I rediscovered in the twentieth century.

HIEROS GAMOS

We come to the
  smokey-blue-walled
    Sanctum,
Priest and me.
For the sacred marriage
  At last.

We are directed
  by those in
Temporal and Spiritual power
  Over us.

It is all very simple –
  We give our love,
As we have done before,
  To the People.
    The walls still echo:
      'My Love
      Your loins
      Are like the rivers

Tigris and Euphrates
And where they join
We meet
  Sweet.'

I am in silence –
  Overcome
By the perfect blessing
  Of knowing you
  In this hour.

But will remember eternity
  like a ribbon-thread
Through my lives –
  And etch it
In the cuneiform of the day.

A past-life memory of one who was Enheduanna: Princess, Priestess, Poetess, Prophetess (2279 BC, Ur/AD 1990, Watford)

25 Drawing from Ilse Seibert's book about women in the ancient Near East, based on a fragmentary votive terracotta bed from Susa, Iran; now in the Louvre, c.2000–1500 BC.

4

PLANTS AND PLANETS

Role type: Ishtar

THE MOON PRIESTESSES

Measuring time by the moon goes back to palaeolithic times, if tallies on caveman bones really do refer to moon reckoning as Marshack interprets. It is the heavenly body closest to Earth and is ever linked, like a child, to Mother Earth, Gaia. Its changes of shape can be seen in the night sky with the naked eye, by professional and non-professional alike. The correlation between its phases and the behaviour of fluids on Earth cannot be denied, even by those who discount the rest of astrology! Tides, rainfall, sap in plants and female menstruation all come under its influence.

On Sumerian clay tablets, the moon is addressed in hymns as 'Lord of Ur', 'self-propagated fruit', 'determining the future to the far day', and 'opening the door of the heavens', by ordaining day, month and year. 'He' is hailed as the 'shining barque of the heavens . . . by whom all rivers and canals are filled', delighting the night and making the stars rejoice. This is an emotional expression about the practical measurement of time made through moon observations, central to the working of the calendar.

Due to the signature of the moon on their inner biology, women are clearly most suited to be Moon Priestesses, since their very bodies measure its phases. In this sense they are inevitably married to the moon. How far back in time was women's menstruation used to double-check the passing of the months – especially in the stormy climate often obscuring the skies of southern Iraq? Perhaps it is palaeolithic in origin, or as old as female biology.

I believe month-counting was a

factor in the need for large groups of women to be attached to the temple in a *gigparu* (convent) as brides of the Moon God, as at Ur. For it is a well-known fact that groups of women living together end up with their periods synchronizing. In boarding schools girls in a dormitory will after a month or two tend to start in time with each other, similarly with females working in the same office! Before watches and clocks, the sacerdotal community could make use of such a phenomenon as a rule-of-thumb check on calendrical calculations. Today urban society can choose to put into the background the hard fact that ordering the time phases of the year depends on the four main phases of the moon. But in Babylonian diaries the movements of the moon are charted minutely, beginning with a description of the new crescent, whether high or low, and the time from sunset to moonset; they record the progress of the moon through the month, and which stars it moves against. As the diaries built up over the years, forecasts could be made, and its eclipse, that most portentious event around which so much state life revolved, predicted. As early as the records go we know the completion of each quarter was marked by a day of rest, the *sibitti*, or 'holy seventh' when, in recognition of its pause, no mundane work should be undertaken. (In the same way, Apollo festivals were celebrated any 7, 14, 21 or 28 of the month.) We would lose all sense of time if the weeks were not marked, nor a day of rest used as a spacer.

Indirect confirmation that the menstrual cycle was a tangible contribution to measuring out the sacred year (always the main work of a temple) comes from the monotheistic religions succeeding the Jewish Temple Era. Judaism and Islam, both religions based on the lunar calendar, and both perpetuating many other practices from their ancient forbears, disallow women from saying their prayers or entering synagogue or mosque during their periods. In this way every man knows when they are menstruating and thus is able mentally to mark out the 'dark quarter' of each month and thereby work out the rest, even though long since other devices have made such a method of moon-phase assessment archaic. Similarly, in Hinduism it is not permissible for menstruating women to serve meals to, or even come into the presence of, Brahmin males, not for calendrical reasons but because for some reason menstruation came to be considered an impure state by men. I do not believe it was considered impure in itself, but only inasmuch as the odour reminds men of sex, which for the monotheistic religions is inappropriate in a religious setting. The fear of impurity rests rather in the men's thoughts, therefore.

It is a known fact that women can become mentally unstable during their periods (though it is forgotten men too are affected by a full moon). This is unsettling to the smooth running of a religion, and women themselves would often choose to stay apart from the community at this time in many primitive societies. This is a better reason for staying away from a religious building during menstruation, but by choice of the individual concerned, for not all women are affected, nor all the time. As a side-effect of electing out of the group at this time, women have long been made to think that during their periods they are unclean, which makes them feel sinful, which is preposterous.

Much recent discussion has taken place in women's groups to reconsider attitudes towards menstruation, more towards understanding it as a miraculous physical eruption of cosmic order in the female body than as a curse. From a cosmic point of view, it is to be rejoiced at since, despite practical discomforts, it is linked with the recurrent potential for human manifestation in miniature. All the same, living through it on a monthly basis is full of pain and it is an area of experience women should teach men about in frank terms. Exudation of blood from any part of the body has always held a symbolic place in most religions, as a sign of the divine breaking out into incarnation, almost as if the crushing weight borne by flesh in allowing divine light to use it as a vehicle for its form is hardly containable. There is pain associated with the lost opportunity as the seed has not come to fruition and the womb lining breaks down. But the avoidance of causing carnal manifestation was considered in a positive light by those aspiring to spiritual development (see the discussion of Artemis in Chapter 9). As far as Mesopotamian culture was concerned, it was all bound up with being married to the Moon God, which none of us can avoid!

Finally, on cessation of menstruation, usually a disruptive time of increased, then diminished, blood flow, lasting from a year to 10 years, tradition holds that a wise woman should result. No longer able to channel incarnation, she is free to devote her energies totally to the unmanifest dimensions. This, rather than mere physical age, is the factor giving her spiritual seniority.

In Old Babylonian texts from a later period, we learn that there were different ranks of priestess, some of whose titles it is not always possible to translate: in one list they are given as *entum*, *shugitum*, *zikrum*, *qadishtum*, *ishtaritum* and *kulmashitum*. The first three could refer to singers or attendant officiants who carried out peripheral details of ritual. The latter three were types of hierodule, which is the one English word that best conveys the idea of 'sacred prostitute'. One would rather not use the word 'prostitute' since, as mentioned in the last chapter, it implies a judgmental view of their function which has usually been misunderstood in the West.

Another text distinguishes between *nin-dingir* priestesses of top seniority, who were allowed to have cylinder seals, and *lukur* priestesses, also of high rank and usually royal, who we know on one occasion were entrusted with the guidance of younger girls dedicated to the temple. Second in rank seem to have been *nu-gig* priestesses, who were allowed to marry in the ordinary world and have their own children. Those

recorded by name were married to men of the highest administrative rank and were highly respected.

Apart from all these ranks, we know most about the *nadiatum*, who definitely lived together in a convent (*gigparu*), and seem often to have been dedicated by their parents to the God when still young girls. The remains of *gigparu* have been found at Kish, Nippur, Larsa, Ur and Sippar. At Sippar in Old Babylonian times about 140 *nadiatum* lived together, and included such distinguished ladies as the daughter of King Zimrilim of Mari. These ladies were guarded by three supervisors, and by male officials such as judges and scribes. In the case of the Sippar *gigparu*, the overall supervisor was a male high priest aided by several female wardens and scribes.

However, it emerges that the ladies had their own private quarters within the *gigparu*, and were allowed out to do business in town: their names and seals sometimes appear on clay documents, including the sale of land or other property. They were technically allowed to marry, although they were still not permitted to have children. The word *nadiatum* means 'virgin', in the sense of 'not bearing children', much as the word *parthenos* meant in ancient

Greece the high-born ladies who served Athena, hence the linked importance of avoiding processes of incarnation mentioned above. Altogether, they were a privileged class of woman, usually from the highest ranks of society, and fulfilling many day-to-day business functions, as did male merchants.

One particularly wealthy lady who emerges from the Sippar texts was the royal sister of Iltani of Karana, a *nadiatum* priestess who had a large team of officials running her estates including the organization of harvest workers. Six cowherds tended her herd of over 1,000 head of cattle. Legal records exist of other *nadiatum* acquiring or trading in property, land and slaves, arranging for loans to be made, and adopting young girls as junior *nadiatum* who would be their spiritual daughters, perpetuate their office and care for them in old age.

In the 1930s excavations of the Abrahamic city of Ur (on record as the true original home of the Jewish people), the architectural complex of the *gigparu* was found flanking the ziggurat within the sacred precinct. Here the *nadiatum* lived all their lives, presided over by the high priestess of the Moon God, Nanna, to whom she was quite clearly stated to be 'married', and whose daughter she simultaneously was. She had to remain 'faithful' to her spouse, and thus live up to her description as *nadiatum*, explained above.

Compared to the appointment of other ranks of priestess, dedicated by their family members, it was only the *nin-dingir*, or 'lady of the God' who had to undergo special selection. Having decided earlier that the title *nin-dingir* meant 'high priestess', we presume this was a special epithet bestowed only on the chief *nadiatum*. She was chosen by priests on the strength of a liver omen, which, cut from a sacrificed goat or sheep, would, by its shape signify divine assent to - or disapproval of - her appointment.

Because the high priestess of Ur (in Sargonic times called the Moon Priestess of Ur) was a daughter of Nanna, she automatically qualified to become a mortal sister of Inanna, the Goddess whose father from amongst the Gods was Nanna himself. Thus amongst the prayers and hymns uttered by the priestesses at Ur which have survived, not only do they address the presiding God, Nanna, but also Inanna, Goddess of Venusian radiance, whose main temple was still paramount at Uruk, and whose yearly festal round was sometimes co-ordinated with the Moon Temple at Ur, so close was the link between the two. There is no doubt that the Moon Priestess, as the high priestess came to be called after the Sumerian period, was therefore also understood as a human stand-in for Inanna in temple life, even if the temple at Ur was dedicated to her father/husband, the Moon God.

The effect of the moon on the fluctuations of plant life was closely understood in the hunter-gatherer era, when, it is presumed, women, who best understood plants and what effect each had, tended to be the gatherers. Of all these, the plant that came to symbolize the produce of the land most indigenous to ancient Mesopotamia was the date-palm. Inanna/Ishtar herself and priestesses or ordinary ladies petitioning her (Figure 26) are all represented in ancient sculpture holding a date cluster in one hand to indicate fertility.

The date-palm symbolized the Goddess, as did also the palm branch and the date cluster. As mentioned in the last chapter, a hymn describing the first union of Innana and Tammuz describes them as 'the Holy Date Palm' and 'the Holy Corn'. When asking a question of the Goddess as oracle, the supplicant would carry a palm branch ('the date-branch, mighty in decision, in my hand I hold'). Sometimes palm-trees stood in pairs at the main entrances to the Goddess's temples. A golden palm tree, hundreds of years later, was dedicated at Delphi.

The seal of a woman named Tata, the picto-graphic syllables of whose name are made up of two vases (Figure 27), shows ladies picking date clusters, against a backdrop of other flourishing plants and birds. This Edenic scene is presided over by the

26 Statuette of a woman which commemorates her role in the ritual banquet as the Goddess Inanna; she is depicted holding a cup in one hand and a date cluster in the other. Found in the Temple of Inanna at Nippur; now in the Iraq Museum, c.2700 BC.

crescent moon which, in the Mediterranean latitudes, west or east, at certain times of the year, appears with horns pointing upward. It is usually shown thus on cylinder seals. The picture beautifully sums up the female domain of the Moon God: even the small palm compared to the large one may refer to the counting of time, since a new ring of leaves replaces the old once a year, creating the trunk. It was known then that to ensure fructification, the female flowers had to be hand-pollinated by humans firmly dabbing pollen onto them from the male palms. Ritualized, the entire activity on Tata's seal becomes symbolic both of the female fertility cycle and of the sacred marriage, which adds

another level of meaning to those sculptures of ladies holding fructified date clusters.

A ceremony regularly enacted at Ur in recognition of the power of the moon entailed the watering of a young date-palm in the presence of the God Nanna (Figure 28). On a stone plaque found in the *gigparu*, two phases of the ritual are shown: the first watering shows an empty container with probably just the seed or shoot in it, while the second watering shows how the plant has sprouted in the precinct of the Moon God's temple. I would think these rituals took place at the spring and autumn equinoxes. In the upper scene the priest pouring the water is shown naked which means in real life

27 The cylinder seal of Tata, showing women collecting date clusters, presided over by a crescent Moon, Lord of Plants; now in the Penningkabinett, The Hague, c.2200 BC.

this ritual must have happened in the inner sanctuary, where it was required that in the presence of the God or Goddess humans should return to their state of original nudity or Adamic innocence – a practice continued by the high priest in the Temple of Solomon in Jerusalem many centuries later. In the upper scene it is hard to tell whether he has naturally long hair, or is wearing a wig. Three priestesses look on, facing sideways, wearing either a cloth held in place by an *agall*, a simpler version of the head-dresses of ladies in the royal burials of Ur, or loose hair held in place by a band. In the second scene the priest pouring water has shaved his head, and the participants include a priest holding a sheep for sacrifice, while the front priestess stares out at us, signifying her immediate presence with us now, which usually in Mesopotamian art only the Goddess Inanna is entitled to do.

Think of the number of house plants we have around these days, quite apart from those in our gardens. How often do we really consider the powers that make growth possible, and make a similar connection of propitiation or thanks by a passing prayer, or

think more carefully about their dependence on the watery moon as we water them? Inspired by the pictures of Ur alone, there is so much room in our daily practices for venerating the key influence that regulates plant life and our calendar, the moon. The Green Movement is not only about Gaia, but, vitally, about water, and the moon energies.

On my altar at home I like to put flowers or fruit from the garden, or that I have bought from the supermarket, in front of the image of the God and Goddess, to thank them for nurturing me, but even a prayer of thanks as you store provender in the freezer would be acceptable to them. You can think beyond, to consider the

28 Upper and lower halves of a commemorative plaque found in the gigparu *at Ur showing the ritual of watering a young date-palm shoot before the Moon God Nanna and his temple; now in the British Museum, drawing from P. Amiet c.2500 BC.*

moon energy and feel united with it consciously, as daughter bride. As happened with priests and priestesses of the past, after standing on the offering table, or in the offering fridge, for some hours - or days - the food can be taken back and eaten, or left to dry up and die, whichever you feel is most appropriate. In either case, it is the symbolic act of recognition and thanks that counts and the subtle results will be noticeable.

༄

Among the finds in the ruins of the *gigparu* at Ur was a round limestone disc which the excavator, Woolley, immediately took to refer to the moon, calling it 'a lunar disc' (detail, Figure 29). Although badly battered, it showed a small ziggurat (probably that at Ur itself), with a plant-watering ceremony being performed by the Priest of Nanna, followed by a woman named Enheduanna (second from the left) whose face was well preserved. Her retinue of two more priestesses was barely visible when discovered, and this picture shows them roughly restored over the traces. The inscription on the back says quite clearly that it was dedicated by Enheduanna, Moon Priestess of Ur. Asher-Grève points out that she raises her right hand to her nose, the normal convention for greeting a Divinity.

Enheduanna was appointed the very first Moon Priestess of Ur by her father, the Semitic King Sargon of Akkad, who had just conquered Sumer and begun a

29 When first illustrated by Woolley, this round object was captioned as a 'calcite lunar disc'. Although found in the gigparu at Ur in a battered state, enough remains to discern the face of Enheduanna (second from left) in full dress as first Moon Priestess of Ur, attending the date-palm watering ceremony; now in the Philadelphia Museum, c.2400 BC.

new era in its history (see Chronological Table). One way to smooth over the transition was to put his daughter into a key temple of the land, which was 'twinned' with the age-old sky temples of Uruk. Since Enheduanna almost certainly also officiated at Uruk in person, not only would she have been seen as the personification of Inanna, but her human father, King Sargon became linked into the Divine Family as 'brother-in-law of Anu', Sky God of Uruk, and 'father-in-law of Nanna of Ur'.

One of Enheduanna's main tasks was not only to continue to worship the Moon God (known to the Akkadians by the Semitic name, Sin, sometimes transliterated Suen), whom both the Sumerians and Akkadians worshipped in common, but, more to the point, to neatly blend Sumerian worship of Inanna with that of the kindred Semitic Goddess, known in their language as Ishtar, *their* name for Venus. To them, Ishtar was at times male, a warrior goddess in armour, sometimes bearded, when she rose with the sun in the morning (Figure 30), but most times female, presiding over the sexual reproduction and perfect formation of all living young, showing herself as the planet Venus when she rose at night as the beautiful evening star. By the theological combination of Inanna and Ishtar worship, Sargon hoped to weld together the empire of Sumer and Akkad, and mask the raw fact of abrupt political takeover.

The special state role given by King Sargon to his daughter was perhaps also in recognition of how much his fate had depended on the female *shakti*: he was, he described, the offspring of a priestess, deserving therefore to be king, because he

30 This fine cylinder seal, dedicated to the Goddess by a stone-cutter from central Iraq, shows Ishtar in many-horned crown and battle array harnessing the lioness of her Venusian energy, with her eight-armed planet behind her. She is greeted with the characteristic gesture by a ministering priestess wearing a single pair of horns; c.2200 BC.

was the Son of a Divine Womb. His autobiography (which is uncannily echoed in later centuries by the story of Moses, for the baby Sargon was also found floating in a reed basket and rescued from the river by foster parents) says he rose to power through another priestess's influence, after he became the 'beloved of Ishtar', meaning that he had performed the sacred marriage - priestesses being the carriers of Inanna/Ishtar's authority to bestow rulership, as obtained from Enki. The idea that the kings of Sumer and Akkad could only gain royal authority by mating with the Goddess in the person of a high priestess was explored in the last chapter. If pleased with the potential king, Ishtar would appoint him by handing to him her lapis lazuli rod and measuring line, the instruments of just and measured rule.

Enheduanna herself was said to be the child of Sargon and a (possibly Sumerian) priestess, and her office of Moon Priestess of Ur lasted for life. But even this task had its ups and downs, for there was a period when Enheduanna was suspended from office, when her father was experiencing setbacks in securing his empire against rebel forces. At this time attempts were made by a temporary usurper to alter the cults of Uruk and Ur, and Enheduanna felt she had been abandoned by Nanna:

As for me, my Nanna takes no
  heed of me
He has verily given me over to
  destruction in murderous straits.
Ashimbabbar has not pronounced
  my judgement.
Had he pronounced it, what is it
  to me? Had he not pronounced
  it, what is it to me?
[Me] who once sat triumphant he
  has driven out of the sanctuary,
Like a swallow he made me fly
  from the window - my life is
  consumed.
He made me walk in the bramble
  of the mountain.
He stripped me of the turban
  appropriate for high
  priestesshood.

Not only was Enheduanna suspended, but it appears from another of her hymns that the person she should have celebrated the sacred marriage with violated his trust and took liberties with her and other priestesses which were of an entirely profane character.

In some of her heartfelt songs she turned from the Moon God to appeal to Inanna/Ishtar, referring to past sacred marriage rites by saying:

Very I had entered the holy *gigparu*
  at your behest,
I, the High Priestess, I,
  Enheduanna!

I carried the ritual basket, I
  intoned the acclaim,
But now I am placed in the leper's
  ward: I, even I, can no longer
  live with you!

When discovered, the lunar disc
showing Enheduanna conducting
the plant-watering ceremony had,
according to the excavators, been
'smashed and deliberately
defaced'. Hallo and van Dijk, who
translated all Enheduanna's
surviving hymns and wrote a
succinct factual account of what
we know of her, wondered
whether this defacement
happened at the time of
Enheduanna's expulsion from Ur,
when, as she herself said, 'the
harp of mourning was placed on
the ground' (referring, they
suggest, to an Inanna myth called
'Enki and the Organization of the
World' where Inanna is described
as 'tirelessly playing an
instrument of mourning' for her
lost lover, Tammuz).

It is hard to tell whether
Enheduanna's ordeal lasted
months or years, but in the end
she and the cults of Ur and Uruk
were restored:

The First Lady, the Reliance of the
  throne room
Has accepted her offerings.
Inanna's heart has been restored.
The day was favourable for her, she
  was clothed sumptuously, She
  was garbed in womanly beauty.

Like the light of the rising moon,
  how was she sumptuously attired!
When Nanna appeared in proper
  view
They all blessed [Inanna's] mother,
  Ningal.
The heavenly threshold called,
  'Hail!'

For that her [Enheduanna's]
  speaking to the Divine Hierodule
  was exalted,
Praise to Her who destroys the
  lands, endowed with the *Me* from
  Anu,
To my lady wrapped in beauty,
  Inanna!

There is a deliberate ambiguity in
the description of the cult image
of the Goddess in all her finery
with that of Enheduanna herself
in priestessly attire as she
celebrates the reinstatement of
the cults of the Goddess and her
father the moon, not forgetting
his own heavenly consort, Ningal,
Goddess of Dream Interpretation
(oneiromancy). Enheduanna
herself described how inspiration
for hymns came to her by night,
and that giving form to them was
as agonizing as labour pains.
Some of the Moon Priestesses at
Ur were dream interpreters,
though throughout
Mesopotamian history this job,
according to Oppenheim, seems
usually to have been exclusively a
male preserve.

By the end of his reign, Sargon
had finally overcome the rebels
who besieged him at Akkad,

inflicting such a forceful defeat on them that they were bound to acknowledge the 'Dynasty of Ishtar' at last. Enheduanna continued in office after the death of her father, who was succeeded by his grandson, Naram-Sin, who only on Enheduanna's death appointed his own daughter, Enmenanna, ruler (note how both names include the name of the Sky God, Anu, at the end). According to an inscription found at Ur, she, in turn, became 'spouse of Nanna, High Priestess of Sin'.

Long after her death, the brilliance of Enheduanna's life and example were remembered as so outstanding that in later literature she was given saintly status. Many other names of priestesses who were her successors were found in inscriptions in the *gigparu*, which was added to, built on and rebuilt over five centuries between about 2300-1800 BC. In other words, for over 500 years the rulers of Sumer and Akkad filled this important post with their own daughters, who continued in it, as had Enheduanna, despite changes of kingship on the political scene, until death. As Hallo in his article puts it, 'thirteen princely princesses held [unbroken] office for an average of 35-40 years during . . . nearly half a millennium'. In the history of Mesopotamia, it was only the Akkadians and their successors in the Ur III and Isin-Larsa periods (up to around 1800 BC) that held the female priestly office in quite such high regard, due to their theological doctrine of royal authority being derived from the Goddess, through the person of the high priestess.

When the Akkadian empire finally fell c.2160 BC, the land reverted to petty princedoms, amongst which that of Gudea's Lagash (2150-2100 BC) stands out for the beauty of the statuary discovered there, mostly showing the ruler Gudea himself. Women played an important role in the succession of the Lagash dynasty, since succession was usually secured through the female line. Ur-Bau was the dynast of the line, having many daughters, one of whom, Enannepada, succeeded Enmenanna as the next high priestess of Sin at Ur. Another of his daughters became the wife of Gudea, who also had a second wife, whom the archaeologist Parrot believes is represented in a damaged but fine sculpture (Figure 31) that conveys a mood of serene balance and purity, though we do not know whether the lady was of priestessly rank.

The ladies of Lagash (up-river from Ur) dedicated vases and sculptures to their local Goddess,

Bau, whose symbol was a dog. A sculpture of her was found at Ur from the time the Lagashites held some kind of hegemony over that city. She is seated on a throne with a dog carved on the side. Interesting is the habit some Lagashites had of dedicating a small sculpture of a lady's coiffure to the Goddess (Figure 32), not unlike nuns dedicating their hair to God when they become novitiates, though without the idea behind it of self-degradation by renouncing 'luxuries' which could lead to fleshly Sin. Even if the stone wig was intended to be fitted onto a complete sculpture, as some experts argue, the fact that it is separately dedicated as 'a woman's glory' as a substitute for cutting off her real hair shows a positive attitude to female beauty in relation to the divine, where personal physical beauty is notionally given back to Beauty. It also gives an insight into one purpose of ancient art.

For the duration of the dynasty that followed, called the Ur III period (2100–2000), there was a Sumerian revival, begun by the king Ur-Nammu, whose name suggests he worshipped the Goddess of the Primeval Waters. His and his son's daughters provided queens and priestesses for a vast Sumerian empire based on intermarriage which, on the Akkadian prototype, stretched again from Ebla and Mari in Syria to Susa and Anshan in western Iran. It was he who rebuilt the ziggurats at Ur and Uruk as they remain today. The foundation inscription of the ziggurat at Uruk reads: 'Inanna, Lady of Eanna: for his Lady has the great procreator, Ur-Nammu, King of Ur, King of Sumer and Akkad, built her house again.'

31 A fragmentary statue of a lady with hands clasped in worship, made of finely worked steatite, from Lagash. It conveys honesty, sincerity, refinement and nobility, but we do not know who she was; c.2100 BC.

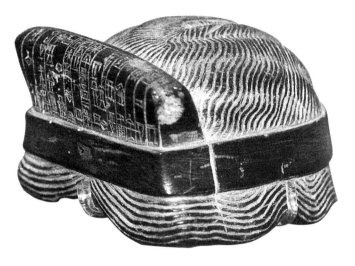

32 Diorite head-dress described by the Lagashite lady who dedicated it in the temple as 'the beauty of her womanhood'; now in the British Museum, c.2100 BC.

The kings of this dynasty, like Sargon of Akkad, extolled the sweetness of marriage with the Goddess, whereby they perpetuated their political sway over a vast kingdom. The poems of kings like Shulgi and Shu-Sin are full of tenderness, blending erotic with heavenly delight, showing how they sometimes became personally attached to the priestess involved. Ibbi-Sin was the last of the neo-Sumerian line before Aramaic-speaking Amorites poured into the kingdom, introducing, after a brief neo-Sumerian interlude, a harsher brand of Semitic culture and language, labelled the Isin-Larsa period (2000–1800 BC) which is sometimes called the Early Old Babylonian period because it turned out to be a prelude to the Old Babylonian era.

In the Old Babylonian period, a king of truly international character, Hammurabi, welded the Sumerian, Akkadian and Amorite peoples then living in Mesopotamia into a new kingdom: Babylonia – which name it was to bear until Classical Greek times. Despite some changes in life, still the ancient tradition continued of appointing the king's daughter as high priestess of Sin at Ur.

We will return to Moon Priestesses again in Chapter 8, for their importance increased again in Babylon under Nabonidus in the 6C BC, after a gap from 1800 BC onwards where we have no clear record of continuing practice in succeeding centuries, possibly because they did not enjoy such high status as they had for those 500 years for which we have so many living names and faces.

From the insights we have of that time I believe we can consider how to work in the world as Moon Priestesses. We may have our altar at home, but today, as in Sumerian times, the world of offices and shops is the domain that needs our gentle touch, linking in sympathy with other females we find ourselves working with. At all levels the first step in priesthood can be made by nurturing those around us, having first replenished ourselves through communion with the Gods in the privacy of our home. Men especially need to be watered like plants. Some people need to be nurtured in a motherly way as if you are Ningal, others in a sexual way as if you are Ishtar. Some people need to be fed physical food, others spiritual food. Don't be taken in by the outward mask: try to sense the hidden need. The moon has an energy that sensitively picks up change and fluctuation in other people's emotions: open out your woman-given receptiveness while at the same time protecting yourself with Ishtar's commanding vitality.

The most vivid symbol of lunar receptiveness is the mirror. Often the Goddess herself is shown holding a mirror for this reason. It is also a symbol of purity, or virginity. Though reflecting everything around it, the mirror itself is untouched by the reflections it contains. This is a true analogy whereby to understand the Immaculate Conception, which is nothing to do with physical sex, but with how the *Materia Prima*, or original Substance of the Universe, holds all forms, even the Universal Man Himself, while Herself remaining untouched. The *Materia Prima* is The Mother. A mirror on the altar can remind you that this is the detached yet sensitive state you wish to retain in order not to be carried away by all that you reflect and are required for.

Starting from today, you can begin to appreciate that all material things around you, fine and coarse, are held in The Mother, and that she is their substance. You can act as a replica of the Great Mother - all women can do so by nature without having to try, but this faculty has been severely damaged, even though it is what is subconsciously expected of them by others. In India that fine tradition is still retained whereby all women older than your own generation are called mother, those of your own generation sister, and those younger, daughter. This recognizes that all women are reflections of the universal *Materia Prima*, and that through their different modes according to age, the Goddess Herself can be contacted.

Thus identifying with the *Materia Prima*, you feel yourself as the virginal substance behind all things - this is the best use of the root chakra. See how it changes the way you treat people. Let The Mother shine through your particular physical form, and your choice of dress, and give your radiance to all. Because we live in such fallen times people will at first misunderstand you, in some contexts thinking you are making improper advances! Persist, keeping your inner intention in mind and gently correct people's distorted responses. The basic idea to keep in mind is that, like the moon, you open up to mirror other people's needs in order to find out what they are, and then, with the power of Venus, you radiate life-giving support. But, just like the moon and the planet Venus, who are both visible by virtue of the sun's reflected light, you can only make use of their light if you keep the right distance away. By trial and error learn through all the languages at your disposal to enable people in turn to keep the right distance from you. In Muslim countries this is done by completely covering the body in shapeless drapes, but it can by done by purely psychological means, and manners and social customs are there for a purpose: to form demarcation lines upholding dignity, but not as barriers to friendliness!

Working at putting your chakras into proper alignment is of key importance in the process of recognizing which zone is the best tool to use in a given situation. The rebuilding of your internal hierarchy is well summed up in the Babylonian version of the return journey from the Underworld of Inanna (now firmly named Ishtar), so, with slight changes from the Sumerian version to the items which marked her chakras, I reproduce below the relevant section from William Sladek's translation. Ereshkigal, Queen of the Netherworld (or Netcherworld, World of the Inner Workings of the Gods in the Psyche, as Normandi Ellis has well pointed out in her Introduction to *Osiris Awakening*), gives permission for the release of her sister Ishtar to return to the earthly plane. Gate by gate, the *Me* are returned to her:

Then Ereshkigal opened her mouth and spoke.
She said to Namtar her vizier:
'Go, Namtar, and knock at Egalgina,
Decorate the thresholds with cowrie shells.
Bring out the Anunnaki [the Gods and Goddesses] and seat them on the golden thrones.
Sprinkle Ishtar with the life-giving water and take her from my presence.'

Namtar went and knocked at Egalgina,
He decorated the thresholds with cowrie shells.
He brought out the Anunnaki and seated them on the golden thrones.
He sprinkled Ishtar with the life-giving water and took her from

Ereshkigal's presence.
He brought her out through the
first gate and returned the
beautiful dress for her body.
He brought her out through the
second gate and returned the
rings for her hands and feet.
He brought her out through the
third gate and returned the girdle
of birth stones from her waist.
He brought her out through the
fourth gate and returned the
pectoral for her breasts.
He brought her out through the
fifth gate and returned the egg-
shaped beads for her neck.
He brought her out through the
sixth gate and returned the rings
for her ears.
He brought her out through the
seventh gate and returned the
great crown for her head.

'As for Dumuzi, the lover of her
youth,
Wash him with pure water, anoint
him with fine oil;
Clothe him in a red garment, let
him play on a flute of lapis
lazuli!'

This excerpt ends on the sad note
that Tammuz is being prepared to
take Ishtar's place in the
Netcherworld, since either one
sacrifices to the other their
opposing position in the realm of
the Gods as they affect Gaia, just
as one star sets in order to let its
opposite rise. In the story of
Ishtar/Tammuz as a year myth,
this means that as Sirius/Ishtar
rises, so must the stars of
Capricorn, the Goat
constellation, start to set.

Gradually, letting your mind work
well, your heart open out, your
action centre act (the sexual
centre is linked by association to
hands and feet), subtly you interchange energy with other people
(as love, as information, as
wisdom, for example) at each and
all chakra levels. Don't let the
Gods of the Netcherworld use
you in their clouded and
confused form: by cleaning up
your inner roses you become
their mistress as well as a true
servant of whichever combination
of Gods and Goddesses suits your
type best! While allowing your
psyche and spirit to stroke the
psyches and spirits of others in a
thousand different ways according
to their needs, you can keep
physical intimacy in bounds, at its
proper place on the chakra tree.
Think carefully which chakra you
actually need to use before
activating it: will it be the
pectoral or the crown, the girdle
or the ear-rings – or a
combination? What does the
person you are exchanging with
actually need? Do not adulterate
the chakras by confusing them.

Possibly, like Enheduanna, you
will be moved to place the
overflow of your outgiving into
songs, poems, pictures and
dancing. Keep these same ideas in
mind however you decide to
radiate the Universe to the world
as a Moon Priestess.

BABYLONIA, OASES AND SEA PEOPLES

MEDITERRANEAN

5

ABSTRACT STONES AND HUMAN SACRIFICE

Role types: Anat/Astarte/Ellaat

By the beginning of the second millennium, as Babylonia was forming a consolidated empire in Mesopotamia, the countries on the eastern seaboard of the Mediterranean, peopled by Canaanites, come more fully into view in the historical record of the Bronze Age, mainly due to one discovery. In 1928 an Arab peasant digging his field at Ras Shamra, in present-day Syria just beyond the Lebanon border, came across remains which initiated decades of yearly excavation. The first archaeologist involved was Claude Schaeffer, who from the 1930s onwards displayed to the world second-millennium Ugarit, as it was then known, with its port of Minet el-Beida (White Harbour) beyond.

Ras Shamra-Ugarit is the star of this chapter simply because it gives us the most information – named personalities and a vast cache of broken clay tablets revealing a complicated mythology, in writing ancestral to both the Hebrew and Phoenician alphabets. These were mostly found in the priests' quarters next to the temple of Baal, where the priests (*kohanim*), under a high priest (*rabb kohanim*) lived. Attending in the temple itself were the *qadeshim*, those set apart from the world because of their purity, who could be male or female. On a scale later perfected by the Hebrews there were deemed to be four levels of purity: *tame* (impure); *tahor* (pure); *qadesh* (holy); and *qadesh-qadeshim* (holy of holies, or sacrosanct). Only a high priest or priestess would attain the last level of purity.

The word *qadesh* derives from the Semitic root 'to stand apart', which results from a purification of mind, body and spirit, whose result is holiness, the literal meaning of the word *qadesh*. As Dussaud expresses so well, respect for the priestess in Canaan originally derived from her activities in the utter sanctity of the holy of holies (in Mesopotamian times the *giguna*), but with the passage of time, in both Babylon and Canaan her role diminished, to the point where by the beginning of the Iron Age (*c.*1000 BC onwards) she was becoming an object of scorn.

While the priestess retained sanctity, and her proper position in the hierarchy both spiritually and socially, anything out of place would immediately ring false: 'And the stranger shall not come nigh unto you . . . and the stranger that cometh nigh shall be put to death' (Numbers 18:4/7). But things began to lose their proper order, and for some reason the decline was not scotched at the outset, perhaps because the Land of Canaan rarely came under centralized administration. I hope this chapter will give an inkling as to why the *qadeshim* lost their sanctity, though they and the Goddess whom they represented continued to be called *qadesh* well into Classical times. By this time the Greek Goddess Artemis was sometimes also called *hiera*, the Greek equivalent, as were her priestesses.

The reasons for the spiritual fall of priestesshood could be explained in terms of the Sephirothic Tree of the Kabbalah, an ancient wisdom which is as old as Sumer and which the Hebrews have preserved as a universal esoteric teaching, for it is a metaphysical Tree of Life that describes an elaborate chakra system concerning not simply the body, but also the Four Worlds of Matter, Psyche, Spirit and Divine Qualities. But as this book is based on archaeological evidence, I will have to leave you to work out for yourselves where the Two Pillars, male and female, which hold up the Tree, started to get seriously out of kilter. (For good books on the Kabbalah I suggest you read Warren Kenton/Z'ev ben Shimon Halevi.)

As well as in Ugarit, *kohanim* and *qadeshim* probably served in second-millennium Byblos, further down the coast, where, too, there was a temple to Baal, the Bull God. Nearby was the temple of Baalat Gebal, the female half of Baal usually known as Anat (they were later to emerge in the Greek world as the brother and sister diarchy of Apollo and Artemis). One text calls Anat 'the beloved sister of Baal who with him celebrates the sacred marriage'. Because of the frequent interchange between

Egypt and Byblos during the Old Kingdom in the third millennium, it is probable that Baalat Gebal was a Canaanite form of Hathor. Planted round the inner sanctum of her temple was an impressive cluster of conical stones, so the archaeologists named it the temple of the Obelisks. However for Byblos we have little to go on concerning priestesses for the second millennium (though we do for the Late Period; see Chapter 10).

As well as the striking finds of Ugarit, we cannot dispense with the information on priestesses culled from many other hundreds of seemingly minor excavations undertaken by Americans, English, French and then native archaeologists. They have contributed to our ability to conjure up the highly localized and eclectic kaleidoscope of life in the Bronze Age Levant. Even so, many spaces between the shifting jigsaw pieces still remain blank, and the picture never unifies into one broad perspective, as it can for long reaches of Mesopotamian or Egyptian history. Hence any attempt to reconstruct from slivers of evidence the activities of priestesses is going to be even more fragmentary and speculative than it has been so far. Nonetheless, gleaning through the information, the overall impression is gained that there were large numbers of priestesses of the lower ranks, and a highly colourful royal priestess or two steps briefly into the limelight.

Then, as today, the territories on both the coastal and hinterland stretches of the Land of Canaan (which is a good blanket term to use for the region at this period since its borders were continually in flux and we are not trying to write a precise political history of each petty kingdom) were playthings in the hands of surrounding empires. Though some priestess traditions had been kept alive from the time the Sumerian civilization of Uruk had reached as far along the Euphrates as Ebla in Syria, and Anatolian/Hittite contributions from what is present-day Turkey to the north had some hold, the most striking influence was Egyptian. This was certainly not one-way, however, for during the first half of the second millennium Caananite culture had infiltrated into Egypt, especially via the nomadic Shepherd Kings, the Hyksos. In reaction, in the second half of the millennium (c.1500-1000), the Egyptians started to move into Canaan in order to create a buffer zone ruled by native princes or even Egyptian resident governors to protect the country's borders from the Semitic invasions that had been so successful in Mesopotamia, and had actually penetrated Egypt itself in the First, then Second, Intermediate Periods.

Priestesses continuing the practices of the third-millennium north Syrian/Mesopotamian type, often in a somewhat provincial way, must have adapted to these new political facts of life, for this is expressed in the visual mixture to be found in the iconography of cylinder seals which depict them. Through the international nature of life at this time, Canaanite priestess practices gradually diffused into Egypt. By the end of the millennium, especially during the reigns of Hatshepsut, Akhenaten and then the Ramessides, first at Thebes, then Amarna and the Delta region, the introduction of Canaanite gods and goddesses, and of priestesses who ministered on the Canaanite/Mesopotamian model, came to transform Egypt's temple life permanently (see Chapter 7).

In the records left to us from the Land of Canaan, we thus find represented, in writing and pictures, a fascinating mixture of local rulers in native or Egyptian dress (or combinations of the two), who worship Mesopotamian, Hittite or sometimes Egyptian divinities, separately or together. Take, for example, the Amorite ruler (signified by the crouching gazelle behind him) who appears on a seal which perhaps was his own personal stamp for commercial transactions, rather like a credit card (Figure 33). It shows him in

33 A haematite cylinder seal from northern Syria showing the mixed religious influences of the second millennium in the Land of Canaan, as Venus is worshipped by an Amorite ruler both as Anat and as Hathor; now in the British Museum - photo courtesy The Trustees of the British Museum, seal no. WAA 129585; c.2000–1500 BC.

Anatolian-style round felt cap and padded coat paying his respects to the Goddess of Life in two forms. As a Levantine Goddess she is Anat/Ellaat/Astarte, with her hair done up in tubular rolls, wearing looped ear-rings, and parting her transparent veil ringed and girdled with beads, accompanied by a bird. In her Egyptian form she is Hathor/Baalat Gebal, with ram's horns, holding out two conical objects which could either be stones or cakes (the significance of both will be seen later). She is preceded by her own sign, the Egyptian *ankh*, hieroglyph for 'Life' which is retained in present-day astrology as the sign for Venus.

It was at the beginning of the second millennium (*c.*2000BC) when the rise of the Babylonian empire brought an end to prosperity in Sumer, that Abram left Ur to travel to Harran, and on to the Land of Canaan with its mixed cultural background. Harran was a Hittite town at the edge of Canaan where the Mesopotamian Moon God Sin and his wife Ningal were wor-shipped on the same lines as at Ur. Moon Priestesses continued to minister there even into the Archaic period (see Chapter 9). Then Abram, now named Abraham because of his covenant

with God, slowly moved south with his successors and their flocks into Canaan. They still required their wives to be Hittite, but were starting to mesh into a new, Canaanite context. The Bible shows how in these pioneering days the proto-Jews (Hebrews) did not find Canaanite beliefs incompatible with their own version of Mesopotamian cosmology: according to a text on clay found at Ras Shamra, their own God, Jahweh, was in the Canaanite hierarchy the son of El and Ellaat, the Universal 'Him' and 'Her' (which is the literal translation of these two words). There is no doubt that at that time, as attested both at Harran and Ugarit, priestesses of the Ur-related variety were admitted as an acceptable part of Hebrew sacerdotal life as well as those with the mixed background just described.

Around the time Akhenaten and his father Amenophis III ruled Egypt (known as the Amarna period, see Chronological Table), a king of Ugarit named Niqmepa married an Egyptian princess in order to forge good relations between himself and Egypt. It is probably he and his wife who are shown on a fragment of an alabaster vase found at Ugarit (Figure 34a). The row of gazelles indicate Niqmepa was a Canaanite nomad in origin, since gazelles were symbolic of nomadic desert life under the aegis of the God Amurru, while bulls stood for those Gods and their peoples who followed the more settled life required for cattle raising.

In a similar cosmopolitan mix, an Ugaritic queen, who might have been Mesopotamian (since her name, Sharelli, is composed of the words 'Shara' and 'El', referring to the Goddess and the God), used a stamp seal with her name on it in rough Egyptian hieroglyphics (Figure 34b). Schaeffer, however, interpreted it as belonging to the very Egyptian princess who married Niqmepa and who, although changing her name to Sharelli, still clung to the hieroglyphics she could read, even if carved clumsily by locals (and thus its decipherment, apart from her name is problematic, though it depicts Baal in his Egyptian form as Seth/Anubis, the crouching jackal).

In the same way, by the beginning of the first millennium, the Jewish King Solomon made diplomatic marriages with foreign princesses, allowing them to practise their own religions. He was visited by the famed Queen of Sheba, endowed with wealth, power and knowledge, to whom was ascribed by the scriptures of all the monotheistic religions both an exotic aura of romance and supernatural powers. On the pattern of later Arab priestess queens recorded more firmly in Assyrian annals (see Chapter 8), the strands of information we have about her point to the fact that she was such an august person herself, and the apocryphal account of the encounter between her and King Solomon has all the hallmarks of a sacred marriage. Something was transmitted between them that warranted the permanence of the story in scripture thereafter. She was his equal and could not be tidily put away into his international harem. If we know her kingdom was Saba, we know from the Qur'an that her own name was Balqis, and that she came from the matriarchy of Saba, which had been founded in the heartland of northern Arabia and gradually moved south until it was best known in Classical times as forming part of present-day Yemen. Balqis is credited with founding two dynasties, those of the Himyars in southern Arabia, and the imperial line of Abyssinia. The fact that she was a queen ruling in her own right was not unusual for Arabia, then or later (see Chapters 9 and 11) – an ironic contrast to the present situation.

Taking this eclectic culture into account as a background, scenes on cylinder seals used in Canaan between the time of Abraham and that of Solomon show female temple personnel mediating in rituals alongside rulers and the Gods or Goddesses they address. They are most usually shown as priestesses of the Mesopotamian tradition, retaining the same flounced dresses and semaphoric hand gestures to address the Gods as in the previous millennium. The one appearing in Figure 35 stands with the Goddess's lion behind her with junior worshippers on a smaller scale joining in. She pays obeisance to the Anatolian Storm God Teshub (known further south as Baal or Haddad, the equivalent, later, of Jupiter), who flourishes a mace and double axe and stands on two mountain peaks. He contemplates his sister Anat unveiling herself as she

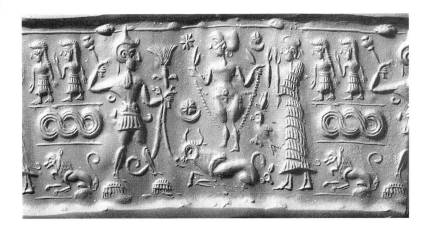

stands, with her bird, on a cow giving birth, while he holds its nose-ring and a lion's tail. Planetary signs fill the space between them, indicating they are Gods, not mere mortals.

As this seal was bought on the market and has no inscription we do not know the precise place it came from in Canaan, nor who its owner was, whether a priestess or some other official. The Mercurial coiling snakes, which can be traced back to third-millennium imagery, representing the mating vipers of spring, are now stylized into a running guilloche. In Canaanite art Anat/Ellaat/ Astarte is always shown as un- ashamedly naked and sexually invit- ing, often holding the snakes of Gaia in her hands to suggest the com- municative convul- sions of life itself, as well as its eternal renewal due to the snake's ability to shed its own skin for a better replacement (Figure 36). By analogy with Astarte's journey to the Netherworld, domain of spirits dwelling in snakes, by being shown naked with snakes the Goddess was overwhelmingly associated with her stay down in the womb of the Earth, where, stripped of her dress, she hung dead like a piece of meat on a wooden stake (see Chapter 2). As a Triple Goddess, her other names referred to her dominion over the stars (the zodiac) and the sky (the planets), apart from her dominion over the Earth. The Canaanite Goddess/priestess of snakes is contemporary with Minoan counterparts, and their Under- world cults were probably related.

Snakes seemed to slither about as chthonic guard- ians of sacred sites, as they did later at Delphi and Athens (see Chapters 9 and 10).

This helps to understand why in Canaan there was more of an Under- world flavour to the practice of religion which, on the model of the self-sacrifice of Tammuz enabling his beloved's return, involved human sacrifice itself, the price to be paid for their mutual love. Both these

36 The Underworld character of the priestesshood in Canaan was based on the behaviour of the Goddess Anat/Astarte, usually shown nude, holding serpents and standing on her lion, as on this charac- teristic gold neck pendant; now in the Louvre, c.1450–1350 BC.

realities contributed to the Canaanite priestess's relative instability due to operating only at dangerous borderlines, to her tendency to concentrate on sexual tantrism at the cost of the serenity given by the suffusion of the higher worlds to regulate Underworld rites.

The savageness of the Canaanite world is shown by a myth from Ugarit which describes a battle between Baal and his rival Yam, God of the Stormy Sea, in which his sister Anat makes herself up with henna, coriander and purple murex dye and gets down to shedding the blood of the worshippers of Baal in the valley of the two cities Ugarit and Minet el-Beida until 'heads were like balls beneath her' and she 'plunged her knees in the blood of the guards, her skirts in the gore of the warriors, until she was sated with fighting in the house'. (This scene has been compared with the description, in the book of Kings, of the prophets of Baal on Mount Carmel who danced around the altar, lacerating themselves until the blood ran, to propitiate the God for rain.) Later in the story Anat colours El's beard red with her gore, thereby rejuvenating him.

Throughout Canaan and her colonies in north Africa and islands in the Mediterranean and Atlantic (Bel and Astarte are still alive in Britain in Bel- and -Star placenames, and Druids dimly remember their Phoenician links with stone circles) evidence for the practice of human, and especially child, sacrifice is overwhelmingly strong. If priestesses officiated at sacred marriages throughout the country as representatives of the Goddess, then on the bloodthirsty image of Anat given above (which resembles that of the Indian devourer, Kali), it is quite likely that they also played a part in the killing of children in its ritualized form, as a supreme blood-spilling to ensure the renewal of life in the uncertain conditions of the Holy Land.

To kill a baby is a desperate rite symbolically, fusing the dual concepts of death and life. A visit to the *tophet*, or cemetery, of ancient Carthage as first rediscovered by the archaeologists would have presented a vista of funerary stelae, or *hammanim*, which marked the spots at which human sacrifice (*mulk*), usually of babies, had been carried out in order to attract the blessing of Baal and his consort Tanit, the latter usually depicted on slabs as a conical stone with little arms and head. Most remains are datable to the Classical period.

Even at Jerusalem the *tophet* (a Hebrew word referring to the brazier in which the body was half-burned before burial) of the Valley of Ben-Hinnom bears witness to the hundreds of child sacrifices that took place here long before Carthage was colonized. It was indeed the Valley of the Shadow of Mot, or Death. As Solomon's son David emotively described it in Psalm 106:

Yea, they sacrificed their sons and their daughters unto devils, and shed innocent blood ... whom they sacrificed unto the idols of Caanan: and the land was polluted with blood.

As far as relating to this rite in the twentieth century is concerned, while no-one would want to needlessly kill a baby as part of religious ritual, there are many instances in everyday life where natural death occurs, or abortion has to happen, which could be treated as a rite. Here the thought is to facilitate the return of the little soul to its source and look on the happy side of the fact that it did not have to take on a human body for very long, that it was released from incarnation and its miseries. This is a common event of life where not only doctors and nurses could be present, but also a priestess, to perform an appropriate rite which would also

be of help to the mother and father in accepting what has happened. In fact we do not know whether the many babies found in the *tophets* of Carthage or Jerusalem were all deliberately sacrificed or whether some were babies who had died naturally.

The story of Abraham and Isaac shows how a new attitude was formed towards this practice by the Hebrews, for whom animal substitution was less abhorrent. Even at Carthage animals were found very often to have been substituted for children, and in the later Greek Eleusinian Mysteries, little pink piglets were substituted as a matter of course.

Gradually the Hebrews systematized sacrifices into types. As in Sumerian times, fruit, grains and liquids could be offered. In the killing of an animal, the draining of its blood ensured its soul returned to Heaven, and was an expiatory act. (It remained a crucial doctrine that all the blood be poured onto the earth and not be consumed by humans. This could be due to the high iron content of blood, which is more useful to the earth, as well as the waste matter it carries, which is injurious to human health.) By burning the carcass, in a holocaust, smoke took the prayer to Heaven. If it were only cooked rather than burnt, a communion took place afterwards where the priesthood could eat it, thus joining with God by eating His substance. There is no record of priestesses officiating in these kinds of activity, since by then they were debarred from Hebrew temple life because of the contrast of the Canaanite modes: 'And ye shall be unto Me a kingdom of priests, and a holy nation' (Exodus 19:6).

Alongside such Hebrew codifications, though, overall one could be bold enough to generalize that other temples in Canaan from 2000 BC onwards, in taking over the baton of priestesshood from Mesopotamia, continued to develop the stronger Netherworld associations throughout the millennium which brought it, rightly or wrongly, ever more deeply into disrepute. Even some of the more decadent Gnostic rites recorded from this region many centuries later bear a resemblance to their activities. Lying out of immediate reach of Babylonia, Canaanite priestesses must have had to adapt dignified Mesopotamian ways to the local mentality.

Even in Babylonia itself priestesses no longer enjoyed quite the same position as they had at the time of Enheduanna and her successors, though for the duration of Hammurabi's empire Moon Priestesses still officiated, for worship of the moon did not cease to be of central importance. A Babylonian version of the Gilgamesh myth actually accuses Ishtar of misleading the hero by making him her lover, and having other lovers, where in Sumerian times it would have been understood as his great privilege, and that he could not have obtained his kingship without gaining authority from the Goddess in Inanna's priestess, in the usual manner.

Here in Canaan, Ishtar was known as Astarte, sometimes analysed as meaning 'She who gives Life to the Bull' (ʿash-thawr). Though she was often equated with the local Amorite Goddess Ellaat, Ellaat herself is more often identified as an Arabian Ereshkigal, Queen of the Underworld, her permanent abode, and is not an equivalent to Astarte, who passed through, but came back. Astarte is less easy to distinguish from the Canaanite Anat, described on one stela as Goddess of the Sky and Ruler of all the Gods, which is really the description best suited to Astarte herself, but possibly the Canaanites themselves mismatched the newcomer Goddess to those already existing. Certainly in Ugaritic mythology,

Astarte, Ellaat and Anat are given different husbands, though made to belong to one extended family. Perhaps they are best understood as an early version of the Triple Goddess, whose triplicity is confusingly interchangeable, unseizable as the water they protect.

The name Anat, which has the Semitic sound *'ayn* before the 'A', means 'water source', and indeed the Goddess of Life in the entire region was primarily worshipped at springs and oases, wherever water flowed to bring life. Perhaps because of her association with water she was called 'virgin' (*betoulat*), which is close to the word for baetyl (see below), and is often shown holding a mirror. Her association with the Storm God Baal/Haddad/Teshub is natural, since rain results from his lightning and thunder claps across the mountain tops. Hence Anat herself was later called 'Baal's Name', or 'The Face of Baal', since lightning releases her water from the clouds, making his power show, as a face reflects thoughts and emotions.

In a hot country where agriculture flourished according to the vagaries of rainfall rather than via a reliable irrigation system, the Goddess was viewed as highly capricious, like an amorous woman who might withdraw her favours at the last minute. Thus the smooth running of the sacred marriage between Heaven and Earth was chancy and fraught with danger, manifesting as spasmodic releases of water triggered by unreliably timed thunder and lightning. Indeed the entire psychology of people in the region has ever been strained by the high tension caused by the contradictions of a loving sensuality reined in by deathly barriers, which judgemental Islamic or Jewish rules perpetuate today.

In this area, then as now, life flirts with death constantly, and in Ugaritic mythology the other successful murderer of Baal was the God of Death, or Drought, Mot. According to Sanchoniathon and Damascius, at the beginning of time, Mot was an egg which, when split in two, produced Uranus and Ge, Heaven and Earth, from whose marriage the whole creation ensued. Mot is the original Mother's Womb/Tomb from which all things come and to which all things return, being more a Pluto energy than the Venus energy of Anat. In Canaanite-influenced Egypt, both were blended in the wife of the Sky God Amun, the Lioness Goddess Mut, whose other animal familiar was the vulture, devourer of the dead.

In the Ugaritic text giving the

story of Baal and Mot, Anat goes to the Netherworld to search for Baal, and demands his return from Mot, who in this story is male and has taken the place of Ellaat. He denies he knows where Baal is and as the days pass and the drought gets worse Anat becomes desperate as she searches for her beloved Baal. Then:

She seized divine Mot,
With a blade she split him,
With a sieve she winnowed him,
With fire she burnt him,
In a field she scattered him;
So that his flesh the birds could
   eat,
So that his parts the sparrows
   could peck.

Announcing that Mot has perished (and Inanna never succeeded in doing the same to Ereshkigal, nor did Tammuz come to search for her with the same fervour as Anat for Baal), Anat rejoices that from now on 'the heavens will rain oil, the ravines flow with honey' because Baal will now come back to life.

This is but one text from Canaan which gives a variation on the blueprint myth of the entire ancient Near East, that of the dying God who is restored to life by the Goddess. It was celebrated under many guises, whether the hero was named Tammuz, Baal, Adonis, Osiris, Attis, Dionysius or Jesus Christ. We have to consider how deeply important the rites connected with this particular myth were to local rulers, such as to the ancient king of Moab, who had himself depicted on a basalt stone between Baal and Anat, looking so Egyptian that at first they could be mistaken for Osiris and Isis.

Anat's particular function was to 'feed the Gods' through sacrifices, whether of animals or humans, or even of the God Mot himself as described above, to ensure fertility of the land. Hence in this part of the world the idea that war was a sacrifice to the Gods fits into place perfectly naturally, an attitude perpetuated in the Islamic idea of 'The Holy War', where loss of life is regarded as a spiritual attainment. So Anat is a much more difficult - or perhaps we should say for those with a lurid temperament, a much *too easy* - role model for priestesses to follow than was Inanna/Ishtar or consorts of the Gods such as Ningal. The perfectly balanced and integrated priestess is harder work to achieve, because work is done at the mental and spiritual levels of the Sephiroth, whereas there have always been adherents of Underworld cults among groups interested by the sensational lure of the

Underworld/Psyche, relying more on an oral tradition of magic and gypsy lore passed on for generations. Of course that world must have its due in the scheme of things, but it is a mistake to think that the Netherworld is worth staying in, even if it needs to be explored in order to be understood. I sympathize more with the Inanna/Ishtar who makes the return journey successfully and re-establishes links between Heaven and Earth, thus putting the Netherworld into its true perspective. Even though it is necessary to 'make visits' to the murky domain of the psyche in order to know what is going on, it cannot take the place of such higher dimensions as the angelic powers and divine qualities in everyday life: these all have their position on the Tree of Life. The job of the priestess is to act as a bridge between these invisible worlds and the world at large - the very function which the priesthood these days neglects, for the Underworld has a way of obstructing access. Hence the enormous need to study the universal spiritual language preserved by the Kabbalah or the Sanātana dharma of Vedanta - languages such as number, geometry, colour or music, which lie beyond the clichés of individual religious traditions.

By the end of the Bronze Age in Canaan, the priesthood, through its unrelieved sexuality, had become so dissolute that the priestesses brought scorn upon themselves. The male priesthood even gave themselves over to female sexual practices as eunuchs of the Goddess - on the model of which the present priesthood of the Catholic Church continues.

This was the situation when, soon after the start of the first millennium, a generation or two after Solomon built the Temple, a particular priestess of Astarte Qarnain (the Two-Horned Venus) is recorded in the book of Kings as actively practising the cycle of rites connected with the dying and resurrected Baal - and that is Jezebel. Carved ivories of the time coming from that region show a woman looking out of the window. This has been linked to the Astarte cult and the special look given by the temple priestess inviting the man in to the sacred marriage (Figure 37). Remembering that in Mesopotamian art only the Goddess Inanna or the high priestess was entitled to looked out frontally to the viewer (see Figures 37 and 39), in Canaan the woman at the window motif could therefore show Astarte herself at the window, or a priestess in her service. When

37 One of many hundreds of ivories showing the woman at the window on the model of descriptions of the high priestess Jezebel, a product of the craftsmen of Syria much prized by Assyrians in the early first millennium; this one is in the British Museum, c.900 BC.

used by the shaktic priestesses in Cyprus (see below), this special 'I am staring at you: look at me!' stance was called the *parakyptousa*, or 'sidelong glance through the window'. Before this, 'She who nods at the window' was the epithet given to a Babylonian Goddess whose origins were Sumerian. Jezebel herself is described in II Kings 9:30 waiting for Jehu: 'And she painted her eyes, and attired her head, and looked out of the window.'

To digress for a moment, the theology of The Look thus had roots in Sumer. The Sumerian statues that featured earlier in this book have enormous, staring eyes. Sometimes the eyes appear alone on pottery or stone pots of the period to represent the divine presence, for it is transmitted by human eyes. Through the eyes one connects with the divine in a person - and thus with The Divine. The 'look of the priestess' is thus a most important act, but in Canaan it became degraded into mere harlotry by becoming disconnected from its celestial channels, inviting only to personal sexual experience.

It is worth considering how women use their eyes now. In the Middle East they are often the only thing that can be seen, and as much expressive use is made of them as in the old days at the temple window! In the West we make them up mostly to attract people *to* us. I tried an exercise where I was the one looking at people, radiating out love and interest - how powerful it is to use the eyes to give. Whatever is going on in the brain, the eyes will reflect. That explains the change that happened far away in history now, when the eyes turned into a vehicle for the self-centred ego, instead of looking out on behalf of the Goddess, *at* the Creation. Many versions of · the woman at the window, including the one illustrated here, do indeed seem to look out rather than invite in. Watch yourself in the way you use your eyes - a whole world of spiritual reorientation is there. People will be more attracted when you cease to try to attract! And what should they be attracted to - your body, your mind, or to the divine Goddess looking through you? Monitor the input beyond your eyes, stop playing games and provide a clear channel.

By the time, then, that Jezebel appears in history, the Hebrews had become thoroughly Semitized through staying in Canaan (despite a first visit to Egypt), and for a long time 'there was no king in Israel: every man did that which was right in his own eyes' (last verse of Judges). But as time went on, this particular community began to reject the increasingly licentious shaktic priesthood of Canaan ('there shall be no whore of the daughters of Israel, nor a sodomite of the sons of Israel' Deuteronomy 23:17). At first they had mixed up their own traditions with local practices, which on first sight had appeared acceptable, but after their second stay in Egypt, and the rise of Moses under the Queen Hatshepsut (or was it Ramses II?),

they had finally returned to Canaan, finally wresting from the Amorites that land they believed was now theirs by moral right.

Scholars argue that at this time when a new covenant was made between Moses and Jahweh, their extant body of scripture was overhauled and the Book of Deuteronomy written. When it was rediscovered very much later and taken to Josiah by the scribe Shaphan, it was read out to him. The king was unable to judge its authenticity and sent a delegation to consult the prophetess Huldah, who in Mitchell's account 'pronounced in the name of Jahweh a condemnation of apostasy and heterodoxy', and prophesied a coming judgement on Jerusalem which would be held off until after Josiah's death.

Far more amazing than Huldah's authority in judging Jewish scripture is the assertion made in Bloom's new book called *The Book of J*, in which he claims that the core material of the Old Testament/Torah was written by an enlightened Hebrew woman. In his words:

I am assuming J lived at or nearby the Court of Solomon's son and successor, King Rehoboam of Judah . . . My further assumption is that J was not a professional scribe but rather an immensely sophisticated, highly placed member of the Solomonic élite.

He argues that her view blended Canaanite and Hebrew strands in an all-embracing, if ironic tolerance, and that her imagery is vividly concrete. Only later reworkings by male contributors with a particular dogma they wished to impose on the material, like steel splints to a leg, stifled the original freshness of her anthology.

Despite attempts to hold them at arm's length, however, Canaanite practices continued to infiltrate Jewish life. The mother of King Asa, son of Rehoboam, still worshipped Astarte, and the kings like him who followed after Solomon still sacrificed at the high places, marked by the Canaanite-type pillars and sacred poles known as *asherim*. Even so, pious Jews fought against the continued inclusion of 'foreign elements' and judgements for and against see-sawed for centuries, and are recorded in the Old Testament.

For this reason Jezebel, so deeply disapproved of by Elijah, has a bad press in the Old Testament as we have it today, reworked by many disapproving male pens. This she may not actually deserve – for all royal women seem to have felt more at home with Goddess-based practices. Living in the ninth century BC, she was probably the daughter of Itto-Baal, high priest of Astarte and king of Tyre, who wished to reawaken Astarte worship in the lands beyond his own kingdom. Jezebel, who was her father's daughter in this respect, was given by him in marriage to Ahab, king of Israel, son of Omri.

We are told the princess took with her to her new kingdom all the paraphernalia of her religious worship, together with her sacerdotal entourage. Four hundred and fifty priests of Baal were attached to the worship of that God in Israel and 400 others who served Astarte dwelt in the precinct of Jezebel's palace and were fed by her there until a temple was built for them to minister. Through her persistence, Ahab built both a great temple to Baal at Samaria, and a sanctuary to Astarte at Jezreel, presenting these Canaanite forms as a legitimate religion to the Israelites, such that they apostasized from the worship of Jahweh.

Ahab ruled for 21 years, and Jezebel survived him for a further 14 years, maintaining the practices of her own religion during the reigns of her sons. When Jehu became king of Israel, however, even though she had tried to charm him through the window as he approached, he had Jezebel killed along with most of her line, and the temple of Baal at

Samaria, with all its worshippers, was destroyed. Given the conflicting evidence, we just do not know whether Jezebel was a fallen priestess, using her eyes wrongly, or someone using them rightly and trying to get the Old Religion back on the rails.

Jezebel's daughter Athaliah, also a priestess of Astarte, had been married off by Jezebel to King Ahaziah of the nearby kingdom of Judah, and she in the same way brought the cult of Astarte to that kingdom. When Ahaziah was murdered by Jehu, Athaliah took the throne, killing all those with a claim to it and establishing the Baal cult as the state religion. Later the High Priest Jehoiada put her to death, but after he died the cult of Baal and Astarte returned as before, fostered by the nobility. The prophet Ezekiel was quite certain the fortunes of the Jews failed because they had turned to these practices, bewailing the fact that as he was brought 'to the door of the house of Jahweh which was towards the north; behold, there sat women weeping for Tammuz'. Similarly, Jeremiah said, 'Will ye . . . burn incense unto Baal and walk after other gods whom ye know not?' Then, quite beyond himself, 'Seest thou not what they do in the cities of Judah and in the streets of Jerusalem? The children gather wood, and the fathers kindle the fire, and the women knead their dough, to make cakes to the Queen of Heaven, and to pour out drink offerings unto other gods . . .!'

As late as the end of the nineteenth century, a Mr H. A. Harper, who was on a sketching tour in Palestine, describes how in the neighbourhood of Nazareth he came across about 300 peasant women dancing to the Goddess. Drawn into the jollification, he was presented with two conical cakes of lightly baked dough, marked with a crescent moon! Similarly at Easter to celebrate the resurrection of Christ we make special hot cross buns and give Easter eggs, which originally referred to Astarte/Mot.

All the examples given of the Canaanite worship of Astarte go to show that it was a religion that suited women, and that all through the second millennium BC there was a women-led religion and a men-led religion. If this is so, perhaps the best way to go forward in the second millennium AD is similarly to develop a women-led religion, which men can participate in on women's terms, parallel with religions which are male-dominated which women may participate in on men's terms. This seems much more fair, and also reasonable. Hence it may be fruitless for women to try and get the Church, synagogue or mosque to accept them on their terms, an attempt which so far has meant nothing but humiliation. They will have more success by keeping to practices tailor-made to their own perspective. Easier said than done!

⌒✦⌒

The Easter rite particularly gives clues about the worship of Bel and Astarte even in the Hyperborean countries: it spread anywhere interesting metals could be mined by the sea-faring Canaanites, known in the Iron Age as Phoenicians. The name 'Ittobaal' was for the Jews the name 'Tubal', and the Canaanite word *qayin* meant a metalsmith. Tubal Cain in the Old Testament was the quintessential craftsman clever at fashioning metal, who nonetheless socially was 'beyond the pale'. Such craftsmen helped in the fashioning both of Canaanite or Jewish temples.

The best known of these was the ingenious master craftsman, Hiram of Tyre, who cast all the metalwork for Solomon's temple, built in the tenth century BC, shortly before the time of Jezebel. His masterpiece was the Sea of Brass, which was a large vessel on wheels to contain ablution water,

fed into many spouts. Its bowl was supported by lionesses and bulls - evidently it was impossible to exclude Anat and Baal! (Exodus 38 describes a different font for ablutions made of metal which was cast from the bronze mirrors of women who queued in crowds to make their contribution.)

What did The Temple of Solomon look like? Very like temples of Baal and Astarte, even to the use of horned altars. There are many more archaeological remains today of the Canaanite temples than of Solomon's (now the Temple Mount), but there is a very full, if sometimes ambiguous, verbal description of its construction in the Book of Kings. One could bear in mind, too, that by the time Solomon's Temple was built, the Jews had come and gone from Egypt and spliced further elements into their own religious practices which derived from that civilization. One writer has suggested the best surviving look-alike for Solomon's temple is the Egyptian temple of Khonsu at Karnak, which has an outer court, an inner court and a holy of holies. But the third-millennium Mesopotamian temples, as at Khafaje, are just as close in general layout.

Whichever model Solomon's Temple was based on, both the

Egyptian and the Mesopotamian temple type lacked one vital feature at their very heart which was the unique contribution of Canaan, and was also first adopted then discarded by the Hebrews. A large conical stone was placed at the centre of the inner sanctum, which was usually on the highest point of the area, often on a mountain top open to the sky. This helped to focus worship on the divinity.

Given the difficulties of visiting the more unusual archaeological sites in the troubled Holy Land today, the nearest I have been to experiencing a High Place, as opposed to a straightforward temple, is atop the spectacular rocky city of Petra, in Jordan. This is not, however, particularly associated with any recorded priestess activity, though it has been claimed that the Kanz, the first building one sees blazing in light at the end of the dark rocky defile when penetrating into Petra, was a tomb dedicated by the Nabataeans in Classical times to the protection of Baal and Astarte. David Roberts' lovely watercolour of the Kanz puts the horns back on Astarte, the central figure on the pediment, while the eagles of Baal perch on each end.

In the case of the supreme God, El, the holy of Holies was called the House of El, *Bayt-El*,

but later the conical stone itself came to be called a *baetyl*, literally a 'divine stone'. It was not meant to be made into a statue of a God or Goddess as was the practice in Mesopotamia, indeed it was to be a naturally weathered stone, or at the most split out of a natural rock seam and left unhewn - hence the Jewish Commandment against graven images, or actual statues of divinities. Throughout the Old Testament, oaths and covenants were made standing by such pillars of stone, or *masseboth*. Baetyl worship, which implied the impossibility of confusing an outward shape with the inner nature of the God or Goddess addressed, entailed leaving it abstract, and such worship continued into Archaic Greek times (see Chapter 9), when Apollo, Artemis or Aphrodite were frequently represented by aniconic stones.

For practical reasons, shrines in open spaces were often closed in to keep out sun and rain, and the temenos protected by a wall to keep out the profane, who were put to death if they entered. One of the most intriguing reconstructions of a Canaanite temple (by E. Renan) I have come across shows a late Phoenician cubic shrine to Baal (Jupiter) from Amrith set at the centre of a temenos formed by a previously existing neolithic stone circle, of which there are many still to be seen throughout Canaan. The drawing resembles an account of the ancient temple of pre-Islamic Mecca, which consisted of three upright monoliths dedicated to the three Goddesses, Al'Uzzah, Ellaat, and Al-Manaat, with 360 stones placed round it in a circle standing for the days of the lunar year. Perhaps contemporary with that temple, it is worth remembering that during the wanderings of the Jews in the lands of the moon (Sin-ai) just two items were placed inside their portable holy of holies or Ark of the Covenant between God and Moses: two stones recording the Ten Commandments.

If the reconstruction is valid, perhaps an idea of the exterior appearance of a second-millennium Canaanite temple can be gained from the present-day temples of Malta, especially the magnificent open-air complex at Hajar Qim which overlooks the sea (Figure 38). In a similar temple called Gigantija, on the nearby island of Gozo, a baetyl of Astarte was found still in the sanctuary. The interior plans of the Maltese temples, however, are quite different from the usual Canaanite layout.

The best Canaanite-type temple whose plan can be studied and easily visited on site is that at Paphos in Cyprus, where the Classical temple to Aphrodite, last inheritor of Astarte worship, was built over an earlier Phoenician version, of which only the ground

38 The temple of Hajar Qim in Malta gives a rough idea of how Canaanite temples in Canaan itself could have looked from the outside in the second millennium; c.2000 BC.

plan remains for those with sharp eyes. The treat is to see in the site museum the remains of the conical stone used to mark the Goddess's inner sanctum. Polished, weathered, black and assymetrical, it asks to be stroked, touched and kissed, for it radiates great power. Conical stones from other Phoenician sites of a later period (see Chapter 10) survive from points as far flung in the sea-faring network as Antibes in France, Carthage in north Africa (where the Goddess was called Tanit rather than Anat), Kythera and many places in Greece, where sometimes to avoid all doubt they are inscribed with the name of Aphrodite.

On the Paphos temple site itself, looking from its interior on the hillside terrace across to the sea, a hollow cement replica marks the baetyl's original position, now framed between two pieces of ugly twentieth-century masonry. Legend has it that when it rained on the island of Astarte, Queen of Heaven, it never rained over the sanctuary of her temple. It was Elissa, better known as Dido, a great-granddaughter of Ittobaal (father of Jezebel) who, according to the more apocryphal late Classical writers, was dethroned by her brother, and escaped to Cyprus and then Carthage, spreading the worship of Astarte in the process. The cult of the Paphian Venus in turn travelled far and wide: inscriptions tell of daughter temples in Pergamon in western Anatolia, Cnidos, Crete, Carthage in north Africa, Cagliari in Sardinia, Erice in Sicily, and Naucratis on the Egyptian Delta.

As in Astarte temples in Canaan, it is on record that at this temple Canaanite priestesses – and perhaps co-opted local women – offered themselves for the shaktic rite of union with the Goddess on as large a scale as they did at Babylon centuries later. Clement of Alexandria and Justin both later referred to the organization of the rite as brought over from Tyre and Sidon by Kinyras, priest of Astarte. Here he took on the role of the Goddess's consort as Pygmalion (the original Cypriote name is Pumiaton), who, the later Greek myth goes, fell in love so ardently with her image that she came to life to satisfy his desires (another *hieros gamos*), their son being Adonis.

Although at the time of Moses Cyprus was a possession of Egypt, religion spread here in its Canaanite, or Hyksos, form. The temple at Paphos was founded by the mother temple of Astarte of Ascalon, near Tyre, in the fifteenth century BC, and its Tyrian founder, Kinyras, founded a hereditary king-priesthood of Astarte here, the priestesses being junior to him. Like the priests of Astarte on the mainland, such as Eshmunazar and Tabnit, kings of Sidon, or, earlier, Ittobaal, Jezebel's father, king of Tyre, they, too, were senior to the priestesses and organized them.

At the turn of the first millennium the Assyrian king of Nineveh, Ashurnasirpal, who had had a special bed made for the Goddess, addressed Ishtar of Nineveh as 'Thy priest-king, favourite who never changes'. The expanding power of the Assyrian empire eventually occupied Cyprus itself, and the cult of Astarte on the island was then run on the lines of the Assyrian and Babylonian cult of Astarte of Nineveh in northern Mesopotamia. Certainly at this time the Canaanite and Cypriote priest-kings made sure to enhance their authority through the rite of sacred marriage to the Goddess.

When Canaanites and then Assyrians brought the Astarte cult to Cyprus, not only was Paphos chosen as a useful vantage point for sailing south to Egypt, but temples were also founded at Amathus and Kition; the remains at Kition still known today as the temple of Astarte, though no baetyl remains. During the time of the Trojan War, the Kinyrad

line had been expelled from the island by the Mycenaeans, who in turn stepped smoothly into the eastern rites, already having strong links with Hyksos customs because they had fought as mercenaries for them in Egypt.

Many of the traces of baetyl worship have disappeared, and the stones themselves often been destroyed, smashed to smithereens by monotheists. One baetyl, however, continues in use today, and is regularly kissed and stroked: the Black Stone of Astarte which is incorporated into the Ka'aba at Mecca in a silver frame. It is ironic that Ellaat was originally the protecting Goddess of the tribe of Taqif, based at Taif (just outside Mecca), and indeed of the Tribe of Quraish in Mecca itself, to which the Prophet Muhammad belonged. At Taif before the advent of Islam she was revered in a temple on a white rectilinear base, and as a tree on which pieces of cloth and weapons were hung.

Stony Arabia is the heartland of Semitism, and of the mentality that the divine can only be worshipped in abstract terms. Proto-Jewish doctrine was infiltrated by Canaanite abstract thought, and, like the Islamic centuries later, came to abhor attempts to represent the divine by human images. Even though in developed Judaism and Islam the female half of Athtar was denied an existence, it nonetheless provides a hidden ground swell in the religion. Driven underground, Mot and Anat hold sway in the Middle East as the pull between war and suppressed sensuality; and Ellaat is powerfully hidden in the word for God, pronounced 'Allaah', written with exactly the same spelling in Arabic for both names! The suppressed priestesshood of Canaan, whether Arab or Jew, still knows its craft from centuries of memories locked in every cell of flesh, and it will inevitably step to the fore as the new century dawns.

It is simple and effective to focus on the Ultimate Power in abstract form, and you, too, may wish to use a stone. You may also decide it must be unhewn, and look for a piece from a natural rocky outcrop, or a pebble thrown up by the sea. Like the more familiar (to Westerners) omphalos of Delphi, it becomes symbolic of the Absolute Centre. It could be very large and like a menhir, placed in the sanctuary of your garden, or be small, for your altar or mantelpiece.

You may, indeed, like the idea of having two stones, one male and one female, standing side by side, or fitting like lingam and yoni one into the other. As you meditate on the stones' lack of human associations, the fact that they in some strange way embody the ultimate, unformed substance of God and Goddess before the world emanated from them brings the mind and heart to a complete stop - and rest. By coming to a stand-still and focusing on the virgin, formless baetyl, the vast Divine Peace, the Shekinah, will make itself known, opposites in resolution, the One.

In Canaan the Goddess and her son-consort were, however, also worshipped as trees like cypresses, pines or junipers, either alive within a sacred grove, or as stripped tree poles: one *asherah*, or a pair of *asherim* placed at either side of a temple entrance or framing the doorway to the inner sanctum.

At Christmas the fairy at the top of the tree is a faint reminder that it is the whole tree as Goddess whom we should revere. But in Canaan all through the year they used to sacrifice upon the tops of the mountains, and burn incense upon the hills, under oaks and poplars and elms, 'because the shadow thereof is good' (Hosea 4:13). In Jewish thinking it is the *masseba*, or stylized date-palm (made of stone or of wood), which like the upright Egyptian Djed column is associated with the idea of permanence, and the Everlasting.

Some centuries later Pausanias in his description of ancient vestiges of the cult of the Queen of Heaven (so called because she was born direct from the semen of Uranus/Anu) in gardens on the north slope of the Athenian Acropolis - which probably used to be her sacred grove - describes the history of her advent from Assyria to Ascalon in Palestine, moving then to Paphos, Kythera and finally Athens. Pausanias saw her in Athens as a pillar of stone with a female head, and connected with the name Aphrodite-Baalat (the female Baal). Although a late sculpture, this seemed to commemorate the ancient roots of her cult many centuries earlier, especially as later excavations were to discover some 200 skeletons of sacrificed babies buried beneath it, which cannot have happened in Classical times.

But the earliest representation of Athena herself, also born direct from the Sky God Zeus, is described as a *xoanon*, simply an aniconic piece of wood, standing for the Goddess in the sacred olive tree. The Classical writer Nonnus described how, further east, the island of Tyre floated in the sea and sheltered the olive tree of Astarte, guarded by an eagle and a serpent. The distinguished priestesshood of Athena (see Chapter 10), probably derived from a priestesshood of the Astarte type at a time when transmission from Phoenicians to Mycenaeans was taking place at the turn of the first millennium.

❧

Similarly, you could reinstate the worship of God and/or Goddess as trees. While writing this chapter, I looked out of my kitchen window and realized I had in my back garden a sycamore tree which I used to curse because of all the seeds and seedlings I have to weed each year. I looked twice on this occasion and thought, 'That is Hathor/Astarte, and I have been ignoring her all these years!' All of a sudden the tree became both majestic and mysterious, and I realized the Goddess has looked over my garden to remind me of Life, or the Axis of the World, day in, day out, without my connecting. But you may prefer to move more deeply inwards and use the Sephiroth, or the chains of Sephirothic Trees, from the Kabbalah, for this is the Body of Astarte in its entirety.

❧

One of the most beautiful scenes to be saved by the spade from Ugarit (Figure 39) shows the now

familiar meeting between ruler and priestess, either side of a stylized date-palm - or Tree of Life, since it has a carefully carved *ankh* floating above it. Compared to the raunchy meeting between a provincial Amorite ruler and a sexy Venus in Figure 33, this encounter is refined and restrained. The ruler raises one hand, and one muscular leg steps forward from within his Syrian fur-bordered robe to greet the priestess, who herself raises her arms in a gesture of intercession. Possibly she has just accorded him the boomerang of authority as used in that part of the world. The sacred marriage between male and female energy has once more been celebrated, and controlled growth means that one more layer can be added to the tree of the state.

The war between priests and priestesses, as it began in second-millennium Canaan (or did it begin with Adam and Eve?), and yet rages in its new form, threatens the Tree of Life. But renewed co-operation between the sexes - in the knowledge of its occurrence in ancient history - will revive It, and the Serpent of communication and transformation will convulse once more, connecting the higher and lower dimensions, as if an electric current has been switched on after replacement of a blown fuse.

39 Haematite cylinder seal from Ugarit showing an Ugaritic ruler facing a high priestess who represents the Goddess, standing either side of the sacred tree, or Asherah; now in the Louvre - photo courtesy Musées Nationaux, Paris.

6

DRAMATIC
PERFORMANCES

Role type: Potnia

CRETE AND MYCENAE
By Michael Duigan

It should first be admitted that little is known about the religious beliefs of prehistoric Greece. It is very probable that the numerous images on engraved rings, seal stones and frescoes illustrate religious subjects, but the substance of their beliefs must forever remain conjectural. The problem is not helped by our present inability to decipher the Minoan tablets written in Linear A script.

Nevertheless, the uniform character and recurring iconographic themes of Cretan art must reveal something about the essence of Cretan religion and its priestesses. The most striking quality is its gentle, feminine nature – in sharp contrast with male-dominated, Indo-European religious beliefs.

In common with many other peoples of the ancient Near East, the Cretans' religious concerns focused on fertility and rebirth in the form of a creative maternal Goddess, but in a form unique in the ancient world. Originally this Goddess was depicted naked, for example on a vessel found at Mallia. Later she is represented in the elaborate robes of a court lady, but her fertility is still emphasized by ample breasts (see Frontispiece). The numerous and varied images represent what was essentially a single deity in three main aspects: a domestic Goddess (Figure 40) holding snakes (an ancestress of Athena), a Goddess of vegetation and rebirth dancing in wild places (associated with Ariadne) and finally the Mistress of Wild Animals – the Cretan Britomartis, later to reappear in Classical times as Artemis.

What was it about Minoan religious belief that gave a special place to women in spiritual matters? The supreme act of creation is birth, and the religious awe inspired by this awareness shaped their view of the natural world. Just as the creative power of women ensured the continued existence of the human species, in like manner Gaia, the Earth, created an abundance of grain and fruit to ensure survival. In this scheme of things nature is a Great Mother and the vegetation which, in the cycle of the seasons, dies only to be reborn, is a young God seen as her child and later her lover. A gold Minoan/Mycenaean signet ring must illustrate this belief in which votaries mourn the shedding of leaves on deciduous trees in autumn and joyfully greet their return in spring. To secure the continuity of this cycle of fertility, sexual procreation must have had an important ritual significance. At Palaikastro in a temple of Dictaian Zeus, a hymn was written, possibly dating from the 3C BC though the content is much older, supporting the view that sexual rites formed part of a spring festival to bring about rebirth. As elsewhere in the ancient Near East, this uninhibited and natural view of sexual matters pervades Minoan religion and is reflected in the costume of both sexes.

It was this emphasis on the creative feminine principle that gave a dominant role to women in the religious cults of Bronze Age Greece, and their works of art leave us in no doubt about this. The painted clay Haghia Triadha sarcophagus (Figure 41) depicts a religious funerary rite which, while giving a detailed and vivid illustration of the ritual, cult objects and sacred costume

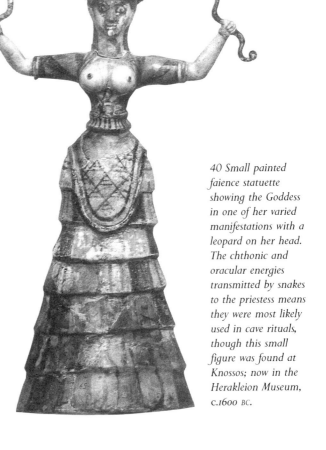

40 Small painted faience statuette showing the Goddess in one of her varied manifestations with a leopard on her head. The chthonic and oracular energies transmitted by snakes to the priestess means they were most likely used in cave rituals, though this small figure was found at Knossos; now in the Herakleion Museum, c.1600 BC.

41 Detail from the painted clay sarcophagus of a Mycenaean prince buried at Haghia Triadha, Crete, demonstrating conclusively that priestesses played the lead role in Cretan religion; now in the Herakleion Museum, c.1400 BC.

Bronze Age Crete there was harmony and consistency on this point, unlike modern times, where there is a growing mismatch between the role women are winning for themselves in secular affairs and the anachronistic position allocated to them in religious matters.

What did the Cretan priestesses look like? The statuettes and paintings show sophisticated women with their hair elaborately styled in coils and ringlets, wearing tight jackets with puffed sleeves supporting bare breasts. From their narrow waists heavily flounced skirts descended row upon row to little shoes. This elegant costume was enriched by elaborate gold jewellery. When performing ceremonies, ritual hats were worn in the form of a round flat cap with rosettes round the edge, and plumes, tassels or a beast placed on the centre. Another ritual addition took the form of a sacred knot worn at the back of the neck. For many ancient peoples the knot had magical healing and binding qualities and Cretan images sometimes show priestesses, or Goddesses, confining griffins with these knots. The discovery at Arkhanes of the tomb of a woman who may have been a queen/priestess fills out this picture. Her robe was enriched

used, shows women taking a leading part in the ceremonies. That they should continue to do so in Mycenaean times (the date of the sarcophagus, when religion was more male-oriented) only makes it certain that women played the leading role in Minoan religion. There is more to say about this sarcophagus later.

We do not know the legal and social status of women in general in ancient Crete, but the pre-eminence of women in their religion must reflect a basic attitude in their society. The Goddess, her cult images and symbols, were everywhere and must have enhanced women's self-esteem. Cretan paintings show them mixing without constraint with men and taking a leading part in the activities of palaces or religious shrines. Then, as now, society's attitude to women at large determined their role in spiritual matters. In by pieces of gold and she was wearing necklaces and rings of the same precious metal. One of the latter was engraved with a picture of a Goddess wearing a dress similar to her own. An interesting feature of sacred costume is that priests, in order to participate more fully in this female-dominated religion, practised ritual transvestism. This custom survived in Asia Minor where the priests of Kybele wore women's dress in later times.

The lives and careers of the Minoan priestesses will forever be lost to us, but the names of some of the royal priestesses survive in Greek mythology, including Pasiphae, Ariadne and Phaedra, and we can make informed speculations about their ritual activities in honour of the Goddess.

It is probable that the royal family - whose lives were proscribed by ritual - enacted the role of Gods, with the queen, seated on her alabaster throne, presiding over the religious drama. There is considerable archaeological evidence to support this notion of a queen-priestess as the occupant of the throne of Knossos, before the era of King Minos, which belongs to the later, Mycenaean age. In Cretan iconography the central figure is always a Goddess,

dominating a junior male deity. She is sometimes seated on a throne and even (on a seal found at Psychro) flanked by a pair of griffins. This provides a close parallel to the ritual throne at Knossos, likewise supported on either side by griffins. Opposed to this theory is the fact that the Knossos throne room in its present form dates from Mycenaean times and a similar arrangement exists at Mycenaean Pylos. Nevertheless, the decorative scheme may date from earlier times when a queen held temporal power, and she may have retained her ritual position as high priestess to the end of the Bronze Age.

The ritual drama probably took the form of libations, bull games, sacrifices and a sacred marriage. The queen/priestess, associated with the moon (Pasiphae means 'Full of Light'), was the sacred cow fertilized by the bull, the king, associated with the sun which also fertilizes the Earth. Their offspring, the heir, was called Asterion. As the child of the sun he was associated with the starry sky. In earlier times the death of the bull, the sacrificial animal, may have been as important ritually as that of the Bull of Apis, his counterpart in Egypt.

This construction provides an explanation for that strange

42 The bull-leaping games were closely associated with a Cretan fertility cult of the Goddess, and women played an equal role with men in this dangerous ritual, as is shown by contemporary paintings and this ivory and gold statuette of a leaper/catcher, possibly from Knossos; photo courtesy The Royal Ontario Museum, Toronto, c.1600 BC.

manifestation of religious life in Crete - the bull games. This was a fertility rite in which female athletes/priestesses, as well as males, encountered the virile bull. In the famous bull-leaping fresco from Knossos a man vaults over the bull's back while a woman grasps his horns in order to do likewise. The significance of this religious drama in Minoan belief is probably reflected in the myth of the love of Pasiphae for a bull.

Many other ceremonial acts, including prayers, were performed for the Goddess. Clay figures from late Minoan shrines suggest the attitude adopted by priestesses while praying was to have their arms outstretched parallel to the body and bent at the elbow so that the hands reach to the sky in supplication.

Offerings were also brought to a cult image by priestesses. One of the loveliest depictions of this is in a fresco from the 'House of the Ladies' at Santorini. Here the Goddess is seated before large sea-daffodils while priestesses bring offerings including a *peplos*, or robe (as their descendants did to Athena Parthenos). In another house on the same site a young priestess wearing a saffron-coloured dress is painted on a wall, offering a gold and silver bowl which contains either a cake or incense. The palace of Mallia still contains a circular ritual vessel, or Kernos, for the reception of such offerings. Containing a bowl at the centre with rounded hollows round the circumference, once filled with fruit, it formed a kind of wreath of 'First Fruit' offerings. We know that in later times Demeter received such offerings including oils, milk, wine, honey and cereals. The Haghia Triadha sarcophagus also shows offerings being made of fruit and wine to a sacred tree (Figure 43).

Using ritual vessels called rhytons, the priestesses poured libations into lustral areas which flowed from there to Mother Earth. The liquid poured may sometimes have taken the form of blood from a sacrificial animal – the rhyton in this case could be modelled on a bull's head. The detail on the Haghia Triadha sarcophagus depicts this ritual pouring, of which more will be said when discussing funerary rites. Priestesses also presided over, or participated in, ritual communion services. In a fresco fragment young men, wearing flounced robes, pass a two-handled goblet between them, accompanied in all probability by a priestess wearing a sacred knot – the famous 'La Parisienne'.

As we cannot read Linear A we do not know the meaning of inscriptions written on the inside of several cups. They may have imparted magical qualities to the contents or have been used to constrain spiritual powers. The priestesses may have used them for exorcism or to achieve magical ends. They could simply be dedications or declarations of ownership. Perhaps drugs were used by these priestesses to induce visions and trances: in Minoan art they are sometimes shown holding poppy seed

43 The other long side of the Haghia Triadha sarcophagus shows further rituals including sacrifice and libations carried out by priestesses assisted by male musicians, to ensure the resurrection of a dead prince; now in the Herakleion Museum, c.1400 BC.

flowers and one priestess is crowned with three seed heads which have been cut in order to extract the opium.

Natural or drug-induced states of ecstasy may have been a factor in that most typically Cretan form of honouring their Goddess: the dance. The surviving pictures make it certain that it is mainly – but not exclusively – women who are performing and that they rejoice in the ecstatic movement of their bodies infused by religious fervour. The famous gold ring from Isopata shows priestesses in a field of lilies engaged in an orgiastic dance, their bodies swaying, snake-like, in a state of trance. Another image shows two dancing priestesses flanking the Goddess who holds flowers in her hands. A fresco from Knossos shows dancing women (Figure 44), all with their right arm raised as they move in unison (forms of these ritual dances still survive in Crete). The very area in which this dance may have taken place still survives in Knossos in the form of a stepped area flanking a paved floor (Figure 45). This must be 'the dancing floor . . . that Daedalus designed in the spacious town of Knossos for Ariadne of the lovely locks . . .' celebrated by Homer in *The Iliad*. The famous reference also tells us about the form of the dance:

44 Later Greek legend attributed the invention of the sacred dance to ancient Crete, and priestesses are often shown in Cretan art worshipping their Goddess in movement, as in this restored fresco fragment from Knossos; now in the Herakleion Museum, c.1450 BC.

45 This famous theatre area at the site of Knossos may be the 'dancing floor' which Homer tells us Daedalus constructed for Ariadne at Knossos. The stepped area - too shallow for seats - may have been designed to vary the heights of performers as on the modern stage.

Youths and maidens were dancing on it with their hands on one another's wrists. The girls garlanded and in fine linen . . . here they ran lightly round, circling as smoothly as the wheel of a potter when he sits and spins it with his hands: and there they ran in lines to meet each other.

Book xviii

Dance was so important in Minoan religious life that later Greek legend credited them with the invention of this art form. The famous Crane Dance was performed by Cretan priestesses and witnessed by Theseus, who introduced it to Delos. A fascinating group of pottery figures from Palaikastro shows dancing women who circle around a female lyre player, which may illustrate the ancient Cretan dance known as the *hyporchema*. Intriguingly, a form of this dance still survives in Crete where dancers hold each others' shoulders and form a circle around a central musician in the manner of the Palaikastro group. It is reminiscent of Homer's description: 'A large crowd stood round enjoying the dance while a minstrel sang divinely to the lyre.' R. W. Hutchinson in his *Prehistoric Crete* suggests an - admittedly tenuous, but fascinating - connection with a dance of Spanish origin now performed in Guatemala. Here two groups, dancing in circles, actually wear bull masks, looking like Minotaurs. Could this derive from the Mediterranean, and ultimately Crete, as some scholars have suggested was also the case for toreador sports?

Music must have been an integral part of many Cretan rituals (in later times the Cretans were credited with introducing many musical forms to mainland Greece). We can assume that it formed an accompaniment to the singing of hymns by the priestesses. Reference has already been made to the hymn discovered at Palaikastro. Like so much in prehistoric Crete the music is lost forever, but we do know some of the instruments used. One carving shows a priestess blowing a conch horn. As the range of notes that can be achieved on this instrument is limited, she may be calling people to a festival. She may also be summoning the Goddess to attend a ritual. A triton shell carved from stone was found at Haghia Triadha. Other instruments include a bone horn discovered at Phaistos, resembling those still used in Crete. A pair of bone tubes may be the remnants of a Pan pipe or set of double pipes as shown being played on the Haghia Triadha sarcophagus. This painting demonstrates that the music was sometimes performed by men to support the priestesses in their ritual performances. One plays a lyre with seven strings, the soundbox formed from a tortoise shell (see Figures 41 and 43).

Even in Crete man was mortal, and the Mother Goddess prescribed funerary rites for recalling the dead to herself. We are fortunate to have in the Haghia Triadha sarcophagus an illustrated ritual guide in which priestesses - supported by priests - return a Minoan noble to the Earth. The first side (see Figure 41) depicts offerings being made to the deceased with the corpse standing before his tomb and facing a sacred tree. He is approached by sheepskin-clad priests carrying a boat and a bull. Simultaneously a lyre player accompanies the pouring of libations by a priestess who empties what is possibly bull's blood into a large two-handled vessel. Her assistant carries further buckets of this liquid suspended from a shoulder bar. On the panel on the opposite side (see Figure 43) other stages of the ritual are enacted to ensure rebirth. This is carried out to the music of a double pipe and the focal point is a shrine crowned with horns of consecration from which grows (or is reborn) a sacred tree. Before this a priestess stretches out her hands over an altar while gazing at a bird perched on a double axe. Behind her is another sacrificial bull accompanied by two goats, doubtless destined to share its fate. Five processing priestesses concluded the scene, but unfortunately only the first of these has survived intact.

The settings in which priestesses worshipped their Goddess, and the ritual furniture and sacred objects they used, have sometimes survived. Shrines in palaces and large houses took various forms. One design consisted of three connected rooms, the central one higher and surmounted by images of 'horns of consecration'. Stamped gold foil images from Mycenae suggest that doves - a symbol of the Goddess - lived amorously in the rooftops. Frescoes from a shrine in Santorini suggest the decorative scheme on the interior walls. Priestesses worshipped the Goddess surrounded by a painted landscape of luminous colours showing nature flowering at springtime, lilies coming into full bloom and graceful swallows darting through the sky.

Archaeology has also revealed a number of important pillar crypts including one at Knossos itself. A krater from Cyprus, dating from Mycenaean times, now in the British Museum (no.C391), is decorated with repeated images of this form of shrine, with flanking priestesses adoring a pillar in each case. We know that they left offerings in small cups or poured libations onto the pavement at the base of the pillar. These were often carved with sacred symbols like the double axe or trident.

A third form of shrine was the lustral basin reached by a short flight of stairs. A number of these existed at Knossos - one directly in front of the throne. The ceremonies conducted there must have included libations and ritual purification.

An interesting historical development in late Minoan times was the appearance of communal shrines. All of the shrines found in Crete were small, intimate buildings. This feminine religion preferred close, private communication with their Goddess to the grandiose projection of divine power characteristic of contemporary religions. In contrast to Mesopotamia or Egypt (or present-day religions) they had no monumental temples, and their cult images were on a small scale. Portable and fragile faience or ivory statuettes of the Goddess make an eloquent contrast with the contemporary massive granite Gods of Egypt.

Surely a consequence of the feminine character of Minoan religion, and the leading part played by its priestesses, was its sensitive love of nature. They preferred to worship the Goddess in her natural settings of caves, mountain peaks and other wild places: a lesson for us today.

The cave is an obvious female image of the womb and one in particular at Amnisos was dedicated to Eileithyia, Goddess of Childbirth. Two stalagmites were seen as images of the Goddess and her divine infant and were protected by a low stone wall. Until the 6C AD women seeking or expecting a child left offerings of milk and honey to the Goddess. The inferior pottery found in the cave shows that Eileithyia extended her care to the poor.

At the end of the 19C, D. G. Hogarth explored the famous Cave Sanctuary at Psychro, which is the most splendid in Crete and one of the most famous anywhere. Candlelight revealed hundreds of bronze knives, women's ornaments and miniature double axes of gold, concealed in the stalactites. Hogarth concluded that 'among the holy caverns in the world, that of Psychro, in virtue of its lower halls, must stand alone'.

Even today the mountain peaks of Crete are remote and supernatural places. The priestesses came here to perform their dances and to witness the Goddess, locks of hair floating skyward as She descended to her little sanctuary. Wind and rain have swept away much of the evidence, but a stone libation jar from Kato Zakro preserves the appearance of a peak shrine covered with running spirals and surmounted by graceful ibexes. We know that the worshippers on mountain peaks lit huge fires into which they threw clay figurines of supplicants together with models of limbs in order to bring about magical cures. Ignited close to Heaven, these fires may have been intended to restore the dying strength of the winter sun.

The celebration of the natural world in the religion led by these priestesses is expressed in the sensitive depictions of flowering plants and creatures of the sea. This empathy with their physical surroundings, pregnant with divine, symbolic meaning, made impossible the exploitative and destructive use of the environment characteristic of modern times. The refeminization of modern religion must surely include a view of nature as sacred and would prevent her being used for the sole purpose of 'man's use and benefit'.

The objects used in the cult of the Goddess by priestesses and worshippers are richly symbolic and relate to the Goddess or her divine child/lover. Examples have been found in the various shrines of Crete. These include models of sacred pillars, horns of consecration, doves, snakes, flying fish and, most famously, the double axe (Figure 46). Images of the Goddess (or priestess impersonating her) have been found wearing the axe on her head or holding it in her hands. Its design, based on the double triangle, signified 'woman'. Its cutting edge was slightly curved and the surface was sometimes decorated with incised lines. Made of bronze or even gold, the larger examples were fixed on stands and placed beside altars in the sanctuaries of the Goddess. In the Haghia Triadha painting we see a pair of these axes mounted on tapering shafts standing on stepped bases which flank the priestess pouring a libation.

After the Mycenaeans had taken over the government of Crete, at a time which is still debated, possibly during the second half of the 15C BC, they adopted its beliefs. The material evidence would suggest that they espoused them completely, without trying to make much alteration to them. Some archaeologists even speak of a Minoan/Mycenaean religion, for the art, symbols and religious artefacts can be indistinguishable from each other, leading to disputes as to which culture they belong. However, the dramatic decipherment of Linear B Mycenaean tablets by Ventris force us to reject the view that

these religions were entirely identical. The hundreds of clay tablets from Pylos, Mycenae and elsewhere contain no theological writings, but rather accounting lists which in passing reveal much about Mycenaean beliefs. These record offerings to various deities, including precious vessels, oils, honey and slaves.

The revelation is not only the names of the Gods mentioned, but their relative order of importance. They show the male Gods of Mycenae, including Poseidon, Zeus, Ares and Dionysos in prominent positions. What misled earlier archaeologists was the absence of images of these masculine Gods in their art. This can be attributed to the aniconic tradition of the Mycenaeans, together with the lack of suitable protypes in Minoan icongraphy.

46 Symbolic of the Goddess, the double axe, of gold or bronze, was placed in large numbers in her shrines and was engraved in sacred pillar crypts; this particular one was painted on a storage vase from Knossos c.1450.

It seems now that when the Mycenaean Greeks came into contact with the Minoan religion they grafted on those elements which did not conflict with their own beliefs. The Great Goddess of fertility and vegetation and her attendant priestesses were therefore retained. The Linear B tablets make numerous references to these priestesses: there are 'slaves of the priestesses', 'a Priestess of the Winds' and 'a priestess . . . in the service of Potnia (Our Lady)'.

We know little about the real status of Mycenaean priestesses apart from these brief mentions, but for over 200 years they must have retained the costume of their Minoan predecessors. A faience replica of the Sacred Knot has been found in Mycenae. From this site also, a fresco shows a priestess, sheaths of corn in her hand, wearing the traditional flat circular cap with tassels hanging from the centre. The fortress of Tiryns contained paintings of these priestesses with elaborate hair, wearing the full skirts and jackets of Minoan times.

The Goddess continued to enjoy the dancing of her priestesses as shown by a carnelian seal stone from a tomb at Vaphio. She also received, as formerly, processions of offering bearers. A gold ring found at Mycenae shows two priestesses and a young girl, who could be a novice, bringing flowers to the seated Goddess. Libations to her continued to be poured. The tablets tell us that these consisted of water, wine, oil and honey. The Goddess showed the same aversion to monumental cult images and temples, and priestesses placed leafy boughs perfumed with oil on her altars.

We do not fully know what part Mycenaean queens played in the religious ceremonial of their courts, but there is reason to suspect it was a significant one. At this period the Goddess is sometimes referred to as a *wanassa*, which means 'queen', suggesting that the king was seen as son and consort to the Goddess, embodied in the queen. Minoan traditions are more likely to have lingered on in the religious life of the royal courts than elsewhere and Homer tells us that Alcinous' queen, Arete, is honoured 'as no other woman is honoured . . . Thus she hath and hath ever had, all worship from her dear children and from her Lord Alcinous and from all the people, who look on her as a Goddess.'

Despite the decline of Mycenaean power and the onset of the Dark Age, the worship and memory of the Great Goddess lived on. Herodotos acknowledges that the oldest

Gods of Greece were Hera, Hestia, Themis and the Graces. Hestia was believed to have founded Knossos. When Pheidias made his wonderful chryselephantine (gold and ivory) statue of Athena for the Parthenon several hundred years later, he equipped her with a snake, a bird, a pillar and a shield - all Minoan religious attributes (Figure 47). By then Athena had triumphed over Poseidon in their struggle for sovereignty over Attica.

47 In Classical Athens, Pheidias created a majestic image of their patron Goddess in ivory and gold. Like her Cretan ancestor, Athena's attributes included a shield, a pillar and the guardian snake of the Acropolis, as in this detail on a Roman marble copy of the famed original; National Museum of Athens, c.438-432 BC.

EGYPT

NILE

7

SPIRITUAL GOVERNMENT

Role type: Isis

QUEENS AND PRIESTESSES
By Michael Duigan

The priestesshood was the most important of a number of professions open to women in ancient Egypt and represented the highest status to which most women in that society could aspire. Throughout Egypt's history there were priestesses of a wide range of deities, the most popular being Hathor. Their ministrations however, were by no means confined to female deities alone, as the records mention priestesses of other cults including those of Thoth, Min and Amun.

From the perspective of our modern society, it is easy to misunderstand the nature of the priesthood and its place in the life of men and women in ancient Egypt. No sharp distinction between sacred and secular was made - every aspect of life was the concern of the Gods - with the consequence that it was not necessary to have a separate category of persons who were priests. The titles of the 'priests' reveal that they participated in a range of varied activities that mingled our discrete categories of religious, political and domestic life. This fusion of - or rather refusal to separate - secular and religious life is reflected in the organization of the priesthood overall. These servants of the Gods formed four groups, each responsible in different ways for administering the temple and conducting the ritual for one month, on a rota basis. Each group of priestesses within the hierarchy was headed by a woman of high status, the wife of a nobleman or chief priest, and was called 'The Great One of the Musicians'. Unlike the men, it appears that the women were not required to be celibate during their term of office. Unless protected by the privileges unique to a specific temple, they were subject to the same duties, however, such as taxes and state services, as all other members of society. Their payment was a share in temple revenues, or in the food which reverted to the staff after being offered to the cult images.

There must have been a number of Egyptian priests who were responsible for researching and compiling the theological systems (and who approximate to our present idea of a priest), but they are not easily identified. It is interesting to note, in this context, that it was a Goddess – Sheshat – who was worshipped under the epithet, 'She who is Foremost in the House of Books'.

The generic Egyptian concept of the priesthood, however, is quite different from our own. They conceived of the Gods as princes resident in their temples, commanding a major share of the lands and resources of Egypt. The priests and priestesses were members of the Gods' household and, as in any other domestic establishment, their duties ranged from attending to the Gods' personal needs such as food and entertainment, to the administration of their vast agricultural estates. With significant exceptions (to be dealt with below), priestesses carried

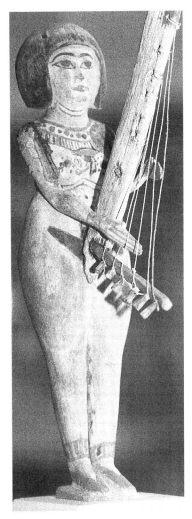

48 Wooden statuette of female harpist. The harp had great symbolic meaning in Egyptian funerary rites, where it evoked regeneration; British Museum, Late Period after 850 BC.

out the lower grade functions, with some supervisory roles such as 'Overseer of the Storehouse'. The Gods, like other earthly princes, maintained an extensive harem, and such women are referred to as 'Concubines of the God'. They held varying degrees of rank, like their earthy counterparts, and were headed by

49 Boundary stela of Tell-el-Amarna, depicting Queen Nefertiti and her daughters with Akhenaten offering to the Aten sun disc. The unique status of Nefertiti allowed her to carry out priestly functions hitherto the sole privilege of the king; Hermopolis, Eighteenth Dynasty, c.1370 BC.

'The Chief Concubine'. However the role must not be misunderstood, and the translation 'concubine' is now rejected by many authorities. Theirs was a priestessly function, and it was their duty to provide musical worship of the Gods. They entertained their deity by playing a variety of musical instruments (Figure 48), and by singing and dancing.

In this context, the archetypal Egyptian priestess personifying the female 'Singer of the God' is a figure named Meret. Wearing a vulture crown and associated with the queen, she raises her arms to sing when the sun rises.

Nefertiti, queen of Akhenaten, is referred to as 'the one who pacifies the Aten with a sweet voice' (Figure 49).

The priestesses would sing rhythmically, chanting or reciting while clapping their hands and clicking their fingers. Contemporary images and surviving examples demonstrate a range of stringed and percussion instruments used by these women to enhance the ritual. These include clappers of wood or ivory decorated with images of Hathor, harps, and tambourines and heavy bead necklaces which were shaken to create different textures of sound. The most

notable musical instrument was a sacred rattle, the sistrum (Figure 50), which was widely used in the cult of Hathor from the close of the Old Kingdom. Formed like a sceptre, there were two variants. The earlier was in the form of a little cubicle, or *naos*, the later type a loop resembling an *ankh*. In both cases wires supported metal discs to create a tinkling sound, and the handle was decorated with the head of Bat, a form of Hathor. The sistrum shaker continued to be used until modern times in the Coptic Mass.

The priestesses also worshipped the Gods through dancing. Many images and some of their titles illustrate this. A block from a shrine of Hatshepsut at Karnak shows female dancers moving rhythmically and in unison and seems to illustrate two stages of the movement. An inscription on a later statue of a queen, possibly Tuya, mother of Ramesses II, calls her a 'dancer of Horus'. Yet the mummy of a singer of Amun showed no wear to the feet (they did not wear shoes while dancing), which would be expected if she had also danced for the God. Possibly they were separate professions, or her title may have been honorary only. Dancing priestesses would have begun their training from childhood, a necessity, as they had to master elaborate

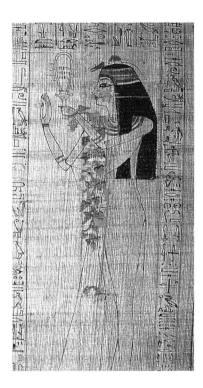

50 *Painting in the papyrus* Book of the Dead *commissioned by the priestess Anhai who, garlanded in leaves, shakes the sistrum of Hathor in a ritual of passing through the Underworld ruled by Osiris; British Museum, Twentieth Dynasty, c.1100 BC.*

movement requiring great acrobatic skills. A lovely drawing on an ostracon from Deir-el-Medina shows a young girl performing a somersault, her body arching backwards to form an almost complete circle.

Egyptian ritual consisted, to a significant extent, of the dramatic enactment of ritual events. At Abydos, for example, the Death of Osiris was avenged ritually by human actors as part of the religious rites at the site. Masks worn by priests while impersonating Anubis still survive in various museums. When she impersonated a Goddess, the priestess carried out one of her most important functions and at this sacred moment she actually became the Goddess. In an important ritual scene from the tomb of Kheruef, Amenophis III is identified as the Sun God Ra and his Queen Tiye becomes the Goddess Maat.

We do not know much about the actual ceremonies in which these priestesses played their part, but some of them can be identified. The ritual of coronation was carried out in two pavilions. In the 'House of Flame' priestesses impersonating Nekhbet, Neith, Isis and other Goddesses exalted the new king. Meanwhile in the 'Great House' a priestess in the form of a Snake Goddess waited to 'embrace' the new king as prescribed in the ritual formula. Priestesses played a significant part also in the ritual of the Heb Sed festival which in part involved a re-enactment of

the king's coronation. Temple reliefs and carvings in private tombs show these women shaking sistra or pouring libations.

Funerary rites designed to bring about rebirth by means of self-generation also required the participation of priestesses. In these ceremonies they played the part of Isis and her sister Nephthys mourning at the head and feet of the corpse (Figure 51). Their musical performance had sexual connotations in which the harp played an important role. In the tomb of Mereruka his wife plays this instrument while they sit on a bed. Numerous tomb paintings show priestesses playing this harp, called a *bnt*. In Egyptian *bn* or *bn bn* meant 'to copulate, join'. In modern times Mace described how he witnessed the survival of a Hathor funerary rite. He saw a number of women processing to the cemetery while singing and holding red handkerchiefs. On the way they

51 Drawing made by Mariette of a relief on the Chapel of Osiris in the temple of Hathor, Denderah, showing Isis and Nephthys mourning the corpse of Osiris on his bed next to the scarab of resurrection, an omen of his revival; photo courtesy the British Library, Ptolemaic period, 4/3C BC.

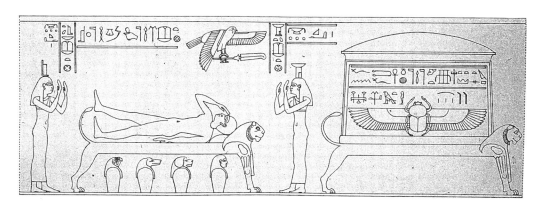

regularly formed a circle to chant, dance and perform acrobatic leaps while beating tambourines.

Royal women performed a priestessly role in the consecration of temples, maybe in the guise of the Goddess Sheshat. Characteristically they carried a special sceptre on these occasions, known as the *hts*. A relief fragment from Hatshepsut's temple at Deir-el-Bahari shows her daughter, Neferure, bearing this sceptre.

The most important rite carried out by royal women was that of priestess in the cult of the Pharoah. As the bearers of life and as the mothers and wives of kings, they played a central role in the birth and rebirth of the Pharaoh. The queen was closely identified with Hathor, mother of Egypt's kings before Isis, and her role was established through ritual: she represented the feminine aspect of kingship and was its means of renewal. The importance of the creative, erotic relationship between the king and the royal women may explain their burial in the royal funerary complex, most famously in the case of Mentuhotep II. This is doubtless also the basis for the famous love scenes of Akhenaten and Nefertiti. The relationship between women of the royal household and the king was modelled on that of priestesses to their God – that is, they functioned as priestesses to their royal husbands. In an important scene from a gold shrine of Tutankhamun, his queen, while holding a necklace weight (*menat*), shakes a sistrum before him, in the manner of a priestess worshipping a God. While this interpretation has been questioned, the roles do appear to have been allocated along these lines in Ramesside times. A title of royal women appearing then was 'Chantress of Horus, Lord of the Palace'.

It is difficult to say more than this in general terms about Egyptian priestesses as, despite popular misconceptions, Egyptian religion and women's involvement in over 3,000 years of its development was not static. The extent and nature of women's cultic activity changed over time and this subject must therefore now be examined chronologically.

From the prehistoric period, we may have a statuette of a priestess in a clay figure found at Mamariya. The figure has been interpreted as dancing with her arms arched over her head to simulate the horns of the Goddess Hathor. This pose has definite symbolic meaning, as it recurs in numerous vase paintings of this period. Evidence for priestesses in the later Thinite period takes the form of an ivory plaque found at Hieraconpolis. Carved on its surface is a row of women bearing what look like sistra resembling the *ankh* sign. In the Old Kingdom annals we find the mother of King Djer referred to as 'Musician of the Apis Bull'. However throughout the Fourth and Fifth Dynasties, the cult in which priestesses dominated was that of Hathor (Figure 52), the most prominent being Queen Meresankh III. In this period – in contrast to the New Kingdom – the priestly status of women was much higher: they did not serve only as musicians and could function as high priestesses. We know that in the Fifth Dynasty a daughter as well as the sons of a noble served, in turn, as high priest(ess) of Hathor.

At the close of the Old Kingdom we meet an intriguing event which occurred only four times in Egypt's history, when a queen ruled as Pharaoh in her own right. This queen, Nitocris, was, according to Manetho, 'the noblest and loveliest of the women of her time, of fair complexion'. By virtue of her high office she was high priestess of all the cults in Egypt. This raised political and theological issues – still alive today – which will be examined more fully for the reign of Hatshepsut.

The Middle Kingdom was inaugurated by Mentuhotep II, whose burial complex at Deir-el-Bahari was one of the major cult centres of Hathor. Women were interred with him, and it is now accepted that they were not mere concubines, for they carried out important religious functions as members of the royal household and priestesses of Hathor, as is clearly shown by their titles. During this period also, in the great semi-dependent provinces, the female members of the princely families served as priestesses of the local Gods. As in the Old Kingdom, these

52 Detail of a stela showing a priestess. Her description, in hieroglyphs above her, is: 'Sole Royal Favourite and Priestess of Hathor'; British Museum, First Intermediate Period, c.2000 BC.

noblewomen could attain the highest religious positions, and at Beni Hasan the wives of the Nomarch served as high priestesses to the Goddess Pakhet.

Later, at Thebes, a woman called Imeretnebes became high priestess of Amun, whose cult rose in importance in line with the political fortunes of Thebes (Figure 53). From this period, if not earlier, the office of 'God's Wife' appears, first held by non-royal women.

Only a few women of the royal household bear priestessly titles during the Twelfth Dynasty. However, at Medinet Maadi, an interesting image has been found of Neferuptah worshipping the Goddess Renenutet in what may be the earliest instance of a royal woman shaking the sistrum before a God.

At the onset of the New Kingdom there were interesting changes in the role and status of priestesses. On the one hand the priesthood in general became more widely disseminated throughout society, this being one aspect of the democratization of religion which began at the end of the Pyramid Age (Figure 54). No longer the preserve of aristocratic women, the priestesshood was now open to almost every woman in the land, including the wives of artisans. The other, possibly

inevitable, development was that the status of priestesses declined, the higher offices being exclusively a male prerogative, while the women mostly remained singers in the temples.

At the beginning of the New Kingdom, when royal women rarely held other priestessly roles, the position of God's Wife was assumed by Queen Ahmose Nofretari. With the takeover of

53 Wooden statuette of Imeretnebes – the earliest representation known of a high priestess in the cult of Amun at Thebes; Leiden Museum, Twelfth Dynasty, c.1900 BC.

54 Painted wooden stela showing a woman of relatively minor status conducting a priestessly ritual, adoring Rehorakhte (the sun on the horizon), surrounded by the starry body of the Sky Goddess Nut; Liverpool Museum, Late Period, c.1000–800 BC.

this sacerdotal title by such a prominent royal person, the office assumed great significance. A fragmentary stela (known as 'the Donation Stela') found at Karnak documents this important event. As part of his policy to promote the cult of Amun after the difficulties of the Hyksos wars, Pharaoh Ahmose may have given exceptional powers to Queen Ahmose Nofretari. In transferring these responsibilities to the queen, it says on the stela, the Pharoah granted her the title of Second Prophet of Amun. The

Donation Stela records either the granting or the return of this office by Ahmose Nofretari - but in either event it gives her the title of God's Wife, together with extensive properties and revenues which henceforth were attached to that position.

The function of God's Wife - which has been much misunderstood - was to perform ritual acts in the cult of Amun, and it has now been established that it has no relationship to the royal succession or any dynastic significance. The purely cultic nature of the job is made clear in the images which survive of the God's Wife carrying out ritual acts in the temple. Before entering, she was purified in the sacred lake and then performed a range of ceremonies alone or with other priests. She appears, for example, in a procession of priests in funerary ceremonies. She calls the God to partake of his food offerings and in rites of sympathetic magic she burns images of Egypt's enemies to ensure their destruction.

But the principal role of this High Priestess in her capacity of God's Wife was to represent the Consort of the Sky God Amun. So, by means of ritual, she was responsible for reviving and bringing about the self-generation of the God. This involved the establishment and administration of a school of singers to provide the necessary musical rites. The erotic character of these musical performances aroused the God to recreate himself. Texts give some idea where this college of priestesses was located, and a man named Senu was appointed as steward of the foundation. The Donation Stela contains a list of apparel which was probably intended for these priestesses. Ahmose Nofretari achieved great distinction in her own and succeeding ages, and in contemporary images was depicted on the same scale as the king or Amun Ra.

This high honour contrasts with the physical reality. Her mummy, discovered at Deir-el-Bahari, shows that she tended towards baldness, a defect remedied by strands of hair interwoven with her own, and, even more than her grandmother Tetisheri, she had pronounced buck teeth. She was an elderly woman when she died, perhaps 70 years old.

A number of women in the royal family held the office of God's Wife later in the dynasty, including Queen Meritamun, daughter of Ahmose Nofretari, Queen Hatshepsut, and her daughter Neferure. All of these occasionally used the title on its own, and probably carried out the duties of the office like others before them. Subsequent royal women only used the title God's Wife as part of a string of titles, and in all probability delegated the ritual obligations to other priestesses, with a consequent loss in prestige to the office.

The singers of Amun were now controlled by 'Divine Adoratrices' and 'Overseers of the Harem [singers] of the God', who carried out the ritual functions of the God's Wives. Non-royal God's Wives reappeared in the Eighteenth Dynasty.

With the accession of Hatshepsut to sole rule *c.*1490 BC, we have a woman who as Pharaoh was in theory the high priest to every God in Egypt. She claimed this status, being depicted on her monuments in royal sacred regalia offering to all the deities (Figure 55). It is possible to justify sovereign rule by a woman in ancient Egypt in terms of the mythological importance of procreation, the androgyny of the Creator and the female as well as male elements of kingship. But while a case can be made in theological terms for a female occupant of the supreme royal and priestly position, this was made impossible - not for the last time in history - by the political and social male-dominated power structure of the time. Hatshepsut's rule was abnormal and this probably explains the

55 Sandstone block from a dismantled shrine of Queen Hatshepsut, showing her in her capacity as Pharaoh performing the priestly duty of offering incense to Amun in his barque shrine; Karnak open-air museum, Eighteenth Dynasty, c.1503-1482 BC.

ferocity of the later destruction of her monuments.

The great queens of the Eighteenth Dynasty increased in importance, though the career of Hatshepsut itself was exceptional. Their priestessly roles increased likewise, and this development reached its apogee in the Amarna period. There can be no doubt that Nefertiti's status was unique (Figure 49). She regularly used the sole title of 'Mistress of the Two Lands', in contrast to her predecessors, and she played a central part in the worship of the Aten. The blocks of Akhenaten's temples retrieved from the ruins of Karnak show her offering to the God, a position hitherto reserved exclusively for the king. It is now recognized that there was even a separate temple for Nefertiti containing scenes where she alone worships the Aten. Furthermore, of 12 offering tables discovered, 10 are inscribed with her titles alone, combined with those of the Aten, with no mention being made of the king. As priestess she played the same female role in relation to her God as her predecessors had done.

Throughout the New Kingdom the high priest of Amun's wife was given the title of 'Chief Concubine [or Head of the Singers] of Amun', in which capacity she superintended the musician priestesses of the temple. In the Twentieth Dynasty Ramesses VI personally attended, at a great state occasion at Karnak, the installation of his daughter as 'God's Wife of Amun and Divine Adoratrice'. His mother and Vizier also attended. In a stela from Coptos his newly installed God's Wife proclaims to Rehorakhte, 'I play the sistrum before Thy Fair Face!'

In the succeeding dynasty the high priests of Amun increased their power, even occasionally claiming royal titles. Their wives held the title of 'Chief of the Concubines/Singers', and continued to preside over the sacred college of priestesses, wielding great authority and influence. One of the most significant figures of this female sacerdotal dynasty was Henttowy, who married her cousin, the high priest Pinudjem I. In an inscription she claims that she was present when her husband repositioned the sphinxes at Karnak. Her mummy - which was not an embalmer's success - reveals that she wore an elaborate wig made of strands of plaited black string.

A daughter of Henttowy named Makare assumed an even more important position in the hierarchy than her mother. A carved relief in the temple of Khonsu shows her wearing more elaborate regalia than Henttowy, and boasting the title 'God's Wife of Amun'. Her death and burial has long puzzled Egyptologists. It is thought that she was required to be celibate, but her mummy indicated an early death in childbirth. She was accompanied by the mummy of her 'child' which seemed to confirm this interpretation, until X-rays established that it was a female hamadryas baboon. Theories range from a substitute child to accompany her into the next life

to the interment of this animal for ritual purposes.

Later in the dynasty, the career of a Chief of the Concubines/Singers of Amun has considerable personal interest. Istemkheb, daughter of a high priest of Amun, was married to the contemporary holder of the office, Pinudjem II. She appears to have been a formidable woman, and the evidence suggests that Pinudjem divorced her. He stripped her of her priestessly titles to confer them on his new favourite, his pretty young niece, Nesikhons. The latter had a graceful narrow face and long dark brown hair. Her early death was followed by strange decrees arranged by Pinudjem. These were designed to protect his children by her, and the post-mortem welfare of Nesikhons herself, from the vengeance of an unnamed person. A plausible conclusion is that the girl's untimely death was suspicious and we know that Istemkheb, as her coffin shows, subsequently regained all her privileges and titles.

A God's Wife of the next dynasty also deserves special mention, as she commissioned what has to be one of the finest works of art produced in ancient Egypt. Queen Karomama, wife of Takelot II, had made for her chapel at Karnak a magnificent bronze statue of herself, in the role of Isis perhaps, shaking sistra (Figure 56). It is a masterpiece of metalwork, inlaid with gold, silver and electrum to create a broad collar and an embroidered feather design on her gown. By a most appropriate accident of history, the name of the artist, Ahtefnakht, survives.

The Twenty-Third Dynasty witnessed a new development in the history of Egypt's priestesses, when additional significance was given to the office of Divine Wife of Amun. King Osorkon III imposed his authority over the Thebans by reducing the power of the high priest to that of officiant in the temple and obliging them to accept the rule of his own daughter, Shepenwepet I. As God's Wife and local ruler, this priestess was given all the prerogatives and symbols of royalty. She received a coronation and was given royal regalia, including the uraeus and double plumes. Her throne name was enclosed in a royal cartouche, and in Thebes she was depicted offering to the Gods. Finally her death was announced in the ritual formula reserved for Pharaohs.

The ritual duties of this God's Wife must have included at least the nominal direction of the priests, temples and properties of Amun. Her theological role as Wife of the God would have remained as before. One of her titles was 'Hand of the God', which must refer to her regenerative role and creative power.

The following priestess-rulers of Thebes were, however, required to live out their ceremonial lives in ritual virginity. It has been remarked that in the history of religion, ancient and modern,

56 Bronze statuette of the God's Wife, Queen Karomama, which she commissioned for her own chapel at Karnak; Louvre, Twenty-Second Dynasty, c.860–835 BC.

where celibacy is required, there is also an imposition of power, a concern for property rights and an inferior status ordained for women. Theological considerations may provide the rationale, but are rarely the determining factor in imposing this ritual requirement. This pattern is certainly true for the office of God's Wife in the Late Period. The reigning Pharaoh secured his power in the semi-autonomous Theban area through his agent, the God's Wife, who was always his daughter, and was nominated by him. Through her, the hierarchy of Thebes acknowledged the sovereignty of the ruling dynasty in the north, and the childless ruler could not create an independent centre of power to challenge his throne.

It is difficult to know to what extent the God's Wives exercised actual political power within Thebes itself. Theoretically they were sovereign, but the excessive splendour of the tombs of their male officials suggests that the real power still lay with these 'servants'. On the other hand, the spiritual authority of these Divine Wives - through their control of the Oracles of Amun - must have been great, and perhaps their effective power was what individual holders of the office made of it.

Shepenwepet I, who left evidence of her reign in a temple of Osiris at Karnak, also built the first of a series of funerary chapels dedicated to the God's

57 Chapels of the God's Wives. Two only of the four originally constructed now remain, positioned before the temple of Ramesses III at Medinet Habu, Thebes; Twenty-Fifth–Twenty-Sixth Dynasty, 8–6C BC.

58 Statue of the God's Wife, Shepenwepet II, priestess-ruler of Thebes, whom King Piankhi installed as his sister's heir in 710 BC. During her reign the Assyrians sacked Thebes; Louvre, Twenty-Fifth Dynasty, c.700 BC.

Wives at Medinet Habu (Figure 57), under the floor of which she was finally buried. These mortuary shrines are a major source for the history of the priestess-rulers of Thebes.

When, in the middle of the 8C BC, the Kushite dynasty from Nubia imposed its rule on Egypt, Pharaoh Piankhi, like his predecessor, took measures to secure the loyalty of Thebes. So Shepenwepet I was obliged to adopt the king's sister, Amenirdis I,

as her heir. A number of beautiful statues of this priestess survive, one in particular being an alabaster statue from a chapel of Osiris at Karnak. The fine details of wig and jewellery have been carefully picked out in the flesh-like, semi-transparent stone. Though idealized, the plump, Nubian features of the God's Wife can be detected. An extremely interesting statuette of her now in the Cairo Museum gives a sculptural representation of her theological role. She is seated on the lap of Amun and they embrace each other lovingly. Amenirdis I was likewise buried at Medinet Habu in her own chapel. Though the grave was completely looted, a number of her funerary objects still survive in museum collections.

Amenirdis I had adopted Piankhi's daughter, Shepenwepet II, who now succeeded her (Figure 58). She built the funerary chapel of her predecessor, and carved it with reliefs, which are a fine example of the art of the period. It also contained the standard request of worshippers to recite an offering formula, but added an ominous threat that those who failed to do so would fall sick, and their wives likewise would be afflicted.

An enigmatic building constructed at Karnak during the reign of Taharqa gives a fascinating insight into the ritual activities of the God's Wife at this time. Carved on the lintel is an image of the priestess – unfortunately without a name – wearing the traditional close-fitting wig and fillet with streamers, a tight dress and broad collar. She is shooting arrows at four circular targets, which may be loaves of bread, in the shape of the Egyptian hieroglyph for 'town'. These symbolize the four cardinal points, the foreign territories subject to Egypt and the four rebellious children of Ra. The God's Wife is protecting the tomb of Amun-Ra, eliminating his enemies to clear the way for his rebirth and re-emergence. The accompanying text explains this: 'The Wife of the God, she has taken the bow, shooting towards the South, the North, the West and the East, according to his own account which he has transmitted to her.' The ritual prescribes for the priestess 'the words to be recited: "Fall on your faces, enemies, rebels! Make way for me." '

The ritual did not succeed against the most terrible of Egypt's enemies when in 663 Assurbanipal's Assyrian army sacked and burned Thebes. The 'young children [of that city] were dashed in pieces at the top of all the streets . . . and all her great men were bound in chains'

(Nahum 3, 8-10). Shepenwepet II must have witnessed this disaster, as she retained office throughout the occupation. However, it affected her closely, for following the collapse of the Kushite dynasty, her adoption of Amenirdis II, daughter of Taharqa, as her heir had to be set aside. A new native family from the Delta under Psammetichus succeeded in reuniting Egypt under their rule and Thebes, which still acknowledged Kushite rule, was persuaded to change allegiance to him. To secure this regime, the king's daughter Nitocris was appointed as the new heiress to Shepenwepet II, to become God's Wife on her death. Psammetichus protested that he would not displace a legitimate heir, but it is likely that Amenirdis rejoined her family in Ethiopia, as she is not buried at Medinet Habu with the other God's Wives. Therefore this dynasty began, as did the previous one, with a politically motivated appointment to the post of high priestess at Karnak. Once again, real power lay in the hands of the Pharaoh and the local princes, the most notable being Mentuemhat.

The arrival of the 15-year-old Nitocris in Thebes, in the ninth year of the king's reign, 'to be Divine Consort, to play the sistrum before Amun's Beautiful

Face', is told on a six-foot high stela of red granite. Wearing fine linen and splendid jewellery, she was conducted to the southern city by a great fleet 'laden with every good thing of the King's palace'. Stone blocks excavated in the temple of Mut by the daughter of an Archbishop of Canterbury are carved with scenes of this ceremonial progress.

Sixteen days later Nitocris arrived at the city of Amun and was received by throngs of rejoicing people, and by Shepenwepet. The young girl must have been relieved to meet her adopted mother, who 'was satisfied with her and loved her beyond anything'. Nitocris was then brought to Karnak to be received by her Divine Husband. A broken limestone statue bought from a dealer at Luxor depicts the chief steward of Nitocris holding a small stela. The inscription describes her coronation and subsequent journey to her palace carried on a palanquin. The poles were of silver and gold inlaid with costly stone. The main purpose of this adoption and coronation is boldly stated on the Karnak stela as if the God Amun speaks: 'We have given to thee [Nitocris] all our property in field and in town. Thou abidest on our throne forever and ever.'

Later events in the life of this priestess are recorded by her chief steward, Ibe. Her palace at Karnak started to fall into ruin, and Ibe was commanded by the king to rebuild it. The walls and pavements were of stone and the ceiling lined with electrum. Ibe also administered the priestess's everyday affairs, ensuring the collection of her revenues and payment of her taxes. The steward tells us that he spent a day with her in the temple of Karnak looking over her papers and sealing her documents with her. At Medinet Habu Nitocris completed the funerary chapel of her adopted mother and added another for herself. Her death, recorded on a stela now in the Cairo Museum, tells us that 'She joined the Sun, the divine limbs mingling with Him who made her.' But her tomb was rifled in antiquity, and her sarcophagus reused for another's burial in Deir-el-Medina.

After waiting until she was in her eighties before appointing a successor, Nitocris adopted Ankhnesneferibre, daughter of the reigning king, to be the next priestess-ruler. On arriving at Thebes the reigning God's Wife 'came forth to behold her beauty', and together they went before Amun to confirm the adoption. An alabaster stela from Karnak records this event, informing us that in addition to God's Wife Ankhnesneferibre was simultaneously given the title of 'High Priestess of Amun'. Her ascendancy over the hierarchy of Thebes was complete.

Twelve days after the death of Nitocris, the new ruler proceeded to the temple of her Divine Husband. Surrounded by ranks of senior priests, 'she fastened on all the amulets and ornaments of the Divine Consort', and 'was crowned with the two plumes . . . to be the Queen of every circuit of the Sun'. The portrait on her sarcophagus lid (Figure 59) preserves this moment for eternity. She wears the vulture crown and double plume with the sun disc set between horns, while holding the royal crook and flail. Her titles provide a wonderful commentary on this image:

59 Bas-relief of the God's Wife Ankhnesneferibre, from the lid of her sarcophagus: simultaneously created high priestess of Amun, the office of God's Wife died with her when Egypt was annexed to the Persian Empire; British Museum, Twenty-Sixth Dynasty, c.525 BC.

Hereditary princess, great in amiability, great in favour, mistress of loveliness. Sweet in love, queen of all women, divine consort, divine votaress . . . Divine Hand, Ankhnesneferibre, who lives, King's daughter of the Lord of the Two Lands . . .

When Ankhnesneferibre was at least 80 years old, Egypt had to endure the conquest of Cambyses, king of Persia. We do not know how long the priestess survived this invasion, but there were to be no more God's Wives of Amun.

The end of Ankhnesneferibre's career, like its beginning, was not determined by her. It is important to acknowledge that power in Egypt was almost exclusively in male hands, and the importance of the female principle in theology and myth does not alter this fact. In ancient society, as today, the inferior status given to women limited their participation in religious affairs.

THE ARCHAIC CONTINUUM

DNIESTER, OXUS,
PACTOLUS AND DON

8

HEAVENLY MUSIC IN TENT AND CITY

Role type: Kybele

From the time intermarriage between the royal houses of Egypt, Mesopotamia and Canaan began to politically harmonize the entire ancient Near East at the end of the Bronze Age, the mountain-dwelling Hittites appear on the international scene, providing high-born brides first to Akhenaten and later to Ramesses II. This heralded an era in the Iron Age (roughly 1300-500) when new blood from nomadic peoples flowed into the atrophying body of an ancient Near Eastern urban civilization whose map fluctuated, amoeba-like, according to nuclei shifting from Assyria to Babylon, and then to Persia.

Ladies remaining on home ground in the kingdom of Hatti (eastern Turkey), at the capital Hattusas, wielded much more power than those princesses who became brides in foreign harems, even though these were allowed to continue to practise their native cults within the heart of Egyptian court life. The most notable Hittite queen, or *tawannana*, who stayed on her own soil was Pudukhepa, wife of King Hattusilis III (1289-1265), a contemporary of Ramesses II. As it happens, this king, whose title in that country was *tabarna*, wrote an autobiography which was found amongst the clay tablets excavated at Hattusas. From it we know that Pudukhepa was the daughter of a priest from the coast of Anatolia opposite Cyprus, and had herself been a priestess, her name meaning 'Servant of the Goddess Khepa' (the Hittite Ishtar). Hattusilis was himself an ex-priest, and married her on his return from military campaigns in Egypt after the death of his elder brother. 'The God assigned me to her in a dream,' he wrote. Similarly Ishtar had appeared to Pudukhepa in a dream predicting her husband's rise to high office.

By the time Hattusilis came to the throne, succession to kingship was along the male line; up to the reign of King Telepinu, who lived around 1500 BC, succession had been through the royal females. However, ladies continued to wield immense power on administrative and state religious occasions, as can be seen in the case of Pudukhepa. When a peace treaty was concluded between the lands of Hatti and Egypt, the seal of the king appeared on the front, and of the queen on the back, and the latter sent a message of congratulations to Ramesses II's queen, Nefertari.

Although at the end of her life Pudukhepa spent more time as a talented political administrator, continuing to rule alone as

tawananna after the death of her husband, she nonetheless performed top-level religious rituals as well. Royalty and priesthood were combined in the roles of king and queen, as before in other countries, thus avoiding the split between politics and religion that causes divisions between temporal and spiritual matters. Pudukhepa's rituals would have been of the kind shown in the line drawing from a relief sculpture found at Alaja Hüyük, near Hattusas (Figure 60). Although here the top of the queen's head-dress is damaged, from other examples it is likely to have been high and pointed, like later Scythian examples. Both peoples, like the earliest Greeks, spoke Indo-European languages and were from the same stock.

Another country in the early Iron Age which contributed much to top-level international marriage was Babylonia under the

60 Drawing after a basalt relief from the wall of the Hittite town of Alaja Hüyük, said to show Queen Pudukhepa and her husband King Hattusilis adoring the Bull God; now in the Ankara Museum, c.1400–1200 BC.

rulership of the Kassites, who exchanged correspondence with the Egyptian court (clay tablets with their letters written on them in cuneiform have been found at Amarna; later there are records of the names of Egyptian scribes living in Babylon whose skill was in writing cuneiform). Further to the north the Hurrian kingdom, whose economy was based on horse-rearing, saw one powerful king, Tushratta, who went to the lengths of sending their famed statue of Ishtar of Nineveh (whose Hurrian name was ᶜAshtaj) all the way to Egypt, on loan only, to help cure the ailing Amenophis III, father of Akhenaten. This kingdom in later centuries dissolved into Assyria.

A charming relief on a baetyl now in the Louvre, originally carved to mark the donation of land to his daughter, shows the Kassite king Melishpak presenting his daughter, Shannubatnanna, to the Goddess Inanna, enthroned in her usual flounced robes, witnessed by the sun, moon, and the eight-pointed planet Venus herself. Like all princesses of high birth, Shannubatnanna was trained to play the harp, which she brings with her to the presentation, possibly to signify a priestessly role (her name ends with the name of the Moon God).

From as far back as the harp-playing ladies of the Royal Tombs of Ur, stringed music implied calling up the Harmony of the Spheres, or tuning into the inaudible (to the human ear) music of the planets. This knowledge is as old as music itself and was certainly not 'invented' by Pythagoras. As Inanna was the Queen of Heavenly Harmony, it was appropriate that, of all offerings, the young woman should bring her harp. All weights and measures in ancient Mesopotamia were fixed according to the whole numbers of planetary ratios, and these in turn dictated the string lengths of lyres and harps. The Mesopotamians were without doubt alive to the significance of Divine Number (each God was a Number), but to prove it would take too long here.[1]

❦

The lesson to be drawn for us is that truly heavenly music is one of the most potent instruments of the priestess. Its harmonies, when bringing out the vibrations of cosmic law, heal the soul of the sick and troubled, and link the soul of ill or whole alike to Divine Order and Beauty, without the need to preach. It is not anything to do with noise, cacophony or dissonance, which clairvoyants can see tearing the human aura into shreds. Cosmic number is discussed in several outstanding books on number and music but shortage of space forbids a long digression here.[2] Plato understood the effect of music in creating good government. Today, as the twentieth century closes and a new century dawns, that ancient knowledge of heavenly music is being sought out by those who can see it alive in the cosmos and wish to channel it by voice or musical instrument to restore people to their right mind. If this is one of your gifts, it could be used as it was by the temple singers and priestesses of old. Praise of the Gods is nothing less than making their rhythms audible, and benefits humans as well.

❧

Opposite the coast of Anatolia, in Cyprus of this period, ritual scenes appear on copper stands on wheels for holding buckets (Figure 61). These have been said by one scholar to be miniature versions of the Sea of Brass in the Temple of Jerusalem (this was a large wheeled bowl used for ablutions; see Chapter 5). On the panel shown, the lady with the harp is being ministered to by servants carrying to her the sacred drink, signifying her high position as priestess or queen. On the side panels are a lion killing a

swan and a male winged sphinx, and at the back is a warrior in a chariot. A bottom band shows sporting dolphins and, above, lions killing their prey – symbols respectively of proto-Apollo and proto-Artemis, The God and The Goddess without name later referred to in the Eleusinian Mysteries.

The Kinyrad priest-king dynasty

61 Bronze wheeled cauldron holder from Cyprus, showing cultic scenes and divine symbols, including a servant offering the sacred drink to a priestess playing a harp; British Museum, c.1200 BC.

who introduced the cult of Astarte to Cyprus brought oriental sacred music with them (the word *kinnor* is related to the word 'lyre', and Knr was their Lyre God, like Apollo). In fact the Goddess Anat of Canaan was credited with being the world's first musician and is described playing a lyre in one of the Ugarit texts (as Goddess of Harmony one would expect Venus by any name to be associated with music).

While the Kassites ran Babylonia and Pudukhepa and Hattusilis were ruling neighbouring Hatti, the Assyrians had already started to establish their own kingdom as they annexed Hurrian territory. At first they kept within their own province, but by the 9C BC they had started to move beyond their borders and establish an empire, based at one shifting capital in the north, depending on who was ruler at the time, and a fixed capital, Babylon (the religious centre), in the south. Thus by 876 Ashurnasirpal was exacting tribute from the kings of Tyre, Sidon, Byblos and Arwad: the Assyrians had started to encroach on the territories formerly disputed by the Aramaeans, Hittites and Egyptians, and eventually controlled even Egypt itself. The golden age of Phoenician

independence was over, which helps to explain their own far-flung colonization of the whole Mediterranean basin – and beyond, to Britain – in the Iron Age. Nonetheless, their culture was absorbed by the conquering Assyrians, and notable people from Phoenicia and Syria found their way to the Assyrian court, including priestesses serving Ishtar at Nineveh.

One such was Sammuramat, known better to us as Semiramis, who would have dressed much like the lady on an anonymous Syrian ivory sipping a ritual drink (Figure 62). Many artists have painted pictures of her, including Delacroix, who imagined her giving instructions to architects and engineers as she founded yet another a great city. A stela was found at Ashur, the earliest capital of the Assyrian kings, which reads: 'Stela of Sammuramat, Mistress of the palace of Shamsi-Adad, King of the World, King of Assyria; the Mother of Adad-Nirari, King of the World, King of Assyria; and of Shalmaneser, King of the Four Quarters of the World'. Reference is also made to her on two guardian figures found flanking the entrance of the temple of Nabu (the God Mercury) at Nimrud, now in the main Assyrian Gallery of the British Museum. The two male figures,

The fullest account of Semiramis, given by Diodorus Siculus, appears to be a part mythical, part historical. Siculus relates that Sammuramat was the beautiful daughter of the Syrian Fish Goddess, Derceto, and a handsome youth enflamed with passion for her by the jealous Astarte. Ashamed after their love-making, Derceto killed the young man and threw herself into the sea, leaving Sammuramat exposed in the wilds:

But about the region where the babe was exposed a great multitude of doves had their nests, and by them the child was nurtured in an astounding and miraculous manner: for some of the doves kept the body of the babe warm on all sides by covering it with their wings, while others . . . brought milk in their beaks and fed her.

As the baby grew older the doves pecked off pieces of cheese lying in farmer's dairies, until the farmers started to keep watch to see where the birds went. They discovered 'an infant of surpassing beauty'. One of them brought her up as his own daughter, and gave her the name of Sammuramat, a Syrian word for 'doves', birds which in that country have always been associated with the Goddess. The cylinder seals illustrated in

62 Fragmentary ivory carving on part of a small box from Phoenicia found in Assyria, showing a lady of Sammuramat's time with a North Syrian hairstyle and richly woven robe taking the sacred drink; British Museum, c.800 BC.

made in the name of Adad-Nirari III, refer to his mother, Sammuramat, and enjoin those who enter the temple to trust no other God but Nabu, the God of Intelligence. Historically, scholars have concluded Sammuramat must have been married to the Assyrian king Shamsi-Adad V (824–810), and have brought with her that Syro-Phoenician expertise in religion and the crafts which made her competent to administer the construction of the city of Nineveh, though others have interpreted the records differently.

Chapter 5 nearly all show Astarte accompanied by such a bird. Indeed, the name, when broken down to a simpler linguistic form, 'Shamu-rabbat', translates as 'Lady of the Heavens', Astarte herself.

One day, when Sammuramat was grown up, an Assyrian officer, appointed by the occupying powers as governor of Syria, caught sight of her as he passed through the village to inspect the royal herds, and fell in love with her. He asked the farmer for her hand in marriage, and in time two sons were born. Later her husband was summoned to Bactriana (north of present-day Afghanistan) on a military campaign with the king of Assyria, and in due course he sent for Semiramis to join him. On arrival at the scene of battle in this mountainous region bordering the Himalayas while a siege was under way, she noticed a weak point in the defence and, leading some of her own soldiers, occupied part of the citadel herself. In this way she came to the notice of the king of Assyria, not only for her beauty, but also for her abilities, and he told his governor that he wanted Semiramis to be his own wife. The governor killed himself in grief and the new marriage was consummated, but soon after, the king died, and Semiramis was left

to rule Assyria.

At this point, Diodorus' account of Sammuramat is probably telescoped into the story of another queen, the Babylonian Naqi'a (whom he also confused with Nitocris of Egypt). It was Naqi'a who in neo-Babylonian times was the administrative genius behind the building of Babylon as it was later famed in the writings of Herodotos, where it assumed for the contemporary Greek world the role of Mecca or Jerusalem today as a sacred capital. Naqi'a was probably in fact the wife of a later king of Assyria, Sennacherib (704-681), mother of Esarhaddon (680-669, and grandmother of Ashurbanipal (668-626). Her name is Aramaean (north Syrian), but she also had an Assyrian name, Zakutu. A bronze tablet exists showing Esarhaddon with his mother, an indication of the high esteem in which he held her, for she truly was the power behind the throne. On his accession it was Naqi'a who had a palace built for him at Nineveh. Dedications made by her survive on cult objects, as do reports and oracles made to her on military and religious matters.

Esarhaddon is particularly known for his reliance on oracles delivered by women mediums inspired by Ishtar of Nineveh or Ishtar of Arbela. For instance, it was for Esarhaddon that an oracle was written down that was made through the woman Baia of Arbela (no formal title is given to her, but she must have been an oracular priestess like the later ones at Delphi), acting as the mouthpiece of the Gods:

Fear not, Esarhaddon: I, the God Bel, speak to you. The beams of your heart I strengthen, like your Mother who caused you to exist. Sixty great gods are standing together with me to protect you. The god Sin is at your right, the god Shamash at your left; sixty great gods stand round about you, ranged for battle. Do not trust men! Turn your eyes to me - look at me! I am Ishtar of Arbela: I have turned Ashur's favour unto you. When you were small, I sustained you. Fear not: praise me! Where is the enemy that blew over you [in curse] which I did not notice? The future is like the past! I am the god Nabu, lord of the tablet stylus: praise me!

The tradition of oracle giving, speaking when possessed by the God or Goddess, which is more fully described in Chapter 9, had a long history in the ancient Near East.

Sammuramat/Naqi'a, although clearly associated with Ishtar too, through the miraculous protection given her in babyhood, is not recorded in clear-cut priestessly activities, but she may be a symbol of the spread and establishment of Goddess worship itself, from Syria, its original home. Naqi'a organized the reconstruction of Babylon, because her husband Sennacherib had, in taking it, devastated it. According to Hildegarde Lewy, this would have been between 683-70 BC. Diodorus describes her enormous task thus:

After securing the architects of all the world and skilled artisans and making all the other necessary preparations, she gathered together from her entire kingdom two million men to complete the work.

The fabled Babylon with its gates and walls and canals and temples came into being. A full description of its construction is provided by Diodorus, including the colourful bricks used to decorate the processional way for the New Year Festival exiting at the Ishtar Gate. He describes how Naqi'a was herself portrayed on a glazed brick wall decoration in the palace adjoining the Ishtar Gate, riding on horseback, aiming a javelin at a leopard and accompanied by the king killing a lion.

When this palace was excavated by Koldeway early in the twentieth century, he found amongst the faience fragments one white female face, and pieces of a hunting scene. The face, which could be a portrait of Naqi'a, still exists in either the

Berlin or Baghdad Museum. Of the bronze statues of Naqi'a and her husband, the Assyrian king, alongside Bel (the Babylonian Baal, or Bull God of the Sky), described by Diodorus as originally placed in the courtyard outside the palace, the archaeologists found no trace.

Naqi'a also had a great temple built to Bel, which, according to Diodorus, quoting Herodotos, included a ziggurat from which 'the Chaldaeans made their observations of the stars, whose risings and settings could be accurately observed by reason of the height of the structure'. At the top of the structure, Naqi'a had placed three statues in hammered gold of Bel, Beltis and Ishtar (translated by Diodorus as Zeus, Hera and Kybele). Bel was shown in a striding position, while Beltis stood holding a snake by the head in her right hand. Ishtar was seated on a lion throne wound about with two serpents of silver. Before them was a table made of hammered gold upon which rested two drinking cups, three golden mixing bowls, and incense burners.

It is further described how Naqi'a founded other great cities all along the Tigris and Euphrates, re-establishing the irrigation and trade networks that had formerly linked the Asiatic territories of Mesopotamia, Syria,

Persia, Anatolia and the Scythian tribes beyond. On home territory, she is thought to have been the influence behind the revival of the Aramaean form of the cult of the Moon God Sin. This trend was later consolidated by a later branch of her family under the mother of Nabonidus, and was always connected with the ancient Mesopotamian practice of a priestesship incarnating Ishtar, daughter of Sin, as the bride of the God.

The work of Naqi'a in sheer networking conjures up the picture of a vast continuum of people and places, mostly across inhospitable nomadic terrain of mountain and plain, linked by rivers presided over by the Great Goddess. From time to time, surviving into the twentieth century to meet the archaeologist's trowel, comes evidence that even in these harsh nomadic conditions, priesthood in the service of the Goddess still occupied a prominent place. One of the most interesting examples comes from the remote site of Hasanlu, in present-day Azerbaijan. There the remains of a temple burned down in the 10C BC rendered up the skeletons of young women who were evidently priestesses in the service of the Goddess, since their robes had been pinned at one shoulder by one, two or three bronze lions cast over an iron pin shaft (the latest technology of the time).

❧

Taking a lesson from this, most women have administrative tasks, whether in the home or in the office, and inevitably they build up networks as a result. I believe that at present networking is one of the most potent ways in which women can strengthen their spiritual influence. Ideas are spread from desk to desk, from oven to oven, and gradually the network starts to activate the people criss-crossed on it. There may be an old boys' network which excludes women, but women can create connections just as well, partly creating their own webs, and partly creating synapses with those already existing. Women are notorious for turning this practice to self-centred use, trapping people in their webs, which is an abuse of the gift. Yet strength in a solitary situation comes from the network. Do not underestimate your small part in the total fabric, and keep it serviced, for changing others' attitudes comes from knowing your own.

❧

In time the native Babylonians wrested Babylon back from grip of the Assyrians, and the neo-Babylonian era began (605-539). After a lapse that had lasted 1,000 years or so, the high priestesship of the moon was reinstated in Mesopotamia (now called Babylonia) by Nabonidus, last king of Babylon (555-538) who prided himself on his descent from the Queen Naqi'a who had built Babylon. This act was partly inspired by Nabonidus' excavation and restoration of the temple buildings at Ur. He came across a clay tablet deposited in the foundations of the *gigparu* (convent) which recorded that the Akkadian king Rim-Sin had remodelled the ancient sanctuary in order to make it suitable for his sister, Moon Priestess of Nanna, Enanedu. On a clay tablet which he added to the foundations and which was later dug up by modern archaeologists, Nabonidus described how he also discovered a stone carving placed in the foundations by a more recent predecessor, Nebukadnezzar I, showing a divine bride carved in relief alongside an inscription, when he re-established the *gigparu* for the sacred marriage between deity and mortal. Thus when Nabonidus had rebuilt the *gigparu* and came to dedicate his daughter, Bel-shalti-Nanna (these days transliterated as Ennigaldi-Nanna) as Moon Priestess, Nebukadnezzar's carving of the divine bride served as a model for her own dress for the ceremony. Sadly, we have no sculptural record of the neo-Babylonian event.

Shumuadamqa, Nabonidus' mother, was said to have lived to the grand old age of 104, and Nabonidus often visited her in the vicinity of the moon temple, named Ekhulkhul, at Harran. In an inscription from this temple, Shumuadamqa described with particular joy how her son, 'the offspring of my heart, the king of Babylon, reinstated *the forgotten rites* of Sin, Ningal, Nusku and Sadarnunna' (my italics). Since she was his mother, her influence in reviving the old cults was probably fundamental, though Nabonidus tells that it was in a dream that he was told to rebuild Ekhulkhul, just as Gudea before him dreamed his temple plans, which were interpreted to him by the Goddess/priestess. Although priests were usually dream interpreters, women sometimes also performed this function, for Tammuz' sister Geshtinanna dreamed of his future fate, Gilgamesh's mother was a dream interpretress, and in the Hurrian myth of Keshshi, seven of his dreams were interpreted for him by his mother.

In fact, so old was Nabonidus' mother that she could remember having been placed as a vassal queen of Harran under the suzerainty of the Assyrian empire, probably according to current Arab practice, since she may have been priestess of the moon in the Ekhulkhul temple, which was served by a Babylonian colony, at the same time. For this part of the world it was not unusual for a queen to be appointed to rule, since Arabians in general were used to having queens.

In exactly the same way, when the Assyrians had first started to extend their empire and subjected the northern Arabian kingdom of Dumat, they found it less troublesome to leave the priestess-queen Tabua in power as vassal under Assyrian observation than depose her. The kingdom of Dumat had always had priestess-queens, and Tabua's great-great-grandmother, Queen Zabibi, then her daughter Shamsi (worshipper of the Sun Goddess), had had to adopt a similar vassal position with regard to the earlier Assyrian king Tiglath-Pileser III (745-727). Tabua's grandmother, Iati'e, got herself into trouble for allying herself with the Babylonians as they started to fight back at the Assyrians, and Tabua's mother, Ta'lkhunu, was actually defeated by Sennacherib and taken to Nineveh. But it was under Sennacherib that Tabua was restored to the priestess-queenship of her kingdom when the king realized it would give him less trouble that way.

There were other Arabian queens, who, if the model of Dumat is anything to go by, simultaneously served as high priestess. As Esarhaddon encroached upon Syria and Nabatea, he defeated Baslu, queen of the Ikhilu people, as well as Iapa, queen of the Dhikrani tribe. Assurbanipal captured Queen Adia in Moab, and sent her to Nineveh, no doubt to join his harem. He also encountered a queen of the Lihyanites, whose name is unrecorded. Present Arabian attitudes towards women may be an over-reaction to the life they used to lead under these forceful female spiritual leaders.

Nabonidus himself was deeply involved with northern Arabia, and after his preoccupation with reviving the cult of the moon at Harran and at Ur, presided over respectively by his mother and daughter, he proceeded to Taima in Arabia, which was believed to house the primordial moon temple whence long before, in the third millennium, the daughter temples at Ur and Harran had been founded. The fact that year after year Nabonidus failed to turn up at Babylon to celebrate the New Year festival, preferring to stay in northern Arabia at Taima and the chain of towns stretching as far south as present-day Mecca and Medina, is thought to mean that he could not put his heart into the worship of Bel/Marduk in Babylon, preferring to revive the much earlier, primitive practice of the original Semitic peoples of the Arabian heartlands. His neglect of the Babylonian cult of Marduk (Jupiter) meant his son, the crown prince Bel-Sharra-Usur (Belshazzar), had to govern Babylon for his father, ultimately facing the onslaught of the Persians who took Babylon in 539.

From his inscriptions it is clear Nabonidus was a man of emotion, and it was due to his sensitivity that the role of God's bride was revived. In this his intentions resemble those of the Akkadian king Sargon in appointing his daughter to the first high priestesship of Ur, or the Egyptian Pharaohs of New Kingdom Thebes the Divine Adoratrices of Amun. Both kings understood the need for the female power within temple life to offset the outside political world of action and administration. In the same way, men today who understand the balancing of male and female energy are as forceful in their enthusiasm to restore women to positions of spiritual authority as the women themselves, and turn out to be their greatest allies, knowing that they in turn will benefit.

A beautiful scene on a neo-Babylonian seal of this period (Figure 63) sums up the mood of moon-priestesship under Bel-shalti-Nanna, daughter of Nabonidus. The God Sin appears inside his own crescent, and is held up by the supporting figure of the atmosphere. A priestess, draped in a tasselled robe spiralling round her body like a sari, her hair carefully dressed in a series of loops and ridges, raises her hand in greeting. She is mirrored on the other side by a partner, who may also be greeting the God or uttering an oracle. The hardness of the image conveys something of the obsessional attention to detail which by now rigidly fixed all religious observance at the great religious capital of Babylon, perhaps symptomatic of that lack of flexibility which led to the downfall of Babylon at the hands of the nomadic Persians.

Herodotus, writing in the 5C BC, after Babylon had been occupied by Persia, described how by then every Babylonian woman had once in her life to go and sit in the temenos of the temple of Ishtar, daughter of Sin. The rich would arrive in closed carriages; the poor would openly sit in the large outer courtyard. Lines of cord would mark out paths in all directions amongst the women, and men would pass along, choosing the one who took his

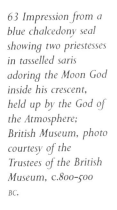

63 Impression from a blue chalcedony seal showing two priestesses in tasselled saris adoring the Moon God inside his crescent, held up by the God of the Atmosphere; British Museum, photo courtesy of the Trustees of the British Museum, c.800–500 BC.

fancy, throwing a coin at her and saying, 'The Goddess Mylitta [referring to Kybele/Ishtar] prosper thee.' 'When she has gone with him and so satisfied the Goddess, she returns home . . . A custom very much like this is found also in certain parts of the island of Cyprus.'

This of course is not priestesship, but rather an initiatory rite for female worshippers who offered to the Goddess an act in the most direct way related to that divinity's power. (The name Mylitta has been linked etymologically to the Arabic root *walada*, which is the root for all words to do with giving birth. The Arabs therefore called her Alitta, and the Persians Mithra, though her son-consort came to take her name in the later cult of Mithraism.) This obligation was often undertaken before marriage, and it was required of married women who had not yet performed the duty. The reasons behind this requirement are explored in the next chapter.

The Medes and Persians who captured Babylon adopted this Babylonian practice and considered it crucial for their women to perform this rite. They, too, dedicated their daughters to the service of the Goddess Anahita in her temples at Babylon and Ecbatana. It is said that

Persian women considered their status to be enhanced by fulfilling such a role, and according to Curtius and Strabo were thereafter 'received with greater regard and affection by their suitors'.

The Persians were close relations of the tribes of the Medes and Parthians, who in turn were related to the Scythian tribe of the Sacae. Indeed, during this period, in the 7C BC, a Scythian empire briefly extended ephemeral tentacles even into Palestine, but was kept from Egypt by the Pharaoh Psammetichus. Its peoples consisted of tribes named after their leaders, such as the Sacae, the famed Massagetae, the Arimaspi and the Sauromatae. We can imagine these horse-loving peoples moving about in the lands surrounding the Caspian and Black Seas, jostling for power and place, relying on the products of their hunting and craftsmanship, and acting as trading middle-men, thus gaining increasing prestige in the eyes of the settled nations. Peissel, who tracked down the beautiful, flower-wearing Minaro people in Zanskar in the northern Himalayas in the 1980s, believes they are a survival of such tribes. The Minaro women run everything, living polyandrously with related males. The key divinities are Goddesses, though a male God was brought in by the men who got tired of being run by women.

The oldest historical accounts of such peoples come from Assyrian documents of the reigns of Sargon II, Sennacherib, Esarhaddon and Assurbanipal, i.e. from 750 BC onwards, during the time of Sammuramat, since the Assyrians tried to conquer the Kingdom of Van (present-day Armenia), and cultural interchange took place between this great empire and surrounding nomadic peoples of mountain and plain in the process of securing borders to the north. After tribal movement and ravage had calmed down, 'there came in Scythia a period of revolutions, in which the sovereigns were women endowed with exceptional valour,' says Diodorus. 'For instance, when Cyrus, the king of the Persians, the mightiest ruler of his day, made a campaign with a vast army into Scythia, the queen of the Scythians not only cut the army of the Persians to pieces, but she even took Cyrus prisoner and crucified him.'

This was in the period after the Persians had become the predominant horse-owning tribe of the Asian plains, and had penetrated south, taking over what we know as Persia today. They supplanted the Assyrians and neo-Babylonians as the grand rulers of the empires of the Near East from capitals at Babylon, Persepolis, Ecbatana and Susa. They had close dealings with the Saca tribe, and it was their ruler, Zarina, 'conspicuous for her beauty, and remarkable as well . . . in whatever she undertook . . . [who] introduced civilized life, founded not a few cities and made the life of her people happier', much in the manner of Sammuramat. From such tribes arose the Amazons, an all-women tribe, whom we will describe in the next chapter.

Herodotos describes a tomb made for Zarina, pyramid-shaped with a golden statue of her on top. This has never been found, but other tombs of unnamed priestess-queens from other Scythian settlements surrounding the Black Sea have been discovered. One is situated at Great Bliznitsa, on the peninsula of Taman on the Sea of Bosphorus. This priestess's tomb was decorated with an Irano-Scythian version of the Great Goddess of Life and Death, a winged lion griffin attacking as its prey a collapsing horse, thus pointing to her role as priestess of the Goddess of Life and Death among the horse people. Although much of the jewellery and vases buried with her indicate she had adopted Greek ideas, her body was dressed in the ritual costume of the nomadic grand priestess, and in the traditional Scythian manner servants were buried with her, also horses and important males in her life. We do not know whether she served the Goddess under her Scythian name, as the Greek Demeter/Aphrodite/Artemis, the Scytho-Iranian Anahita, or as the Anatolian Kybele, so mixed were the religious cross-currents in this region. From later inscriptions it is known that the land of the Taman peninsula was treated as belonging entirely to the Goddess, and that several temples on it were run by colleges of priests or priestesses led by a high priest or priestess.

In the tomb of a young lady from Karagodeuashkh, also in Scythia, the remains of a funeral cart and horse skeletons were found, as well as those of retainers and a richly dressed male, in other chambers. Along the left-hand wall lay her skeleton, dressed in a full array of dazzling Greek jewellery. But at her head was a great triangular gold plaque which would have been fixed to her high tiara. On its lower part is embossed, in the Scythian style, the enthroned Goddess facing outwards wearing just such a veiled tiara, with two priestesses standing either side of her shoulders. The Goddess offers

a sacred drink to an approaching male worshipper in Scythian dress. On the other side, a beardless male dressed in robes holds more of the sacred drink in a bowl in his hands. Herodotos specifically described a certain class of Scythian males called Enarans (c.f. Peissel's Minaros, above) who consecrated themselves to the worship of the goddess by adopting 'female clothing'. (He does not specify whether they were also eunuchs, since the wearing of robes is not necessarily effeminate. Arabs wear robes and so did men in Europe in medieval times; indeed, robes enhance male dignity, where trousers can look ridiculous, especially if the wearer is fat.) The drink offering made by the Goddess is repeated on small plaques that were sewn on the dress of the lady of Karagodeuashkh. This underlies the central importance of the Goddess, who presided over oath-taking and initiated royal Scythians into the hidden mysteries.

Similar tombs have been found at Chertomlyk and Kul Oba. The priestess-queen at Chertomlyk was covered by a purple veil on which were sewn 57 square gold plates representing the seated Goddess with a mirror and a Scyth quaffing the sacred drink in her presence (Figure 64). The

64 Drawing after one of many small gold plates sewn onto the funerary dress of a priestess-queen from Chertomlyk in Russia, showing her as the Goddess holding a mirror which is also sun in the moon, symbol of the sacred marriage, while her partner drinks the sacred drink; Hermitage Museum, c.4C BC.

scaffolding holding up the lady of Chertomlyk's veil had decayed, but the shape left on the ground by the remains of the textile and the gold plaques dotted about above her head made a high pointed triangle reaching a foot above her head, with lappets descending down to her breasts, outlining a tiara of high office, rather like that of the Hittite queen Pudukhepa. By her side was a bronze mirror with an ivory handle. Nearby was the body of her consort, and with them were buried around 30 horses, and provisions stored in great vases. The tomb at Kul Oba also had a buried couple and a male servant, all placed over the body of another person, who may have been an ancestor, a practice continued in Thrace.

Not all priestesses were royal, and Jettmar says that poorer women's graves found in eastern Russia show curious funerary gifts, such as small portable altars decorated with animals, which can only be explained as cultic objects connected with shamanic rituals. Apparatus commonly recurs in their tombs that has been interpreted as inhaling censors on which drugs were burned to further aid the 'trips' of the shamanesses. To such priestesses, possession also by an animal familiar would be second

nature, its guidance enabling them to see visions and the inner truths of situations from the world of the psyche. They would lend their energies to bring about events in the world of nature, by drumming, chanting and dancing.

Shamanesses made a vital contribution to Greek religion, shamanism remaining pre-eminent as long as women were given prominence. This meant being open to divine promptings, by self-induced trance, or with the help of natural substances in plants, or naturally occurring gases, including incense at the lower end of the scale. It provided the basis for oracle giving and is discussed more fully in the next chapter. Suffice it to say here that priestesses should still be able to turn to these avenues if it helps their vision and as long as it does not harm their receiver/transmitter (the body). The fact that the queen bee is an especially evolving creature because she feeds on royal jelly was an analogy used by priestesses in the past, who at Ephesos called themselves 'bees'. Real knowledge of the substances involved is a prerequisite, and they serve to crown preparatory work in prayer and meditation, which themselves can never be dispensed with.

Later, the men who took over

as shamans still had to obtain their energy from women. If practices in Central Africa or Lapland are anything to go by, then it would be obtained by sexual intercourse with close female members of the family such as mother, sister or daughter. The shamanic tradition has rarely been recorded in writing, but today a remaining handful of shamanesses still practice what little they remember of their art in Mongolia, China and Native America, many of them now passing on their dying wisdom to Western practitioners.

In Africa, rain-making dances are often carried out entirely by naked female shamanesses, and must on no account be witnessed by males. Sometimes after ritually throwing water over herself, one woman or girl alone performs the dance, being considered for the time priestess of the moon deity who can bring the rain. Again, in modern times, dances are being passed on and revived in the West, caught from oblivion in the nick of time. Those pulled in this direction will be called. Yet although shamanism has always formed a vital underlay to the Mediterranean tradition of priestesshood, it did not provide its main structure, which is inspired by the all-embracing mythic cycle of the dying God

resurrected by the love of the Goddess – and *vice versa*.

The ancient Persians, because so newly emerged from a nomadic and shamanic past, maintained certain shamanic practices, one of which was the system of *khvaetvadatha*, or next-of-kin marriage, initiated by the priesthood (the *Magi*) as a religious duty to ensure that their spiritual tradition was kept within the family from one generation to the next. As Clement of Alexandria put it, 'Magi men cohabit with their mothers: they may also have like association with daughters and sisters.' As in Elam of earlier times, marriages between father and daughter or brother and sister were allowed. The levirate also operated, as in later Jewish custom, so that for instance in the 12C BC the Elamite queen, Nahhunte-utu, a priestess of the sun, had been first wife of the king, Kutir-Nahhunte, and then of his brother Shilhak-Inshushinak. Here a gynaeocracy prevailed for most of the state's history, as in Lycia (see next chapter).

On the premiss that the basic equation of life was Rulership/Sky/Man versus Submission/Earth/Woman, all the rulers of Achaemenid Persia, although possessing enormous harems, married next-of-kin on the king-priest model as the ladies without whom they would have no royal authority. Cassandane, wife of Cyrus, had four children. Her daughter Atossa married her father Cyrus. On his death she married his brother, Bardiya. When a different branch of the family won the kingship in the person of Darius, he in turn married Atossa - an indication that his authority, like that of Egyptian Pharaohs, relied on being linked to her person as shaktic receptacle of the dynasty. He also married her sister, Artystone, and his niece, Phratagune. Atossa's brother, Cambyses, in turn married two of his sisters. Artaxerxes I married his daughter Parysatis, who later married her brother, Darius II, and so the *khvaetvadatha* practice continued until the dynasty was exterminated by Alexander the Great.

It was probably Parysatis who was the power behind the founding of the cult of Anahita in Persia, for initially the Achaemenids had been Zoroastrians, as the religion guaranteed their right to empire, with its polarizing rationale of Light versus Dark, or Good versus Evil. According to the Man versus Woman opposition mentioned above, unlike their Scythian cousins, Persian royal women would be entitled to wield power only from behind the scenes. However, the influence of the Assyrians and Arabians, according to Herodotos, turned the Persians to making sacrifices to the Heavenly Goddess, Mylitta/Ellaat/ Kybele/Nana, often instigated by the practices of women in their harem who came from these lands. The Persian royal ladies themselves seem to have upheld the Goddess religion as appropriate for their sex, though they often gained the full support of their consorts as well. A statue of Hera captured from Greece in the Persian Wars was brought back to Susa and the King of Kings is recorded as prostrating before it.

Thus Parysatis and Darius II between them permanently established the official cult of Anahita (the equivalent of the Goddess in Persian, especially in her form of the pure water of rivers and pools). A temple of Anahita was probably built at Ecbatana (present-day Hamadan); an account exists of its gold and silver bricks, its silver roof tiles and gold-plated columns. A free-born woman, Aspasia, who had been in the harem of Cyrus the Younger, then of Artaxerxes I, was given as a boon to his son Darius II. The latter, a little while after 'appointed her priestess of the temple of Artemis of Ecbatana, who bears the name Anahita, in order that she might remain chaste for the rest of her life'.

Darius II's son Artaxerxes II was himself renowned for his respect for the cult of Anahita, and the Sasanian kings who formed the next native Persian dynasty prided themselves on their ancestry from him, also therefore giving high place to Anahita. A Sasanian rock carving shows Anahita, incarnated as the queen, dispensing the rod and ring of kingship to her husband (Figure 65) according to the time-honoured Near Eastern tradition.

Before this, Achaemenid art had shied away from giving a form to Anahita, other than on a few seals, such as the fine one in St Petersburg which shows her surrounded by a sunburst standing on a lion, adored by an Achaemenid monarch. Accounts do survive of statues of Anahita/Anaitis worshipped in private shrines attached to royal palaces, perhaps next to the harem quarters. Such small shrines have been excavated at Susa, Arinberd and Persepolis.

One lady of the Persian harem who prevailed upon the King of Kings is spotlit in the Bible's Book of Esther. In it is told how King Xerxes (Ahasuerus), son of Darius I, drunken at New Year

feasting, boasted of the beauty of his Chief Queen Vashti, and sent a command to the harem that she should appear before the court to display her beauty. So precious and intimate to an oriental is the inner mystery of a woman's beauty that Vashti knew she should protect it, and had the courage to refuse to cheapen herself, or the king, by obeying his order. For this she was demoted within the royal harem, although Herodotos reports the king had a gold statue made of

65 Carved on living rock of the mountainside for all to witness, a Sasanian king receives the authority of kingship from his queen as Anahita; Naqsh-i-Rustam near Persepolis, 3C BC.

her as Ishtar, in her memory. Through the influence of a Jew at the Persian court named Mordecai, Esther was appointed his new queen, the king not being aware that she was a Jewess from Babylon. Through intelligence provided by her fellow-countryman, Mordecai, she warned Xerxes of an assassination attempt, which increased the king's faith in her.

Meanwhile, Haman, the king's favourite, was using his influence on the king to draw up decrees for the elimination of all Jews in the Persian empire, to spite Mordecai. When Esther came to hear of the decrees which touched her own people, she walked into the king's presence unbidden, which was to invite an immediate death penalty. Fortunately, because of his trust in her, he stretched forward his sceptre and asked her what she wished. She asked that he and Haman attend a special banquet she was preparing for them and then asked a second boon, that her people be not betrayed. Through her courage, Haman was hanged and Mordecai took his place, and all decrees relating to the liquidation of the Jews were reversed. To commemorate the revenge the Jews then took upon

their intending adversaries, the festival of Purim was instituted as a memorial, not only for the saving of the Jews, but also in memory of the courage of Esther.

The strange thing about the story is that the names Mordecai and Esther closely resemble those of the Babylonian divinities, Marduk (Bel) and Ishtar, so that the whole story may be a cipher to convey the interaction of the Jewish and Persian religions at this time, a coming together again in the 5C BC of two branches of the primordial Mesopotamian faith, back to their common Scytho-Sumerian root.

1. Four forthcoming titles explore this area: *The Octave and the Atom: The Natural Measures* by Maryel Gardyne and Asia Shepsut; *The Quest for Apollo* by Anne Macaulay; *Tracking Third Millennium Stars and Planets* by Asia Shepsut, and *The Lion Attacking its Prey in Ancient Near Eastern Art* by Ayeshah Haleem.

2. Just a few titles are:
Bentov, I., *Stalking the Wild Pendulum* (Rochester, Vermont, 1988).
Berendt, J-E., *Nada Brahma: The World is Sound* (London and The Hague, 1987).
Daniélou, A., *Introduction to the Study of Musical Scales* (Benares, 1942).
Kayser, H., *Akroasis: A Theory of World Harmonics* (Boston, 1970).

9

DIVINE
POSSESSION

Role type: Artemis

The rites of priestesshood travelled not only from the Near East via Crete to Greece during Minoan and Mycenaean times, but also in the Archaic period (*c.*700-500) from Anatolia (present-day Turkey) to Greece. In this period there was a common culture stretching from the west coast of Anatolia, Land of Anat, across the Cycladic islands to eastern Greece. It is not surprising to find close similarities in cult between the matriarchal religious centres of Ephesos and Sardis, Delphi and Athens. This continuum was split asunder by the war between Greece and Persia at the great battles of Marathon (490), Thermopylae and Salamis (480), and of Plataea (479 BC) which led to an unhealed break between east and west, along the Aegean Sea, from which 'The West' as we know it today was born, holding at bay the oriental ways it had formerly espoused.

The Gulf War of 1991 represented a repeat encounter between orient and occident across the same divide shifted further east: though roles were reversed, allies around the Mediterranean basin became involved along much the same lines as had occurred in the Persian Wars, and, 1500 years after that, during the Crusades.

Yet despite the caesura, the attraction of the Holy Land has continued to draw Westerners for spiritual replenishment. The further West, the more material: the further East, the more spiritual. This generalization used to hold true. Now a reverse process is under way where the West has espoused the East and the East the West; and those Westerners who travel away from the East find it at the extreme

West, and the Easterners who travel away from the West find it in the extreme East. This is the compensatory Ying-Yang balance at work: it is unavoidable, in whatever sphere of life, and will help the recovery of priesshood.

This kind of give and take was at work during the Archaic period between Anatolia, Greece and Persia, and perhaps the theme of this chapter can be summed up by Plutarch's account of the journey taken to the west coast of Anatolia (Ionia) by the Greek leader of Athens, Themistocles, whose naval strategy later defeated the Persians at the Battle of Salamis. His initial purpose was to clear up outstanding Greek business, but he arrived unaware of the Persian satrap of Phrygia's plans to have him assassinated. Spending the night at a small village on his way to Sardis, Kybele, the Phrygian Great Mother appeared to him in a dream warning him to change his route. In return for her concern, she commanded him to make his daughter her priestess. Themistocles heeded Kybele's warning, avoided death, and 'built a temple in Magnesia in honour of Kybele Dindymene, appointing his daughter, Mnesiptolema, to be her priestess'.

The fact that the Great Mother

spoke in oracular fashion to Greeks as much as to native Anatolians had a history dating back to at least the Trojan War around 1180. Euripides' play, *Iphigenaia in Tauris* describes how, when Iphigenaia was about to be sacrificed by her father as the Mycenaean army prepared to set sail for Troy, she was saved at the last minute by Artemis/Kybele who substituted a doe in her place, spiriting her away to the Tauric Chersonese, the peninsula on the European side of the Dardanelles. Iphigenaia's principal duty there was to act as priestess in the temple 'whose cornice was discoloured with blood-stains', by sacrificing to the Great Mother any shipwrecked or captured stranger that fell into the hands of the local people, probably Scythians.

Her brother Orestes, meanwhile, had been advised by an oracle of Apollo, as well as ordered by Athena, to go to the Chersonese where his sister served, and bring back to Carystus on the borders of Attica (outside Athens) the polished wooden *asherah*/stone baetyl of the Goddess that was said to have fallen from Heaven and had special powers. On arrival by sea he and his friend Pylades were captured and, as strangers, taken to the temple of Artemis to be sacrificed. Iphigenaia recognized her brother, and, helped by Athena, they both escaped to Greece, not only with the image of the Goddess, but also a group of captive Greek women, who no doubt became the new priesthood of Artemis on their own mainland.

The *xoanon* of Artemis was set up at the new temple of Artemis Tauropolos built opposite the rock of Carystus at Halae near Brauron. Probably here, as is recorded for Hermione, none but the priestess might approach her statue. Athena instructed Iphigenaia:

To commemorate thy ransom from death, let them apply a sword to the neck of a man, and let blood be drawn on account of the sacred Goddess, that she may have honour paid to her. And do thou, oh Iphigenaia, close to the sacred terraces of Brauron, be warden of this temple of the Goddess, where thou shalt be buried at thy death; and they shall consecrate to thee as an offering the rich woven vestments which women, dying in childbirth, may leave behind them in their houses.

Artemis was the nearest the Greeks got to translating Kybele into a Greek Goddess. She nonetheless retained her original oriental strangeness. The Anatolian Kybele was the Presence in wild places, especially rocky and rugged mountains, an Anatolian Ninhursag; she took pleasure in the Phrygian mode in music - melancholy and harsh sounds of crotal and tambourine mixed with the sighing of the flute - the howling of wolves or the roar of lions, and the grinding of mountains and ravines covered in forests. None of the sweetness of Aphrodite's lyre for her. Not only were orgiastic rites connected with her, but the opposite, the complete elimination of sexual transmission. For males this meant self-castration at her spring festival at Pessinus, where, in the Late Period and probably centuries before, priests, or *galloi*, buried their genitals in the earth in her honour. Her consort was the young, beautiful Attis, killed like a wounded stag by her dogs if he ventured too close to her dangerous power, yet mourned by her in utter grief - until his resurrection. The mystics who went through her rites would be told at the end of the cycle, as if they were an Attis, 'Take courage, initiate! The God is saved - and so will you be after your trials!', the trials being the willingness to sacrifice both sexual energy, and one's own life - if it meant getting closer to the Goddess. Barnet mentions a more savage variant on the death of Attis by a boar's tusk, while making love to the Goddess, as the drone dies after fertilizing the queen bee, or the male spider the female. This is the real significance of the castration rites of the Goddess's priests.

Like Kybele, Artemis, too, was Mistress of the Beasts, heiress also to the *Potnia Theron* of Crete, often depicted holding a pair of lions, goats or even snakes in her hands, a sure indication of her Underworld affiliations. She was Goddess of the wildlife sanctuaries which were often attached to temples - a memory of neolithic life before urbanism. A sanctuary of hers is recorded as far east as the island of Ikaros just outside the Shatt al-'Arab, in the northern Gulf, original home of the Phoenicians. It was covered in untouched forest and wild game, with a shrine to Artemis in its midst. There were wildlife sanctuaries of hers all over Greece, the one at Cos even boasting a lion.

Artemis and her priestesses were there to keep alive memories of society's more uncouth Stone Age roots, to ever bear in mind human vulnerability before Mother Nature in the raw, who could kill as well as give nourishment. Thus her priesthood faced up to, and was able to live with, not only the rites of passage from death to life and life to death, but also the control, or actual obstruction, of

the natural processes of reproduction and birth. Like the lioness, Artemis was a devourer back to herself of her own products (lionesses can reabsorb their own pregnancies if necessary). What point was there to manifest further into physical form when a soul could return to its prototype with less pain if that stage were by-passed? Human sacrifice was performed to Kybele/Artemis with the idea of propitiating her by returning a creature back to its divine prototype, or seed in the world of spirit. Chastity has its point on these terms. As a heavenly Power, Artemis was the Goddess of the still, unattainable Polar North, virginal because self-sacrificed to become the Axis of the Universe - the pinpoint to which everything else is referred, the Unmoving Centre, Self-Originated, the Black Baetyl.

A priestess of this kind makes a similar sacrifice, which can only be effective if made on these lines of thinking about the meaning of incarnation, rather than on the basis of a disgust or fear of sex. Those who fully appreciate the power of sex are the only ones able to control it beneficially, in the cause of a higher spiritual good. Those who are responsible about not allowing creatures to manifest through them, so that they may care for the already manifest, are priestesses of Artemis. At a more modest level, women who work to protect wildlife, animals, all of nature, are also her priestesses.

⸙

Hittite control of Anatolia had come to an end after the predatory incursions of the Sea Peoples c.1200-1150, of which the Trojan War was an isolated incident. Out of its ashes had grown the Phrygian kingdom founded by Midas, based at Gordion, some miles away from Hattusas. The Phrygian King Midas, rich from local gold, is the first west asiatic king known to have consulted the Oracle of Delphi, and sent gifts there. From Phrygia the Goddess gained the name of Kybele/Kubaba, and her cult spread across central Anatolia.

Perhaps even earlier than the 10C BC, the temenos of Kybele at Ephesos had started simply as an altar in the middle of a sacred precinct. It was then built upon and built around over many centuries. Kybele in turn was a transformation of the earlier Hittite Goddess, Khepa (already referred to in the Hittite queen Pudukhepa's name), whose sacred precinct, according to Barnet, is likely to be elsewhere in Ephesos, though its remains have not been located.

Ephesos, and its mother city Sardis, were both Lydian towns which came to prominence under the Mermnad dynasty who took precedence in Anatolia after the fall of Phrygia to the Kimmerians. Gyges, the first of the line, was the son of a Phrygian nobleman and a Syrian mother, and ran Lydia under a strongly centralized administration, on Mesopotamian lines. Lydia was the first bridge of communication between the lands west of the Aegean and the great civilizations, so the Mermnads rose to prominence because they lay at the end of the main east-west land route from Syria and the Near East beyond, and had a coastline on the Aegean Sea linking with trade routes all over the Aegean. Psychologically, too, Lydia was a Golden Mean linking point between East and West. (With hindsight I think my own direct connection with the Goddess began when I visited Ephesos 10 years ago. Invisibly Kybele/Artemis took me in hand in a most magical way. For all who visit Ephesos and her temple site, she is Opener of the Ways at this spot.)

When the Mermnads set up their shrines to Kybebe (as she was called in the Lydian tongue) in Lydia, Sardis and Ephesos rose to high prominence internationally. The Mermnad king of Lydia best known for his endowment of these two cities, as much as of the Oracle at Delphi, was Croesus, great-grandson of Gyges, famed for his fabulous riches. Kybebe at Sardis was guardian Goddess of Croesus' famous gold, panned from the Pactolus river, and her shrine presided over the goldsmiths' area of her temple.

Sardis was the capital of Lydia and was seen as a world centre; hence its association in mythology with the legend of Queen Omphale, who was served by Hercules. Not only was it the centre of the gold trade, but also that of copper and silver; indeed, the first coinage was struck here. The Dactyls were priests of Kybele famed for their knowledge of the secrets of metallurgy.

The Mermnad dynasty derived its authority from the Goddess, the Mermnads seeing themselves as a Sandonid people, Sandonis being the priest-king ancestor of Hercules, whose symbol was the double axe. Each Lydian king received the double axe as symbol of their authority from Omphale, presumably acted by a priestess. They also had to marry into the female line in order to secure their throne. Related to Thracians, their sphere of influence stretched up to the Chersonese and across to Greece, where at Delphi they set great store throughout their rule by the advice given by the Oracle, an asiatic institution itself. All processional roads to Delphi came from the East.

Croesus decided to rebuild the earlier temple of Kybele at Ephesos with some of his wealth, and since Greece and Lydia were in close contact he chose Ionian architects and sculptors. Most of the sculptures of the Archaic period connected with the Croesus building were brought back by its excavator, Hogarth, to be stored in the British Museum. All that remains of the actual fabric of the temple, however, is a denuded Hellenistic site. Who would have thought that on completion it was hailed as one of the Seven Wonders of the world? Some say this refers to the colonnaded, pedimented and sculptured edifice built by Croesus in the 6C BC as a grand gesture of recognition to the Goddess of the gold-mining centre on the Pactolus river at Sardis, others that this label was given to Alexander the Great's rebuilding of it. The construction of Croesus' temple was interrupted in 546 by the Persian occupation and the temple took 120 years to complete, so colossal was it. There were in fact five different temples built over each other since the Cretan-type altar was erected in 700 BC. It had begun as a shrine to Kybele, with a holy stone marking her presence. With Greek, then Roman administration succeeding the Lydian and Persian at Ephesos, Kybele was, as at Sardis, given the Greek name Artemis even in her own country.

The Phrygian Kybele was shown in sculpture with polos and veil, holding in either hand a falcon and a jug, and this is how an Anatolian priestess probably looked around 700 BC. The high polos was as important a feature of her dress as it had been for the priestesses of Mari in earlier centuries further east on the same latitude. A fascinating life-size clay model of a priestess's polos from 7C Boeotia in the British Museum, with a spiral stuck to the front like a butterfly tongue, shows this helmet was an object of veneration in its own right, as the Great Mother's cult was adopted in Archaic Greece. It continued to feature in the Roman sculpture of the Goddess of Ephesos (Figure 66), where tiers of architecture formed her crown, signifying the higher worlds governed by the Goddess, and to which the priestess was able to journey in spirit. Sappho much appreciated this imposing head-dress, called the Lydian *mitra* (or mitre), and regretted

she could not obtain one for her daughter, since the magistrate of Lesbos, Pittacus, had forbidden the import of luxury items!

Since the Phrygian Kybele was usually portrayed holding a bird of prey in one hand and a

66 *Engraving after a marble statue of the fruitfully abundant Artemis/Diana of Ephesos whose body and dress encompass the higher realms of Heaven and the middle atmosphere as well as earthly manifestation; drawing from Lajard's* Culte de Venus *(1837), of a c.2C AD original.*

ΦΥCIC ΠΑΝΑΙΟΛΟC

67 Two views of an
ivory carving of a
priestess excavated
from the Cretan-type
altar site under the
temple of Ephesos,
holding the falcon and
jug of Kybele; Istanbul
Museum, c.560 BC.

jug in the other, statuettes of her
priestesses found at Ephesos hold
similar objects, both to indicate
the symbolism of the Goddess
they followed and their two main
modes of worship: shamanic
travelling with a bird spirit guide,
and tantric rites in the Sacred
Void. Only quite recently have the
Archaic layers at Ephesos been
redug and all finds thoroughly
sifted by German and English
excavators. Many small objects
were thrown to the Goddess,
such as coins and small ivory
carvings, including these
statuettes, some of which look
strangely European, others still
markedly oriental, like Assyrian
or Phoenician ivories.

The statuettes are of particular
interest, for they seem to be
dedicatory carvings of priestesses
(and one priest) made for their
Goddess. The first (Figure 67a/b)
shows a woman with loose tresses
of flowing hair, dressed in a
clinging chiton and holding a jug
in one hand. From her head a
long pole rises upwards with a
kite or falcon perched on the top,
indicating that she undertook
shamanic journeys on the lines of
priestesses from nomadic tribes
further north. As a result of
flying with her female bird of
prey, which is made to fly higher
in the sky than any other
creature, scrying events on Earth
below from her superior

perspective, as if from the North
Pole looking downwards, she
would be able to heal people's
invisible souls and pronounce
oracles on the shape of things to
come.

Taking inspiration from the
accounts of the raptors that
inspired the priestesses of
Ephesos and the bears those of
Brauron (see next chapter), the
time has returned where those
with shamanic gifts can
reconnect with specific animals
who will teach us the lessons we
need to relearn. Talking to
dolphins is easy, but the other
animals are also waiting to speak
to us, as a spider did to me
recently, quite out of the blue!
Animals have pure and deep
teaching to give us.

A fragmentary second figure,
which is not specifically from
Ephesus but belongs to the same
family (Figure 68a/b), formed part
of the frame for an ivory swan-
headed lyre, and stands on the
broken head of a sphinx.
Although for some time
interpreted as a male figure, there
is no doubt that it is female for,
apart from the breasts, three long
plaits cascade down her back,
trailing down to her ankles. Her
head fits into the phallic cap

forming the base of the swan's neck. The association of this priestess-like figure with divine music, long before it was linked to Apollo's lyre at Delphi, is not surprising when considering how far back the tradition of female lyre players goes, and how the Lydians were famed for their lyre-playing and their Delphic consultations. Royal burials at Ur, including that of Puabi, held many distinguished animal harps, all played by women, and later in history priesthood was overtly connected with divine music, or making manifest the cosmic harmonies which work on the nervous system, as already mentioned in the last chapter.

The third figure, again from Ephesos, echoes the other two in different respects. At first it looks like a matronly person with the same kind of polos head-dress worn by the harp matron, though not so high. On its top a tenon of material indicates something further was slotted onto it – whether a pole like the first figure with a bird atop, or a piece of a musical instrument or furniture, we shall never know. However, looking more closely, it has a flat chest, dumpy arms holding a chain of office, and a tailored robe, while no long hair falls anywhere. Documentary evidence talks of a Persian official, a Grand Eunuch who administered the temple at Ephesos in Archaic times, called a *megabyzos*, and the figure has with strong reason been interpreted as such, the prototype, as it turns out, of Popes, Bishops and all priests of the monotheistic faiths. It could refer to a particular Persian satrap called Megabyzos who had been satrap of Syria and was perhaps particularly associated with the cult of the Goddess in its strongest form at Hierapolis in Syria. A twin figure, which matches it in age and style, is of a woman with a tiered turban spinning wool on a spindle - both are in the Istanbul Museum now.

Some reasons behind the castration/cessation of fertility of those who served this particular Goddess are described later in this chapter, mostly in relation to females. Men had to deal with it in a different and often drastic way, since erections and night emissions usually occur involuntarily. It is on record that the *megabyzos* of Hierapolis took antaphrodisiacs, but physical mutilation was the usual step that served to ensure no lapses occurred in the Goddess's temple where an atmosphere of sexlessness was paramount. I am sure many homosexuals today are reincarnated eunuchs, which gives an entirely different perspective on their situation,

68 Two views of one fragmentary side of an ivory kithara *(lyre) showing a priestess in an Ionian chiton with three long plaits; Berlin Museum, 6C BC.*

and what they need to work through.

Barnett's brilliant insights on the Hittite influences behind Ephesos points out similarities between the beehive organization of its temple, and prototypes in Hittite mythology, to which the cult of the bee can be traced:

The whole machinery of the sanctuary in classical times seems to have rested on the symbolic analogy of a beehive, with swarms of priestesses called bees (*melissae*), numerous eunuch priests called 'drones' (*essenes*), all ruled by a king-bee or high priest called *basileus* [*megabyzos*], a male ruler perhaps because the bee-queen was the Goddess herself [representations on gold plaques from Rhodes in the British Museum show the Goddess as a bee].

In a Hittite myth featuring the hero Telepinush (the Hittite Tammuz), the Goddess sends a bee to search him out in his hiding place in the Underworld. He is brought back by her sting in his foot, and returns in time to visit the flowers of spring. Barnett cleverly traces the etymology of 'Telepinush' to the 'Telephus' worshipped by the Greeks, then to 'Delphinus'. The cult of Apollo Delphinios was common to all Ionians, and the temple of Apollo at Delphi was an outpost in Greece. We should not be surprised, therefore, that it had priestesses as at Ephesos, and that Apollo and Artemis were seen as twins, two halves of one Androgyne.

These twins are first recorded as being worshipped together at Delos. Before the great Battle of Marathon between Greeks and Persians in 490, the Persian navy, led by Datis and Artaphernes, stopped at Delos. On the orders of the Great King they respected the precincts of Apollo and Artemis on the island, seeing them as embodying their own beliefs, for oriental deities such as Atargatis and Haddad also had shrines here. Another source states that the *Magus* Gobryas was sent to Delos in 480 during the time of the battle of Salamis, 'to protect the island where the Two Deities were born'. On Delos the tombs of several priestesses have been excavated, including those of women from the Hyperborean region (Britain or northern Europe). Of these some were buried in pairs, such as Hyperoche and Laodike, Opis and Arge. Their tombstones outside the temple of Artemis are marked 'Maiden from Abroad'. Later their graves became shrines and they were treated as heroines, embodiments of Artemis.

Maury describes how the young women of Delos, crowned with flowers and dressed in their most beautiful robes, would join in a joyous choir around the altar of the Two Deities, representing by dance the birth of Apollo and Artemis, and the adventures of Leto, their mother. The dancers of Artemis were called *karyatids* and wore crowns of reeds with points on the rim. They crowned the statue of Artemis, said to have been brought from Crete by Ariadne, with flowers. This was a festival which was attended from all over the Agean. The Athenians sent seven maidens and youths to it annually. Only on the return of their boat could death sentences be carried out once more, the reason why the death of Socrates was postponed until its return.

The cult of Artemis spread to Sparta, where Alkmeon, the Spartan poet, describes Artemis making cheese from lioness's milk in a golden bucket. In the temple of Artemis Orthia young boys under the supervision of the priestess, who stood by holding up the image of Artemis, were whipped with stalks of an astringent plant called *lygo* before an open-air altar. This could have been a token for human sacrifice, which still happened in other temples, such as at Kondylea. At Triklaria a beautiful young man and woman had to be sacrificed to Artemis yearly after an Artemis priestess had refused the hand of a young man in marriage.

In Kalydon, Patrai, Hyampolis and elsewhere, living creatures were thrown on a pyre to Artemis and the priestess would arrive to witness the sacrifice in a cart pulled by a stag. At Tegea the priestess stood in for Artemis and watched as a young man was chased and captured, but he was not put to death.

However, at Sparta there could have been another reason for the whipping: King describes how the rationale behind this rite was to stimulate the onset of puberty, since the plant is described in Greek medical texts as encouraging menstruation and lactation in young women, though at the same time reducing sexual desire. It encourages conception, birth in a long labour, and the expelling of the afterbirth. Thus the plant reflected the dual quality of Artemis perfectly, being both a repressive astringent used to stem blood-flow, and a promoter of each stage of the reproductive cycle, especially in females. Hence Artemis here was named Artemis Lygodesma, or Artemis Orthia, referring to the stiff, upright stems of the herb.

On the island of Lemnos Artemis was continually propitiated by the sacrifice of young girls on the model of that of Iphigenaia. This could be similar to a ritual which took place at the ancient temple of Athena at Troy where those young girls who wished to serve Athena as priestesses had to run a race towards the temple. Those that were caught were sacrificed to Athena, and those that reached her temple became her trainee priestesses. It also resembles a Libyan festival of Athena described by Herodotos where the *parthenoi*, or unmarried priestesses of Athena, were divided into two groups and fought each other with sticks and stones. Those who died of their wounds were designated 'fake virgins', since a true virgin would be inviolable. The conclusion therefore was that those who survived were the genuine *parthenoi*. This idea was established by association with the fact that a virgin does not bleed, because her hymen has not been broken, either by sex or parturition.

King points out that the woman (*gyne*) who does proceed with the successive steps of the female cycle and its bleeding is explicitly compared by Aristotle with the sacrificed beast which gives its blood to the earth. Pausanias describes another incident concerning the strangled Artemis (also discussed by King) where the conclusion is that 'Artemis is both the goddess who sheds no blood, and the goddess who makes others bleed'.

This is further linked to the idea of the girdle which played a symbolic role in the life of an ancient Greek woman. King summarizes by saying that the first girdle is put on at puberty and is dedicated to Artemis on marriage. Another special girdle tied with a marriage knot is worn on the wedding night and untied by the husband. At the onset of labour the woman unties her girdle. King believes that 'the association between Artemis and the *zone* [girdle], worn throughout the *parthenos* to *gyne* transition, deserves to be seen not as one of many examples of the release of all knots at times of transition, but as a far more specific reference to the powers of Artemis'. In other words, a priestess of Artemis represents a Goddess who 'assists other women to cross the boundaries which she herself rejects'.

On the face of it the Goddess accepted as her priests those men who made themselves into women, and conversely those women who wished to do without men. One theory takes it that the Amazons, described at one point in Classical history as clustering around the great temple of Ephesos, were in fact its founding hierodules, but it is not a simple matter to piece together the conflicting fragments of their history, which date from different centuries. Some scholars believe they first appear in the written record as female queens and warriors of the Sauromatian tribe which lived round the delta of the Don river in the 8C BC. The same social structure was to be found in nearby tribes of the Sindians and Maeotians. The Greeks, in their second-hand accounts of the Amazons, brought back from trading missions, tended to locate them around the Sea of Azov, where they are said to have migrated after their defeat at the hands of the Greeks, pushed out of their homeland on the northern shore of the Euxine sea. But at the Sea of Azov they encountered Scythian tribes and gradually intermarried with them. The Cimmerians, who were also displaced, moved into Anatolia and first brought the Phrygian kingdom to an end, allowing the Lydians to rise to power, then threatened Lydia and the Persians in turn.

As would be expected, the Goddess was the entire object of worship of the Amazons. Possibly the Greek accounts in the end described as 'Amazon' any tribe that worshipped the Great Goddess through a priesteshood. Wherever the Goddess was worshipped society tended to be matriarchal, and this in itself pointed to a survival from prehistoric times of a culture that predated the urban civilizations of the Fertile Crescent. Despite the attempts of the Indo-Europeans (Hittites, Mycenaeans, Thracians and Greeks) to superimpose their patriarchal beliefs, the Goddess could not be suppressed completely, but the true celebrations of her cult were gradually only to be found on the periphery of the urban civilizations. Interestingly, an item on the World Service news of 1 April 1992 mentioned that 'a group of Nicaraguan women have taken up arms against the government' after it continued to ignore women's needs in the country – but it did not say whether they were Virgin Mary followers (which is likely)!

Diodorus Siculus gives further information about the Amazons. Along the Thermodon river in north-east Anatolia there lived a tribe governed by women who bore arms as vigorously as the men. The queen of the day assigned to men the spinning of wool and other domestic duties while the women went out to war. This was the tribe which mutilated young boys so they would not be war-worthy, whilst they seared off the right breast of the girls so it would not get in the way of effective archery – the word 'Amazon' meaning *a-mastos*, or 'without a breast'. Diodorus says that one particular queen was 'remarkable for her intelligence and ability as a general'. She founded the great city of Themiscyra at the mouth of the Thermodon river and finally died in battle. Her daughter equalled her mother and 'exercised in the chase the maidens from their earliest girlhood and drilled them daily in the arts of war', establishing festivals to Artemis and Ares, and extending her power as far south as Syria.

Succeeding queens ruled with distinction until the time came when Hercules (not only a mythical figure, but the name of a Greek migratory tribal unit) was sent to secure the girdle of Hippolyte the Amazon as one of his Labours. He succeeded in capturing Hippolyte along with her girdle (its significance has already been noted), sorely defeating her army. From then on, other enemies of the Amazons almost decimated them, and the remnants moved to west and south Anatolia.

Before this, at the very earliest phase of their known history, the famous freelance Amazon, Penthesilia, fought as an ally of the Trojans, until she died heroically at the hands of the Achilles the Greek. This shows just how far back the Amazonic tradition reaches, and that those described in Archaic and Classical times were but scattered remnants, for Diodorus states that Penthesilia was the *last* of the true Amazons, portraying real valour.

The regions north of Anatolia were not the only ones where matriarchies ruled, for Diodorus reports also on a similar society in western Libya. Here, women served in the army for a time, then spent a period with men conceiving and caring for children, 'but they kept in their hands the administration of the magistracies and of all the affairs of the state. The men, however, like our married women, spent their days about the house, carrying out the orders which were given them by their wives.' When the children were born they were given over to the men to be nurtured and brought up. Here, too, the breasts of the girls were seared at birth to prevent growth. Diodorus proceeds to describe other female tribes further across Africa in Ethiopia, but these accounts border on the fantastic. The general picture is that gynaeocracies were to be found far and wide around the Mediterranean basin.

One Libyan Amazon queen was Myrina, and her followers used armour made from the thick skin of the abundant Libyan snakes. She made friends in Egypt and, moving north, is said to have penetrated Anatolia and the lands around the Black Sea, before moving west again as far as Thrace, where she met defeat at the hands of Mopsus. She had also captured some Greek islands, and dedicated the island of Samothrace to the Goddess. She and her army are said to have invaded the 'Kingdom of the Atlanteans' (which, it has recently been plausibly posited, was situated either side of the Dardanelles), but ultimately to have lived in peace together in the city of Cerne. But these were amongst the Amazons eventually wiped out by the new patriarchal order brought in by Hercules (a different calendar).

Much of Amazon lore is mythologized history which serves to show the pre-existence of gynaeocracy throughout the Mediterranean, not only in the Archaic period, but from many centuries before. In the Archaic period itself, after the victory of Hercules, some of the original Amazons still living on the Thermodon river, according to Diodorus, decided to take their revenge on the Greeks for their decimation. 'They were especially eager to punish the Athenians because Theseus had made a slave of Antiope, leader of the Amazons, or, as others write, of Hippolyte.' The Scythians joined forces with the Amazons, and they all crossed the Bosphorus and advanced on Athens through Thrace. Theseus, meanwhile had had a son by Antiope/Hippolyte, so his wife fought at his side, defeating the invaders, who returned to their homeland.

Despite the predations of Hercules and some Greek colonists, priestesshood at this time was kept alive in a counter-movement throughout the Mediterranean due to colonization westwards by Phoenicians, Anatolian Ionians and Greeks.

It is not surprising, therefore, that the priestesses of the Archaic period have left evidence of themselves in Spain. The tomb of a priestess at Aliseda dating to 625 BC was full of gold jewellery, precious stones and the sumptuous remains of her dress, all of Syro-Phoenician manufacture. The seals, libation bowls and incense holders found with her all indicate she was more than just a rich lady. The sculptures of the 5C BC Dama de Baza and the Dama de Elche show the rich parure which continued to be favoured by these ladies, along the lines of Puabi's third-millennium example, and no doubt with similar symbolism.

69 Painted gypsum statue of an Etruscan priestess found in the Isis tomb at Vulci along with many oriental objects, including carved ostrich eggs; British Museum, c.570 BC.

The Dama de Baza, seated on a lion throne with wings and holding a dove, looks like an ordinary matronly Spanish lady, yet the heavy necklace on her chest imitates, with its breast-like beads, the Artemis of Ephesos (she may indeed be intended as a Spanish version of the Goddess herself). A standing stone sculpture found at Cerro de los Santos of an august lady draped in sober necklaces and plain robe, but with elaborately coiffured hair in ringlets, holding a container before her, may also be that of a priestess making offering and referring to her calling.

In Tuscan Italy, colonized by Phocaians and Phoenicians, the Etruscans practised rituals such as reading the livers and entrails of sacrificed animals, and interpreting animal behaviour for oracular purposes, some of which can be traced back to the Near East. In the Etruscan tomb of Isis at Vulci was found the distinguished statue of an auguress or other kind of priestess (Figure 69) in local gypsum coated with a thin layer of plaster and painted to look more lifelike, as was the Dama de Baza. Her hair cascades in long plaits bunched together down her back, with four tresses coming forward over her breasts, and she wears a surplice over a long plain dress. The austere simplicity of her demeanour commands awed respect. Amongst the rich contents of the tomb was a hollow golden torso of a Goddess holding a bird in her hand. Herodotus states that the Etruscans had sailed from Anatolian Lydia; if they did, they must have sailed almost directly due west, perhaps using Crete as a staging post.

The patriarchal lyre-playing Druids in Gaul are also described as taking omens, like the Etruscans, from the flight of birds, and the Etruscans could have inherited as much from them as from the East. But certainly in southern Italy there are signs that the Sabines and Etruscans fostered an Anatolian-type oracular priesthood which was shamanic in origin. The most famous Sybil, or Etruscan prophetess, was based at Cumae, a Greek colony founded in the 7C BC near present-day Naples. Before the founding of the Roman Republic, the last three Tarquinian kings of Italy were said to have gained their power through a queen-priestess, Tanaquil. She was said to have been the consort and adviser of Tarquinius Priscus, the mother-in-law of Servius Tullius and the mother of Tarquinius Superbus, the last legendary king of the line who reigned 534-510 BC, contemporary with the height of religious activity in Athens, Delphi, Sardis and Ephesos. Her role as the power-giver indicates nomadic origins, and possibly the myth of her greatness is based on those kings' worship of a Goddess who was personified as a queen by the Romans. Under the Republic of Rome, so crucial was the cult of the Asiatic Kybele that in 204 BC a Sibyl ordered the transport of the baetyl of Kybele from Pergamon to Rome, attended by her priestess.

Popov believes the cult of Kybele/Artemis spread from the Great Temple at Ephesos to the Chersonese (when Iphigenaia was priestess of Artemis in Tauris in the Chersonese), and thence to Thrace at the time of the Trojan War, which would explain similarities between religious cults of western Anatolia and Thrace. The painted walls of the 4C BC tomb of the Thracian *wanax* (king) Seuthes depict his spiritual marriage to the Goddess-priestess, a rite that for Thracians can be traced back to Mycenaean practice.

Scholars believe that although in Thrace and further south in Greece and Crete around 1600 BC the temples of the Goddess were destroyed by the male-dominated Mycenaeans, they could not obliterate the Goddess herself, since they had to gain the co-operation of the Minoans, more sophisticated than they in running a palace economy. The Minoan deities were paired off with the Mycenaean, and not surprisingly the supreme Goddess was married off to the supreme Mycenaean God. In this process the Minoan Goddesses were demoted to second place which is exactly what, in their eyes, human marriage was meant to do, in taming that wildness of single women that patriarchs so much fear. Evidence for this comes from the Linear B tablets where the Goddess is named second to Poseidon. Despite this relegation on the divine level, still the tradition of a special personal relationship between the ruler and the Goddess, like that of Odysseus and Athena, remained the most potent means by which the Mycenaeans legitimized male royal power. The Mycenaean palace and temple were one - the word *megaron* translating literally as 'cave', with all its attendant female symbolism, and future significance for the Cave of Delphi. The Mycenaean palace, in other words, was the home of the Goddess and the palace of the king, her husband.

It has therefore been suggested that the legitimization of Mycenaean rule was brought about on these lines, by a marriage between the king, or *wanax*, as high priest representing the God, with a Minoan queen or princess. Stakenborg-Hoogeveen suggests that 'combined with the fact that the *wanax* was the representative of the Mycenaean god and that the Minoans up to 1600 BC celebrated the holy marriage between the Mother Goddess and a god of lower rank to ensure fertility, it is very tempting to think of a holy marriage ceremony in the Throne Room at Knossos between the Mycenaean supreme god and the Mother Goddess, personified by the *wanax*, and the Minoan royal priestess.' This hypothesis is supported by the myth of Theseus and Ariadne, Theseus being an Athenian prince who married the Cretan princess, daughter of King Minos.

Thus in the 5C BC Mycenaean beliefs survived amongst the Thracians of northern Greece, for after the Trojan War it was they who had kept Mycenaean beliefs alive. They also claimed links with the nobility of Athens, which dated back to Mycenaean times. Apart from the cult of the sacred marriage, they continued to bury high-ranking people in beehive tombs, as the Mycenaeans had done, along with their chariots, horses, dogs, precious possessions and sometimes their servants, just as their Scythian-related ancestors had done. They inherited the rites of funeral games and feasting from the Mycenaeans, often depicted on the walls of their tombs.

Furthermore, tombs have been found in Thrace where men and sometimes women of high status were interred over a single female burial, which had also happened millennia before at Ur. For instance, in the centre of Tumulus 4 at Satovca, there were burials reaching forward in time to the 1C BC made over an original burial of a woman from a much earlier period. Gergova believes this is an instance of the development of a tumulus into a 'heroinon' due to the sanctity or other special qualities of the original person buried. In five out of seven burials at this site, the central burial around which others were clustered was that of a woman; a sixth was round a fire and the seventh over a man. In some cases at other sites, double female burials were found, and Thracian women, like their Scythian and Amazon counterparts, were often buried with weapons. Much later in history, as we know, an entire cathedral would be built round the body of a saint, and thus we could surmise these women were at least great queens, if not also high priestesses. Because of so many similarities between the tombs of ancient Ur *c.*2600 BC, and those of the Indo-European nomads, we can also guess that the especially unusual burials of Ur centuries before point to the northern origins, even then, of a mountain-dwelling, metal-working élite who made it to an urban centre on the plain and ruled it for a while.

On the eastern side of the Aegean, in Anatolia, tombs made under Persians who in the 6C BC became Zoroastrians were quite different, for the body was raised up in a chamber so that it could be exposed to the air and the birds until its bones were left clean. One such is that in honour of Harpagus the Mede and his descendants, Persian satraps who occupied Xanthos, capital of Lycia, after they had taken over Anatolia. On one side is carved a relief in the Ionian Greek style showing three maidens, likely to be priestesses, dressed in diaphanously pleated robes and long plaits with coronet headbands, approaching the Goddess with offerings of an egg, a pomegranate and flowers (Figure 70).

Xanthos lies diagonally opposite the island of Cyprus, where famed *shakti* cults continued in the Archaic period. From this time come limestone or clay statues of Cypriot women offering their worship through their harp-playing, making manifest the divine harmony of the Goddess Aphrodite, whose power co-ordinates all parts into a harmonious whole (Figure 71). They may have been priestesses

70 *Limestone relief from the Harpy Monument, Xanthos, in the gynaeocratic state of Lycia, probably showing priestesses in Ionian chitons bringing offerings to Demeter in spring; British Museum, 5C* BC.

71 Clay figure from Cyprus of a woman playing a lyre, making audible the divine harmony of the Goddess Aphrodite; British Museum, 5C BC.

since harp-playing was a sacred function.

Lying so close to each other across the sea, clearly Lycian and Cypriot cults learned much from each other, but most of the *written* records we have are about the small kingdom of Lycia, whose people formed a fascinating society, perhaps a survivor in this mountainous pocket of Anatolia of a tradition hundreds, if not millennia of years older, if Çatal Hüyük further north-east is anything to go by.

Herodotos reports that Lycians were named after their mothers, that only daughters had the right to inherit, and they were bound by law to provide for their parents in old age. (In Cantabria in southern Italy daughters had to provide dowries for their brothers, which we do not hear of in Lycia, said to be the homeland of the Etruscans.) The source of these attitudes was Anatolian and as Bachofen puts it:

The prestige of womanhood among these peoples [referring to the Carians, Pelasgians, Arcadians and other tribes in Anatolia or their colonies in Greece] was a source of astonishment to the ancients, and gives them all, regardless of individual coloration, a character of archaic sublimity that stands in striking contrast to Hellenic culture.

For such societies, matricide could not be atoned for by anything, one's own country was understood as 'motherland', and female sacrifices were more potent than a male offering.

According to Bachofen's arguments, which explain the range of women's possible roles between the extremes of hetairism and marriage:

A bitter surprise is in store for those who look on marriage as a necessary and primordial state. The ancients held exactly the reverse: they regarded the Demetrian principle [of marriage] as an infringement on an older principle, and marriage as an offense against a religious commandment . . . the law of matter rejects all restrictions, abhors all fetters, and regards exclusivity as an offense against its divinity. This accounts for the hetairic practices surrounding marriage. Diverse in form, they are perfectly homogenous in idea. Marriage as a deviation from the natural law of matter must be expiated . . .

What Bachofen means by this is very important, since the efficacy of priesthood as an extra-marital state in honour of the Goddess is explained by it. It also provides the main reason for the absolute necessity made incumbent upon all women in the Archaic period at least once in their lifetime to give tantric service to the Goddess at her main temples, whether in Babylon, Pessinunte, Hierapolis or Paphos. It was to propitiate the Goddess against inviting her disapproval on entering the state of marriage, a state not favoured by Kybele/Artemis's laws! The interpretation of these mass practices as sheer prostitution is therefore a grave misunderstanding, and Bachofen is the only commentator who arrives at something close to a real understanding of this rite. Only a person who can mentally fully enter the world of pagan checks and balances, understanding the inter-relationship between Spirit, Psyche and Body, will see why this particular balance was a necessary factor in the preservation of Cosmic Law.

Bachofen goes on:

The diversity of intermediary states between hetairism and maternalism indicate the ups and downs in this millenary struggle. The Demetrian principle triumphed gradually, and in the course of time the expiatory sacrifice was steadily restricted. The gradations are extremely interesting. The sacrifice which was first performed annually is later enacted but once; originally practised by matrons, hetairism is now restricted to young girls; it is practised no longer during but only before marriage, and even then it is no longer promiscuous but narrowed down to certain selected persons. In keeping with this limitation, special hierodules are appointed - an important step towards a higher morality, since it transferred the obligation of all womanhood to a restricted class and freed matrons from the duty of being generally available. The mildest form of personal expiation was the sacrifice of the hair, which in some cases regarded as equivalent to the body, was generally associated with the chaos of hetairic reproduction [hence the covering of the hair required of Muslim women].

According to Bachofen, as conjugal union became the norm, both hetairism and Amazonism were gradually rejected as the two main perversions of womanhood. Thence the openings to higher development and priestesshood were also gradually closed down by patriarchal influence - even before the onset of monotheism, it has to be admitted! Later, in medieval times, the practice of the *droit de seigneur* was a rare instance of the understanding and survival of 'the expiatory rite'.

In Lycia the pull between hetairism and marital exclusivity was held in perfect balance, and its society was named by Bachofen 'a conjugal institution'. If its society was run by faithful and serious wives, the result was to inspire its men to war-like bravery, their Lycian hero role model being Bellerophon, just as in medieval times chivalry went hand in hand with the idealized cult of woman. Perhaps, Bachofen suggests, Amazonism is female behaviour driven to over-compensate for men who have degenerated and become spine-less. The feminist movement could partly be understood in this light.

The hero of marital fidelity for Attica, and especially Athens, was Theseus. It was he who put an end to the Amazonism, the warrioress priestesshood, by defeating Hippolyte/Antiope, capturing her girdle and thereafter marrying her. This is why the subject features so often in Classical sculpture, even in Anatolia, as on the Mausoleum of Halicarnassus (Figure 72).

Every possible combination of interaction between men and women was to be found in the ancient Greek world, which sheds light on the harm and help the balance/imbalance of the sexes brings to each other! As much as it affected religion in those times, by as much do we ignore the question at our peril today.

72 Part of a marble frieze by Skopas showing Greeks fighting Amazons, a favourite subject in Classical art, from the east frieze of the Mausoleum of Halicarnassus; British Museum, c.350 BC.

Having now looked at how close Anatolia and Greece were in the Archaic period, and at the often shamanic nature of the priestesses of Artemis, and the reasons for their particular marital status, we end at a climax: a consideration of the prophetesses of the Oracle at Delphi, which was uttered as the words of the God spoken through the mouth of the Pythoness (*Pythia*), the Snake Priestess.

The Phocaians of Anatolia had not only colonized religious foundations in southern Italy and France, but also chosen sites closer at hand, one such being Delphi. It was further built up by the patronage of Lydia and then Persia. Here the ancient serpent religion of the Goddess had been grafted on that of northern, patriarchal version of Apollo with his heavenly music from Hyperborean climes. At its very heart was the primitive Oracle of the Earth Mother, Gaia, and it was still her priestess who, when asked questions about the future, sat on a tripod over the fumes steaming from a fissure in the underground cave at Delphi (said in one account to fill her womb). The Oracle of Delphi was delivered in a cave in the vicinity of the temple, not in the temple itself. With the additional stimulus of chewed laurel leaves (Apollo's own plant, as the laurel

was the Goddess Daphne transformed into a bush, which he vowed always to wear as a wreath on his head), or a drink from the underground fountain called Kassotis, she became possessed of the spirit of prophecy (Figure 73). (At Argos the Pythoness drank the blood of a bull sacrificed at night, in order to be possessed by the God). Just as at Ur drains or pipes were found at the tops of most tombs

73 A melodramatic 19C engraving sums up the ingredients necessary for the Delphic oracular priestess to operate: she sits on the Apollonian tripod draped with snakes, over the steaming crack inside the cave at Delphi, while priests and suppliants strain to hear her words; from Klio, 1891.

to take liquid libations, so the practice continued in Greece, from Minoan times, of pouring blood, milk, wine or oil down to the powers of the Underworld.

Resting on a Mycenaian site where in neolithic times a female deity had been worshipped, the temple at Delphi which protected the Oracle housed the navel of the world for that era, the *omphalos*. In the Archaic period Delphi operated as the centre of the entire Greek world, including, before the split caused by the Persian Wars, great cities in Asia Minor such as Gordion in Phrygia and Sardis in Lydia. By means of the Oracle, to which they all referred for guidance, otherwise self-centred and very disparate city states, as much as far-flung colonies, were magnetized into some kind of unity around a centre. Delphi acted as the axis between Heaven and Earth on behalf of that network, in the same manner that in Sumer the ziggurat was understood as linking not only Heaven to Earth, but also to the cave inside the mountain. Some have pointed out the interesting link between the Akkadian word for the planet Venus, *Dilbat*, and the name 'Delphi'. Scholars have argued that at the same period the *omphalos* for Syria was understood as the Breast of Atargatis, which is interesting,

since the word *Ka'ba*, which holds in its fabric at Mecca today's Muslim *omphallos* (here I have deliberately added an 'l' to bring out something more), the Black Stone of Kybele, is related to the Arabic word *ka'uba*, meaning 'full-breasted', or 'rounded, developing breasts'.

We know the names of several priestesses of Delphi, often called *melissae*, as at Ephesos. The first was Daphne (also called Manto), daughter of the seer Tiresias who had counselled Cadmus of Thebes in Boeotia. According to Diodorus Siculus, she 'possessed no less knowledge of prophecy than her father and in the course of her stay at Delphi developed her skill to a far greater degree . . . Indeed it was from her poetry, they say, that the poet Homer took many verses . . .and since she was often like one inspired when she delivered oracles they say that she was also called Sibylla, for to be inspired in one's tongue is expressed by the word *sibyllainein*.'

Another priestess, Diotima, taught Socrates. He described her as 'wise in love and many other kinds of knowledge'. Themistoclea grounded the young Pythagoras in his basic moral views before he departed for southern Italy.

Sadly, the Spartan king, Kleomenes, was said to have used an agent, Cobon, to corrupt the priestess Perialla by trying to force her to pronounce against the man he wished to depose. An enquiry was made, Cobon was exiled from Delphi and Perialla stripped of her office.

On a happier note, Aristonike pronounced ambiguous oracles to the Athenians on their hopes of victory before the onset of the Persian Wars. When the Persian Wars were half-way through, and the outcome yet undecided, the priests of Delphi were still unsure which side to support, Athens or Persepolis. As a result of their preliminary victories, as Plutarch describes, at Delphi 'there stood a golden statue of Pallas Athene, mounted on a bronze palm-tree, which the Athenians had dedicated out of the prizes for valour which they had won in the Persian wars'. The priests of Delphi 'were advised by another oracle to fetch the priestess of Pallas from Clazomenae (on the coast of Ionia) [and] her name when she arrived turned out to be Hesychia, so by this coincidence the Oracle seemed to advise the city to remain at peace' (i.e., not to take sides).

Otherwise, the Pythonesses, as the priestesses were known, remain anonymous for, as Plutarch described, they were the detached instrument of the use of the God, who, after they had taken the necessary preliminary substances, whether gas, herb or treated water, would with their help open their clairvoyance to look into the future. Then, with their own voice and choice of words, they would express the message given non-verbally by Apollo within their being. The priests surrounding the priestess would listen intently and translate her utterances into verse for the querents, to make them more intelligible. It did not matter if the woman herself was of low stock, for the message of the God was what mattered, not the crudeness of the vehicle. In fact illiteracy was often taken as an advantage, since the person then had no preconceptions. (It is said that illiteracy is the criterion of Muhammad's authenticity, since the words of the Qur'an could not have been his invention, but genuinely imparted to him by divine revelation.)

Originally the Oracle was consulted only once a year, and beforehand a sacrificial animal was drenched with libations. Only when it shivered all over was it deemed the right time to call out the Pythoness. The efficacy of the Oracle depended on the purity of the priestess herself. Plutarch described the requirement thus:

They preserve the body of the Pythia pure of carnal cohabitation and her whole life free from all kinds of alien intercourse, a thing untouched, and before the oracular transaction, they take the signs, believing that the God must know when she has the proper temperament and disposition and can so endure the inspiration without injury . . . It is not good for her to go into the shrine and yield herself to the God unless she is perfectly clean, like an instrument properly prepared and fair-sounding.

In his *De Pythiae Oraculis* he describes the woman who filled the position in his day:

Take the woman who at the present moment serves the God; none of the prophetesses here has been bred more legitimately and honourably, and lived a more decent, orderly life: yet brought up as she was in the house of poor tillers of the soil, and bringing with her no special education, no acquirement or skill, when she descends into the oracular chamber - reminding one indeed of what Xenophon says about a young bride, that the less she has seen and the less she has heard before she goes to her husband's house, the better - this woman, untaught and ignorant, one might say, of everything, comes to her commerce with the God a Virgin indeed, a Virgin in soul.

The experience of the Pythia in receiving the oracle of the God was not always pleasant: rather it was overwhelming. Some idea is given in a passage about the Sibyl in the *Aeneid*, Book 6. She first

feels the God descending on her: 'The God, here is the God!' Then, as the inspiration infuses her, she falls into a paroxysm whose physical aspects are described, such as distressed breathing: 'But the prophetess, not yet able to endure Apollo, raves in the cavern, swollen in stature, striving to throw off the God from her breast; he all the more exercises her frenzied mouth, quelling her wild heart, and fashions her by pressure.' Interestingly, accounts of the receipt of the Qur'an from the Angel Gabriel by the Prophet Muhammad are described in the same terms, including perspiration and singing in the ears, such that the Prophet sometimes thought he was going mad. The description of the Sibyl echoes this further: 'Such a rein doth Apollo pull in, controlling her madness, as he turns the spur deep in her breast' (translated by Bevan).

Lucian gives further insight:

At last Apollo gains mastery of the breast of the priestess and never did he invade her body in fuller volume. He drives out her former mind and commands the human person to surrender the breast wholly to his possession. She goes raving through the cavern, out of her own mind, carrying a neck which is no longer hers.

Later 'Sibylline Oracles' fabricated by Jews and Christians imitate the form of the Delphic Oracle and were imitations of the real utterances of women in a trance condition, e.g. 'And now, O King of the world, cause the message to cease: for I know not the things which I speak: it is Thou in me who are the speaker of everything. Give me rest for a little, for my heart is wearied within me of the inspired utterance' (xii, 297), and 'And now, O King, cause my enchanting voice to cease, remove from me the gad-sting and the divine speech of truth, and the terrible madness' (xi, 523). Finally, in the Bacchic orgies of later times, a general type of ecstatic possession was frequent amongst the maenads (Figure 74), usually inspired by wine and sex.

The language of the priestess inspired by the God is the experience of a higher order of *hieros gamos*. Perhaps all along this was the true meaning of the term! As in the Near Eastern civilizations, the physical sacred marriage played an important part in Archaic Greek life, but began to disappear by the Late Period: it is always an indication of Minoan/Near Eastern influence. Zeus and Hera's sacred marriage is described on Samos, as is that of Kore and Pluto at Eleusis (see next chapter). On these prototypes it was known to be practised by humans in Lydia at Sardis (the marriage of Kore with Sabazios), in Thrace (as already described), and at Thebes in Boeotia. More could be described, but the most explicitly recorded example is the yearly marriage of the Queen Archon at Athens with Dionysos, the Bull

74 Part of a marble frieze from the temple of Dionysos at Teos, Anatolia, showing the frenzied dancing of a maenad flanked by centaurs, one ridden by a male celebrant. With the help of wine, music and sex, possession by the God became available to all in some measure; British Museum, 150–100 BC.

God, at the feast of Anthesteria, 'thus securing the fertility and prosperity of the whole Athenian state,' writes Farnell. At Delphi the Pythia was seen as the Bride of Apollo, but the nature of the impregnation was of Spirit into Matter. In Lycia the priestess of Patara gained her inspiration, Herodotos writes, 'by nuptial union with Apollo'.

Among other Near Eastern parallels, mourning for the dead God also features, in a minor key, in Greek cults connected with Apollo, Artemis and Athena. At the tomb of Hyakinthos, an early form of Apollo at Amyklai, Sparta, his death and resurrection were celebrated. The deaths of Palaimon in Greece; Adonis in Byblos, Cilicia and Cyprus; of Eshmun at Sidon and Carthage; and of Melqart at Tyre and Gades show the company to which the Greek version of the rite belonged. Mainly in Greece it was translated into female form as the myth of Demeter and Kore/Persephone (see next chapter). At Delphi the tomb of Dionysos was to be found by the side of the Oracle. As a divine child he was protected by a python, half-man, half-snake, just as the Acropolis at Athens was guarded by an immense python. One of the festivals of Delphi was the enactment to music of the battle between Apollo and the Python, which was never totally vanquished, but remained in its Underworld role at the heart of the Oracle.

The brilliance of Greek organized religion was to channel the highest levels of oracular revelation into state control, at the great shrines of Dodona, Delphi and Didyma, to name the three principal ones. They could so easily have remained as provincial oracles with some international radiance, like the oracles of Apollo at Branchidae, Claros, Colophon, Didyma, Lykeios, Mallus, Patara, Phocis, Telmessos and Xanthos in Anatolia, at Argos, Tegyra near Orchomenos and Thebes in Boeotia, or at Epiros, where its snakes were fed by the priestess (attempts to make Athena an oracular deity at Athens failed); of Ammon in Egypt; or of Almaqah in Marib, Yemen.

Delphi could have stayed in a backwater, rather like Dodona, where the oracle was delivered from under oak trees, guarded by three priestesses called Peleiades, in service of the Goddess Dione. They gave oracles from watching the flights of birds, especially ravens, as well as from listening to the whispering of the oak leaves on the trees, from which they drew omens. Priests helped to run the cult. But the quality and prestige of Delphi's Oracle stood out against the host of other oracles to be found all round the Mediterranean, in north Africa, Anatolia, elsewhere in Greece, Italy, and even Arabia. Croesus of Lydia relied on it so much that he endowed it with magnificent treasures, preferring its reliability over local oracles in his homeland. As the Classical period wore on and rationalism held sway, divine possession was looked upon by the Greek philosophers with increasing scepticism, because it was often faked or abused. But the greatest, such as Plato, Socrates and Herodotos, gave credence to the authenticity of the Delphic Oracle as the Voice of Apollo, channelled by the Pythoness.

A fragment of Heraklitus reads, 'The Sibyl with raving mouth utters things unsmiling, unbeautified, unperfumed, and yet reaches to a thousand years with her voice by reason of the God.'

It is rare to be given the role of prophetess, and it comes from above, for it cannot be learned or taught, though getting in tune can be practised. High prophetesses are chosen by the God, while lesser lights need the help of his natural substances, which are sacred. May oracular priestesses, married to the Divine Maleness, today find a way to speak to us of Heaven's intentions.

THE CLASSICAL WORLD

DELTA AND ILISSUS

10

THE VEIL OF ISIS

Role types: Athena/Aphrodite/Isis

SAIS, ATHENS AND ROME

In the 5C and 4C BC, the entire Mediterranean adopted a mixture of the main cults of the Goddess deriving from Egypt (Isis), Phoenicia (Isis Urania or Aphrodite Urania) and Anatolia/Greece (Athena/Kybele/Artemis). Priestesses of Isis were to be found from the Delta of the Nile to the banks of the Tiber. Priestesses of Love were common at Hierapolis in Syria, Babylon and their respective daughter temples to as far west as Sicily, Sardinia and Spain. Details about them are plentiful and would fill another book. To gain the flavour of the priestess's work in the Late Period, we shall concentrate mostly on women's rites and their priestesses as found in Classical Athens, since they were central to the inhabitants of the entire Mediterranean world well into Roman times, and form a contrast with the other practices, which went on as before.

In the last chapter, it was described how the cult of the Goddess of Life and Death, Artemis/Kybele, was brought to Brauron in Attica by Iphigenaia and her brother Orestes. Here a five-yearly festival was held, in which the pre-teen trainee priestesses danced the Bear Dance in honour of the Goddess, their circumambulation mimicking the gyration of the Hyperborean stars of the Bear constellations guarded by Artemis as axis of the world. The overt mimicry of the bear's movements convey a distinctly shamanic flavour to the ritual, reinforcing the idea that the dance was a relic of palaeolithic times when animals featured much more strongly as spirit guides to their even higher planetary and zodiacal analogues.

Euripides in his play, *Iphigenaia in Aulis*, describes how Iphigenaia at the moment of sacrifice lets her saffron robe fall from her body, and in the same way the young girls at Brauron would approach Artemis's altar in naked purity, in imitation of their ancestral High Priestess Iphigenaia, whose heroon-like tumulus housed her tomb near the temple. Popov quotes an alternative line to the play in Euripides where Iphigenaia utters the words, 'I shed my saffron robe [as I did when] a Bearess in the Brauronian rituals!' The shamanic dance itself was a major event in the lives of the young priestesses and the practice continued well into the Late Period, when some of them dedicated sculptures of themselves to Artemis (Figure 75).

It appears that only girls from chosen families were allowed to enter the Brauron community – those linked to the original inhabitants of Greece, the Thraco-Pelasgians of Arcadia and Ionia. But then the very territory, Arcadia, was linked to the bear totem, since *arktos* is the Greek word for 'bear', and the young priestesses were called *arktoi*. Because of the link with the polar region on the star map, Arcadia was a focal zone in the Greek world, and means 'Bear County'.

Suidas wrote that all Athenian women, before marriage, were required to spend a period as bear of the Goddess. The female bear is always in rut and, with the usual contradictions of sexuality already discussed in relation to Artemis, she was seen both as the animal of Artemis and of Aphrodite. At Hierapolis in Syria, in the wild sanctuary of the Goddess attached to the temple, there were bears, lions, bulls, eagles and goats, all symbolic of deities. On Classical seals Eros would be shown riding

75 *One of many marble votive statuettes presented by young trainee priestesses (bearesses) to Artemis; this little girl offers a hare; Brauron Museum, 4C BC.*

on the back of a bear, or playing with one.

So special was the *xoanon* of Artemis at Brauron that during the Persian Wars it was captured by the Persians and taken to Susa: they were, after all, taking it back to Asia. As mentioned in the last chapter, the Persians were particularly respectful of the Great Goddess, and on at least two occasions during the war between Greece and Persia her temple was spared from being put to the flames by the Persian army.

The first tyrant of Athens after the Golden Age of Solon (640-560 BC), named Peisistratos, came from Brauron. It was probably due to him that the cult of Artemis Brauronia was imported to a separate area of the Acropolis of Athens, just behind the Propylaea (perhaps planted as a sacred grove). At Athens itself, the training for the priesteshood of young maidens taken from the top noble families was carefully undertaken. This was connected to the very ancient ritual of weaving and spinning, which we know was the occupation of temple women in third-millennium Mesopotamia, when cylinder seals with a spider engraved were used to mark their products.

It was said by Plutarch that before the tyranny of Peisistratos, the high priest Epaminondas of Phaestus, formerly a Minoan temple centre in Crete, who was sometimes regarded, with Solon, as one of the Seven Sages of Greece, had been sent for to regulate the religious affairs of Athens. He must have introduced a measure of patriarchy, for 'he immediately introduced certain sacrifices into their funeral ceremonies and abolished the harsh and barbaric practices in which Athenian women had indulged up to that time' (perhaps the Phoenician-based cults, traces of which have been found on the Acropolis - see Chapter 5).

By the late 6C BC, under Peisistratos, Athens sported a Parthenon with pediments sculpted with the most powerful symbol of the Goddess, lions attacking bulls. Priestesses called *parthenoi*, dedicated to remain unmarried in service of the Goddess Athena, ran the temple. The well-known sculptures of *korai* found in the walls of the Acropolis, built from the shattered pieces of the Acropolis precinct after the Persian War, may be statues commissioned by priestesses showing them perpetually offering to Athena an apple or other such gift (cover/Figure 76), as priestesses had done in the ancient Near East long before, and more recently in Lycia on the

Harpagus Tomb. The *korai* are dressed in the same way as the Anatolian maidens who approach the Goddess on the tomb of Harpagus (Figure 70), showing that Athens in the Archaic period, before its tragic war with Persia, was an extension of the Anatolian world, its beliefs and rites. Close links certainly existed between Xanthos, capital of the kingdom of Lycia, and Athens, even after the Persian War, for there was a temple to Athena there, and Athens sided with Xanthos in her fight to retain her independence from the Persians. Lycian and Athenian ideals of marital balance also coincided (see last chapter), and Athenian cults in the Late Period held up the tamed, married woman as the ideal prototype for Greek citizens to follow, even if some priestesses were still required to follow the virgin ideal.

Graindor has some interesting insights to make about the *korai*, or maidens, who served in the Parthenon. He believes that in Minoan times they would have been sacrificed to the Goddess; then that in later times this was commuted into acting as hierodules in the service of the Goddess (the ante-chamber to a Greek temple was called a *thalamos* which literally means 'marriage chamber', the place where the marriage takes place);

but that finally their virginity was accepted as a substitute for both.

Apart from the Parthenon at Athens, there were four other known Parthenon temples named as such: at Apollonia in Caria, also run by priestesses; at Cyzicus in honour of Kybele, from which a portrait of one of her priestesses exists; at Hermione in honour of Demeter, at which in a dedication mention is made of a convent; and at Magnesia on the Maeander (to Artemis). The Church Fathers later called a convent a *parthenon*. Evidence points, therefore, to *gigparu* (the Mesopotamian 'convent') and temple being one at Athens.

Even though Athens was held in the grip of patriarchy, the high priestess of Athena retained an imposing authority. At a time of strife between political factions in the last two decades of the 6C BC, many noble Athenian families were expelled from the city, and at the request of one Athenian political group, their Spartan allies occupied the Acropolis. A popular uprising of Athenian citizens kept them trapped there, however, until they were forced ignominiously to leave. Herodotus described an encounter during that event, between Kleomenes, the Spartan leader, and the priestess of Athena:

76 One of many painted marble statues of what are probably maiden priestesses of Athena, built into the old walls of the Acropolis after the Persian Wars; originally the priestess would have held out an offering to the Goddess; Athens Museum, 6C BC.

For when he went up to the Acropolis intending to seize it, he went towards the sanctuary of the Goddess to address her; and the Priestess rose up from her throne before he could pass through the door, and said, 'Stranger from Sparta, go back and do not enter the holy place; for it is unlawful for Dorians to enter here.'

I visualize a strong-faced, mature priestess of Athena looking like Lysimache (Figure 77) making this

77 Roman marble portrait of an old woman found in Tarquina, Italy, said to be a copy after the famous Greek 4C BC bronze original of Lysimache, a famed priestess of Athena; British Museum.

statement. A famous bronze statue was made of this priestess and set up on the Acropolis, but all we have is a Roman marble copy of her face at the end of her career, full of experience and wisdom.

In midsummer the Athenian festival named the Scirophoria was celebrated at Sciron, on the holy way to Eleusis. The name of the festival was taken from the large white sunshade (*sciron*) beneath which the priestess of Athena, the priest of Erechtheus and the priest of Helios walked to Sciron to make their offerings, the sunshade becoming symbolic of heavenly protection against the fierceness of the Divine Sun.

Soon after the Scirophoria the Arrephoria was celebrated in honour of Athena. Four young girls from noble families, between seven and eleven years of age, were chosen at this time to spend some months in the Parthenon and take part in its rites. Two of them would be given the task of beginning to weave the peplos, the robe (in Egypt it would be the Veil of Isis) which was later completed by the mature women of Athens to dress the statue of Athena on the occasion of the Panathenaic Festival.

On the night of the festival, the two other girls received from the priestess of Athena some containers whose contents were kept secret. They carried these through underground chambers to the part of the Acropolis where the sanctuary of Aphrodite (formerly Astarte) of the Gardens had been in Phoenician times. Here they were given something equally mysterious to bring back to the Parthenon on the Acropolis. These were the two Arrephoroi, or holy offering bearers, described by Pausanias, who said the contents of the containers were not divulged by the priestess of Athena, but must have been similar to those carried in the baskets to Eleusis.

When the Great Panathenaia was celebrated a few weeks later, a key ceremony took place whereby one of the young girls handed over the freshly woven peplos for the statue of Athena to the Archon Basileus, the equivalent of their constitutional monarch. The Parthenon frieze, now in the British Museum, shows this scene taking place in the presence of the Twelve Gods and Goddesses of Olympus, so central was it to the whole ritual (Figure 78). Turning round to greet two more young girls carrying seats and a footstool is a mature woman whom some interpret as being the Basilinna, the Archon's queen-wife, and others as the priestess of Athena herself, who would soon after conduct the sacred marriage rite with the Basileus within the Parthenon. (This seems to be a different occasion from the

78 A marble slab from the Parthenon frieze showing a young Athenian girl handing the new peplos of Athena to the Basileus, while the priestess of Athena/Queen Basilinna turns to take a stool from a parthenos in order to sit in the company of the Gods; British Museum, 5C BC.

marriage of the Basilinna with the Bull God Dionysos mentioned in the last chapter.) The idea behind the handing over of the seats is that both would join the assembly of the Twelve Olympian Gods (the Zodiac) before the magic rite of the conjunction of Heaven and Earth took place.

The enactment of the *hieros gamos* must have survived from Mycenaean times when the king would receive his authority from the priestess in the temple which was one with his palace: excavations on the Acropolis have revealed the existence of such a Mycenaean megaron. The telling resemblance of this ritual to Near Eastern practice points to Athens' oriental roots, about which there is much controversy. It had added aspects to practices derived from the Delphi-Sardis-Ephesos connection which, on Greek historians' assertions, were to be ascribed to cults brought by Egyptian colonists. Their Great Goddess, Isis, under the name of Neith of Sais, is described by Plutarch thus: 'At Sais the seated statue of Athena [Neith], whom they consider to be Isis also, bore the following inscription: I AM ALL THAT HAS BEEN, AND IS, AND WILL BE: AND NO MORTAL HAS EVER LIFTED MY VEIL.' Using the imagery of lifting the veil of the bride to behold her true beauty, Isis conveys the idea that only those who travel

out of physical manifestation, moving beyond the Veil, will find out who she really is. Hence the symbolism of the weaving the veil or peplos for the divine statue of the Goddess was central to the priestess cults of Isis and Athena.

Once the Persian War was over, the Acropolis of Athens, burned and desecrated by Xerxes, was rebuilt. (The smashed priestess statues were used as building blocks in the new Acropolis wall.) It was at this time, during the 5C BC, that the Parthenon marbles as we know them today were carved to decorate the new temple of Athena. On the Parthenon frieze, which ran round the outer wall of the sanctuary, protected by a colonnade, appear scenes connected with the part females played in the cult of Athena. Amongst the horsemen and soldiers making up the main body of the Panathenaic procession walks with majestic steps a group of Athenian maidens from the noble families of Athens (this slab is in the Louvre), some of whom served as priestesses.

Sadly, the flavour of Athenian priestesshood after the Persian Wars became colder and lost its connection with the shamanic vigour of the Anatolian mainland. In combating the Persians, the Greeks in the process suppressed the oriental depth of the

Goddess, and their religion thereafter had a predominantly male ring to it, such that the martial (rather than marital) character of Athena became supreme, at the expense of the wildness of Kybele/Artemis, last heiress of the transmission from Anat, Astarte, Ishtar and Inanna.

If Bachofen's theory is right, Athens in the 5C BC publicly espoused the morality of marriage, and its festival year revolved around two key rites which celebrated those ideals, the Thesmophoria, and the Mysteries of Eleusis.

The five-day Thesmophoria was a festival for women only, in honour of Demeter, who brought agriculture and civilized marriage to society. It partly celebrated the return of spring by a minor reminder of the Descent and Reascent of Kore/Persephone and therefore also of women's menstruation cycle and ability to bear children. The women celebrating the festival kept vigil together for five days (some say three or four), and all men and male animals were banned from taking part.

The archaeological record for the actual area in Athens where this vigil took place has been pieced together by archaeologists of several nationalities working under American sponsorship from the 1930s onwards. From

Aristophanes' *Thesmophoriazousai* it is known that the women collected in the Thesmophorion, a sacred precinct. They probably remained there for the duration of the festival, since they brought tents and equipment for camping in the grounds. Broneer argues that the Thesmophorion was the temporary name for the sanctuary at Athens called the Eleusinion, usually used in connection with the Mysteries of Eleusis, which had in it temples to Demeter, Kore and Pluto.

Two women called *archousai* served under the priestess of the Thesmophoroi, and were in charge of the preparations, for which they had to contribute in kind and in money from their own or their husbands' means. They were chosen by lot from a short-list of candidates drawn up by the married women of every borough (*deme*). An inscription survives which specifies what provisions the *archousai* were to bring for the festival. These were to be handed over to the priestess.

We are lucky to have from these excavations an inscription referring to a priestess of the Thesmophoroi who was honoured by public subscription. Her eulogy (scholarly indications of gaps or reconstructions have been omitted here) was written on marble thus:

. . ., son of . . . kles made the motion: Inasmuch as the Priestess of the Thesmophoroi, Satyra, wife of Krateas of Melite, having been selected by the members of her *deme*, has performed well and piously on behalf of the demesmen all the appropriate sacrifices prescribed by law; and has repaired all the temples in the Eleusinion and made all the preparations in the Sanctuary of Pluto, and furthermore has expended out of her private means more than a hundred drachmas for the annual sacrifices; be it resolved by the Meliteans – with Good Fortune – to commend the priestess of the Thesmophoroi, Satyra, the wife of Krateas of Melite, and to bestow upon her a crown of myrtle in return for her good will and piety toward the goddesses and the *deme* of the Meliteans; and be it further resolved to grant her the right to set up a painted portrait of herself in the temple of Demeter and Kore in accordance with the privilege bestowed upon other priestesses. The treasurer of the demesmen is to have this decree inscribed upon a marble plaque and placed at the approach to the Eleusinion, the cost of this work to be paid out of the common funds.

The Eleusinian Mysteries were much more serious, and although based at Eleusis, were connected to the cult centres of Delphi and even more so of Athens. In the 5C BC Athens made the Mysteries a cult of the Athenian state, in contrast to the Oracular basis of the Delphic authority: to this extent Delphi and Athens were rivals.

The Greeks claimed that Egyptian colonists had introduced the cult and that Demeter and Dionysos were equivalent to Isis and Osiris (the Holy Bread and the Holy Wine). Bernal believes the Mysteries could have been brought to Greece from the reign of Hatshepsut/Tuthmoses III onwards, when connections were especially close between Greece and Egypt. The visit after the Trojan War of Helen and Menelaus to Egypt confirms a link some 300 years later.

The Mysteries comprised several stages, whose aim was to provide a guide to travel through the Underworld by direct experience of it during the rite. The original Eleusinia were celebrated every five years, from around 1300 BC, accompanied by games. Related sub-forms of the festival were the *Chloia*, which was celebrated when sprouts began to appear, and the *Kalamai* when the stalks appeared. This was followed by the *Haloa* directed by the priestess of Demeter herself in January, in honour of Dionysos and Demeter.

To begin with, Foucart explains, apart from the public side of the festival, only married women could be initiated into the Mysteries of Demeter, men being rigorously excluded. From the

7C BC high priests became involved, and men were accepted, at first only Athenians, and then Hellenes from all over the Mediterranean. Proselytes underwent careful instruction, fasting and retreat before the final initiation night in the Cave of Eleusis. During the period of the Mysteries there was a stop to all war, if any were going on. In the Late Period, when all and sundry flocked to the Mysteries, the truce was announced to all cities in the Mediterranean. This was the job of the heralds, or *spondophoroi*.

At the outset of the festival, a procession from Athens followed the holy way to Eleusis. In the earliest stage of the Mysteries, the direction of the ceremonies, the right to sacrifice and to initiate the proselytes belonged to the priestess of Demeter alone. According to Dittenberger, she was involved in an enactment of the marriage of Dionysos and Kore, and from a fragmentary inscription it is known a banquet was served to the ladies involved, which included cakes made in the shapes of the male and female sexual organs.

Even after the appointment of the two male high priests (the *diadochus* from the Kerycid family, and the *hierophant* from the Eumolpid family) when the Mysteries were institutionalized,

the high priestess of Demeter was the person in whose name the sacred precinct of Eleusis was held, and throughout she personified the most ancient layer of the cult, holding office for life. In a special ceremony at her appointment she was given a sacred name, which was secret. It is possible there was a seat of honour for her at the theatre, and several statues were made of office-holders, of which only the inscriptions remain. The high priestess of Demeter also came from the Eumolpid family, who kept the sacred objects, and it was she alone who transmitted the final initiation orally.

Although there was a high priestess of Kore attendant at the Mysteries, she played an appropriately silent and invisible part.

The priestess of Demeter, also appointed for life, came from the Philleidai family. She was probably chosen by lot and had more of a day-to-day executive role. She had her own house in the sacred precinct, paid for by temple funds. The precinct of Eleusis had a high-walled temenos and holy of holies like Egyptian temples. Like the priestess of Athena, years were counted according to the term of the priestess of Demeter's office. She administered the Thesmophorion and Haloa festivals and gave the initiation of the Haloa. When the sacred marriage was enacted, it was between the *hierophant* (high priest) and the priestess of Demeter. Originally on decrees her name came before that of the high priest, but later the *hierophants* disputed her precedence. Once the priest Archias burnt a sacrifice offered by a woman which only the priestess of Demeter had the right to do, so she took him to a tribunal, charging him with impiety.

There was also a college of virgin priestesses whose role was to carry the sacred objects from Athens to Eleusis, besides the usual daily duties. They lived in the equivalent of a *gigparu*/convent at Eleusis, accommodation which was placed under the protection of the two Goddesses and paid for out of their temple funds, like *melissae* at Ephesos.

At Eleusis the temple of Pluto was a cave under the temple of Demeter. This cult was served by a separate priestess, and was linked to the banquet in honour of Pluto held in the Eleusinion at Athens. Those who were to attend were chosen and invited by the priestess herself.

The priestess of Athena at Athens did not take part in the Eleusinian Mysteries, but walked in the procession from Athens to Eleusis to bring the sacred objects at the start of the festival, and was present as a spectator to represent Athens.

The heart of the initiation of the Eleusinian Mysteries was to give firm reassurance of future happiness in the life beyond the body, something that no other Greek cult offered. As the initiates were sworn to secrecy, it is still hard to understand what actually happened which brought about such certainty in the hearts of all who 'saw the vision'. All we know is that they were shown certain symbolic objects after drinking a special potion, called the *cyceon*. Perhaps, as in the cult of Delphi, plants with special psychotropic effects were used which opened the crown chakra to direct contact with the divine world. The Greeks had access to extensive information on such substances, from Babylon to the east, the shamanic lands to the north, across the Mediterranean, and Egypt to the south.

Diodorus Siculus states that Homer must have visited Egypt because in *The Iliad* he describes Helen as possessing the drug which makes a man forget all past evils. This she administered to Telemachus in the home of Menelaus. This drug, according to Diodorus, was known of only in Egyptian Thebes and is mentioned by Homer as having been presented to Helen by the Egyptian Polydamna, wife of Thon. Other drugs were 'discovered exclusively among the women of the God's City [Thebes]', such as those that cure anger or sorrow. From the same period Medea and Circe were both credited with a profound knowledge of herbs and drugs, both beneficial and poisonous.

The sacred drink is a recurrent theme in the priestess tradition of the East. At Ur it featured on cylinder seals and helped the inhabitants of the Royal Tombs over to The Other Side. We can only speculate from the earliest evidence as to what the drink might have been: many Sumerian hymns mention beer in connection with Inanna. It was so coarse that it had to be sucked from the pot through straws above a strainer, to keep out the solid matter still floating in it (strainers were found, along with metal drinking straws, in the Royal Tombs of Ur). But at high festivals of the year I believe something more potent was the ingredient, that would have sent the couple into a prophetic trance, and into the psychic and spirit realms, to commune with the Gods, the planetary and zodiacal powers, enabling them to make predictions on the coming year for the kingdom - in co-operation with the astrologers,

who on New Year's Day 'fixed the tablets of Destiny'.

The sacred drink continued to feature even into Scythic culture, probably an aspect of the Soma drink referred to in all Indo-European sacred literature, whose recipe has been lost. In the same way the Oracle of Delphi was reached through the sensitivity of the priestess who inhaled vapours and chewed leaves. Similarly the Oracle of Trophonius caused visitors to see visions as they inhaled the natural gases emitted in its cavern. Strabo and Pliny both describe the Plutonium of Hierapolis in Phrygia with its fume-filled cave temple of Kybele. Other such caves were merely medicinal and did not induce visions.

Of course, if the drink is not an actual physical substance which, causing cell changes, transports the seer to an invisible level of existence from which to bring back messages, it can be a way of referring to the experience of those realities. The Sufi sage ibn al-'Arabi described knowledge of spiritual states as Wine, pure metaphysics as Water, knowledge of manifested laws as Milk and knowledge of universal principles as Mead (a honey drink). Once these drinks have been tasted, there is no further need for physical substances as a trigger.

To return to the Mysteries of

Eleusis, Clement of Alexandria is supposed to have revealed the most about them when he wrote, 'I have fasted; I have drunk the *cyceon*; I took out of the basket and having worked in it placed it in the other basket; taking it again in the other basket, I replaced it in the first.' This is suggestive, but actually still leaves us in the dark. Some believe it refers to a sexual rite, but it may not do so at all. (A variation on this statement, concerning the Mysteries of Kybebe and Attis, is 'I have eaten by the tambourine and drunk by the cymbal; I have carried the vase with compartments and I have penetrated the Veil.')

The *cyceon* has always been taken to have been a kind of wheaten gruel, but it must have only been the base for other substances. As late as the nineteenth century, Lane describes how Egyptians he talked to knew of four potions made up of different proportions of opium, hellebore (poisonous) and hemp which would either i) make you sing; ii) make you talk; iii) make you dance and, finally iv) give you visions. However, the wheaten drink of Eleusis may have been brewed in such a way that the ergot on the wheat grains (known to produce visions) was optimized.

All in all the Mysteries provided a mild experience of possession, available to all, as opposed to the dramatic journey of the sole Pythoness of Delphi. As Plato describes in *Phaedrus*, there were four kinds of divine vision: that given to the prophetess of Apollo, that given to initiates by Dionysos, that given to poets by the Muses, and that given to lovers by Aphrodite and Eros.

Our social drinking habits in the West have become totally secular and self-centred, but we still attach ceremonial importance to them. I believe this is because of the distant memory of high drinking rituals such as described above. Drinking a sacred substance features also in the Holy Communion of Christianity: in Islam the most precious drink is Water itself, which is Life.

Thus for the priestess, the drinking ceremony is an area of exploration in the light of much ancient precedent, given that alcohol itself (being a depressant) is not as effective a substance for gaining access to higher worlds as others that were known in ancient times. Their reverential and precise use needs to be rediscovered and helpfully used, as in the Mysteries, for the good of all.

The ceremony should not be profaned by getting drunk for its own sake, which is simply a parody of moving outside the body to higher knowledge. Alcohol and smoking are so abused in the West that it is time to bring them back into their full ritual context, in the right proportions that will attain high states of consciousness, rather than mind-numbing and degrading stupor.

THE POST-MONOTHEIST WORLD

JORDAN AND POTOMAC

11

RESURRECTING OSIRIS

Role type: Gaia – or Urania?

THE BIRTH OF THE DIVINE CHILD

The mythological cycle which is the subject-matter of the submerged priestess tradition is the round of life and death, which is indissolubly bound up with the partnership between male and female. In this book the cycle was entered at the point where Inanna made her descent to the Underworld, that transitional realm between life and death from which, unless there is a good technique and a good map, there is no return to physical embodiment. Inanna returned, but only on condition that her lover, Tammuz, go down to take her place. The cycle comes full circle when the Goddess helps to revive her beloved, resurrecting him before the cycle begins all over again. So we shall end this book on the need for the new priestesses to resurrect our men, young or old.

Some basic criteria about priestesshood have emerged during the progress of the cycle, which can be looked at in an overview. The first step is to decide to take back power, just as in the mists of time Inanna took back female spiritual power. Although today women are starting to repeat this story, the rate and quantity of the power's return could now be stepped up. This subject is at the forefront of Church council debates, even if that body has little to do with whether priestesshood proceeds or not – as it turns out.

I have a poignant example of this in the experience of a friend of mine, gifted in the use of colour and crystals, understanding mythology and alive to the Goddess. She joined a liberal Church group which is positive about these things and began to feel the calling to work towards being a 'priest'. She wrote me a long letter about it, saying that at first she 'wondered if the Anglican Church could embrace my extremely liberal views, but decided that possibly it was an opportunity to help "liberate" the Church from all its patriarchal and clerical nonsenses - to sneak the New Age in by the back door'.

She was in a Confirmation discussion group and debating whether to take the next step forward or not:

I really wasn't sure but then I had a very powerful 'initiation' dream. I was faced by a yawning cave mouth with a little train about to go off into it. I knew what this meant and leapt on board gleefully. Inside was an illuminated cavern with a semi-circle of dignified beings. I declared that I wanted to shed my body and be reborn in a new form. I called on Christ and floated upwards towards a circle of light in the cavern roof. For a moment my courage failed. I felt I wouldn't make it and asked for help. A branch from an oak tree was lowered down to me and I was pulled into the open air where I saw the oak tree growing.

On the strength of that dream she was ready to move forward, and was further encouraged by another dream a week later:

I was at the top of a house. Through the windows I could see the top of the church spire on which was a statue of 'Our Lady', except that She had a long crimson veil. As I looked, She turned her eyes towards me and smiled. This happened three times, and I was overflowing with joy!

Then things happened to change her mind:

Last Sunday I went to a local church to see what went on there. It was very High Anglo-Catholic - freezing cold with a handful of people and a priest who seemed to have dried up inside years ago. The impression of decay and hopelessness was so strong that I felt terrible all day. The same evening there was a TV programme on about the new Bishop of London - all the talk of bigotry and anti-women in the Church depressed me all over again - so many institutionalised old men! Then yesterday there was a programme on about the oppressions of the Roman Catholic Church in dealing with priests who wanted to marry. I suddenly began to see the other side of the coin - all the negative things I'd turned half a blind eye to in my enthusiasm.

I got ready for bed and felt impelled to put on some particular music, despite it being late. Then suddenly I felt swept into the music like a powerful current running into me. I danced round the room, feeling as though I was flinging aside everything that had been clogging me up for ages. I can only describe it as a Goddess energy, as though I was being shown my (and everyone's) potential power to be a priest/ priestess. And I felt strongly that, although I should keep linking with the Church, that I didn't want to be confirmed, I didn't like the implications of the Eucharist and I certainly didn't want a misogynistic old bishop putting his hand on my head and telling me that God approved of me!

This is the dilemma: whether to leave one's orthodox religion or work from inside it against terrible psychological odds. Inanna took the step of taking the power and setting up a female temple in Uruk, separate from the male temple of Anu. Perhaps this is a clue for us to follow, whether it is church, mosque or synagogue at issue. Those who do not have an attachment to an orthodox faith are freer in one sense, but may not be aware of what a small patch of the spiritual universe they are working in, often exaggerating it out of perspective. There are traps on either side of the fence.

All in all, to have the confidence to take power, women have to be sure about what it is they are meant to be doing with it. Ancient example has provided a surprising choice of roles, depending on background and temperament, but as a first guide the realities of femaleness provide the starting point and give analogies on which to run life. It

turns out that the priestess's most important quality is *presence*, rather than *action* - a harder lesson for Western women to learn than for Easterners.

In Mesopotamian mythology the Universe is made from the parts of the body of the Original Mother, Tiamat, The Great Waters. In the same way mankind is born from woman and this gives her, by analogy, spiritual precedence, though only in contrast to the arguments that woman was born of Adam's rib. (In fact, neither has spiritual 'precedence' since both form the halves of the androgyne at a higher level!) This is borne out by current genetic research. Dr J. Money, quoted by Brothers, said, 'Nature's programme in differentiating the embryo is to form Eve first, Adam second.' Dr S. Wachtel added, 'You can think of maleness as a type of birth defect: in the beginning we are all headed toward femaleness.' Brothers digests their specialist information and expands on it, noting that an embryo starts female and, if intended to be female, remains so, but if a male is to develop it has to manage the move from female mode into male mode. This is a 'touch-and-go' situation which is dependent on the release of a certain substance from the hypothalamus which gives a signal to the testosterone. On this model, the myth of Eve's creation from a rib of Adam has been well and truly exploded once and for all.

More importantly, the scripture on which the Church bases its idea of male supremacy (Chapter II of St Paul's first letter to the Corinthians) is therefore nullified. It runs as follows:

For a man it is not right to have his head covered, since he is the image of God and reflects God's glory; but woman is the reflection of man's glory. For man did not come from woman; no, woman came from man; nor was man created for the sake of woman, but woman for the sake of man; and this is why it is right for a woman to wear on her head a sign of the authority over her . . .

This is only a misogynist speaking, for he is possessed neither by the God nor the Goddess! The objections to women's ordination are not theological at all, but pure sexual discrimination based, as I have pointed out, on ancient crises. But, as in the case of my friend, it remains to consider whether it is better to operate as a priestess within the Church, or without it. Perhaps it could be said that the nature of the authority given is in a way inoperative, being by now quite ungrounded in any true knowledge of sexual metaphysics.

As female biology is more subject to cycles than the male, the foundation of priestess activity is to provide a sense of cosmic order, first by re-establishing what natural laws are. (These are different from male 'rules'.) In the ancient world, the place calendar measurement played in religion was more overt. When clocks were not common and water clocks or other devices did not tell you when the year was over, the temple existed to measure time (*tempus*) through observation of the planets. Festivals and rituals were used as reminders to mark key time divisions. Some of these could be reused today, and others invented, just as the original festivals were invented spontaneously out of real-life circumstances.

The 'civil service' priestess, who does not need to have special gifts of prophecy or education, is a time-keeper, ever mindful of the inescapable laws of the universe. She helps others to connect with these measures by taking actions that maintain communication with the fundamental frequencies of the universe. These intervals are marked by her day in, day out, year in, year out, and such a priestess forms the backbone of temple life. Her role model could be the Mother who Measures, Demeter. For the new age ahead of us such rites may well turn out to be different from those of the ancient world, but some principles can be carried over, since the universe itself has not changed very much.

For the priestess who wishes to extend her levels of consciousness and her experience of different realms of existence, in order both to develop herself and to help others, the inner journey has to be undertaken. She is the 'operative' priestess who travels in inner space, willing to change and transform in a continual process of learning, and reaching others. She makes a profession of first developing inner vision, then seeing on behalf of others, and teaching others how to see with the Eye of Consciousness, and link up with Cosmic Law. This book has shown some of the modes women used in the past.

The main cycle of the submerged tradition alternates between death and life; in seasonal terms the turning points are at the equinoxes when the sun changes direction across the equator, dividing the year into a death half and a life half. But mid-way in the cycle occurs a cross-diameter to the story, the joyful time of union and perfect harmony between God and Goddess. This is celebrated in spring, and with the birth of the Divine Child, fruit of autumn.

(Different civilizations vary the placing of the festivals of the quarter season points slightly, according to local conditions.)

The job of the priestess is to help people over these four borderlines in a way that opens up their place in the whole cycle: she presides at rites concerned with death, birth, sexual union, and resuscitation. In a nutshell she constantly strives to bring about the union between Heaven - beyond the Underworld - and Earth, which includes the Underworld as a half-way house towards Heaven. Acts of union go on in life at all levels all the time, and in the Old Religion, the blend of Heaven and Earth was potently celebrated by the symbolic sexual act. In the ancient world this was done to imitate, and to earth, the power of planetary conjunctions for the good of the whole country.

Another form of *hieros gamos* was the reception of divine messages by 'prophetesses' or 'Sibyls' in a trance state (however induced), thus channelling principle into substance - the real subject-matter of religion. The priestess is one pole in gender balancing, bringing her qualities of universal femaleness to enable the current caused by its difference from the male pole to flow. It is clear that maintaining a harmonious balance between the two involves gender balancing at all chakras, and that things break down if connection is via one set of chakras alone.

In exploring the role of the Moon Priestess and of the Priestess of Artemis it is clear how much work there is for priestesses in protecting life and guarding the world of vegetation and its uses, as well as animals, with their pure messages for mankind. This is as true today as ever.

Individual priestesses starting out have to decide whether theirs is to be a solitary life or a group life; whether sexuality is to be part of their operation, or whether spiritual connection is to be enhanced by giving up sex - or alternating phases of both. They can decide, according to their situation, how to blend everyday life with spiritual practice. All possible combinations are possible: there is no one formula which makes a priestess qualify. Some priestesses will be scholars, others astrologers or dreamers. The ancient world has shown us how priestesses often held high administrative posts in government, as in Egypt, or blended marriage with rota duty in the temple, as in Babylon or Athens. For some it is family life, for others office life, which will provide the matrix, or the contrast, for their operation. As

pioneers, they are free to write their own agendas and share their experiences to help others build up a common practice. Networking is important for this.

Men and women still innately have a sense of the Old Religion, the submerged tradition suppressed by monotheism. In many ways it is natural and easy to come back to it, though more difficult to do so as partners rather than enemies. All our present concern for preserving Gaia's very life means that the cycles of natural law must be respected - our food depends on it. Drought conditions require Goddess worship.

The last important step for re-establishing priestesshood which I advise in this book is to resurrect our men: they require a great deal of healing. The rebirth of Tammuz required the help of his Goddess; the birth of males, as much as their rebirth, requires the sympathetic help of their female counterparts. The age of the neo-Amazons is over. We could take as inspiration the version of Osiris' resurrection as given in the story of Isis and Osiris.

Osiris had been cut up into 14 pieces by his wicked brother, Seth. His faithful wife, Isis, searched the length and breadth of Egypt for the scattered parts and put them all together again. The body still lay lifeless in the Underworld. She changed into a kite, and lowered herself onto his erect penis, encouraging the semen to flow (Figure 79). He gradually returned to himself, and from their union was born Horus, the Divine Child.

Throughout history, as this book has shown, men have gained their authority from the Goddess through her priestess. They need it no less now. As a team, the Goddess and priestess make men, giving them life and the confidence to take positions of leadership, as well as simply to work. Men are their children and their husbands. Through them Osiris is resurrected, man made whole. That is why women, but particularly priestesses, should command respect from people,

and be given authority. But to gain the authority, and the respect, they must do the job. A priestess knows quite well what to do, and how to do it, even if, in the present state of affairs, she has to take power first!

The fruit of this work is the birth of the Divine Child, an eruption of pure Heaven into the world of matter. On the analogy of the Isis and Osiris myth, the fruit of work done on piecing men together is a birth. This can manifest in several ways. First, as the stepping into life, or resurrection, of the boy or man himself. Secondly, a Horus *product* can result from the union, at any chakra level. It could be a physical baby, but spiritual work is more likely to have as its first result spiritual enlightenment - the awakening of the Higher Self which in religion

79 Basalt and red granite funerary bed of an unknown person represented as Osiris, who is brought back to life by Isis as a kite in intercourse with him, while other bird deities protect his head and feet; Cairo Museum, Late Period.

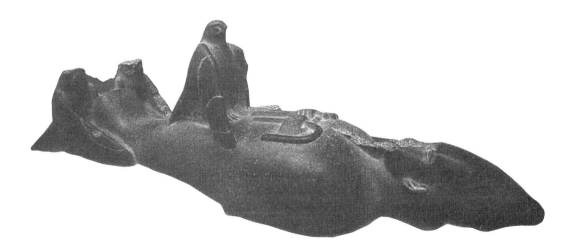

is often understood as a divine, pure baby. At the climax of the Eleusinian Mysteries, it was announced in wonder, 'The Mighty One has borne a holy boy, Brimo Brimos!' Those travelling from Athens to Eleusis would cry, 'Iacchos, Iacchos', referring to the Divine Child to be born. Jesus Christ at Bethlehem repeated the eternal myth. Maybe something more tangible will also result - a man will do his job well, a book might be written, a dance choreographed. Most creation can be traced back to a shaktic union at some level or other - nothing can happen without it. We are most concerned here with what a group of priestesses can bring about - good government, a society reconnected to the cosmos. In small or great ways, a country's leaders were in the past, whether in Akkad or Egypt, submissive to the instruction of the Goddess via the ministrations of a high priestess - it made a vital difference to the efficacy of the great civilizations! If it was invented once, it can be reinvented to suit present times. Before the stage of mutually supportive balancing is achieved, however, I believe a first stage is for women, like Isis, to actively work at healing men so they can operate properly and then give women what *they* require from men. *It will not be easy.*

Amongst Orphic poems inscribed on gold sheets buried with the dead who had been initiated into the Orphic rites, similar to those of Eleusis, the poem of a woman called Petilia is well-known:

During your stay in the Underworld, you will see on the left a cave where a fresh stream flows from the Lake of Memory; in front are its guardians. Say to them, 'I am a child of the earth and of the starry heaven, but know that my origin is celestial. Know this, too. I am consumed by a thirst that brings me to the point of death, but give me without delay of that fresh stream which flows from the Lake of Memory.' And they will give you to drink from the divine source, and from then on you will reign with the other heroes!

As Petilia says, we are both children of the Earth, and of the starry Heaven, but our celestial origin takes precedence. The physical aspects of the priestess's life have been dwelt upon in this book, as a first exercise in looking at primary evidence for their tradition, but it is their rootedness in the celestial that counts. Women have done much in the last decade to celebrate their links with Mother Earth, and with the world of the Psyche. To become a priestess involves adding a further leg to the journey by moving into Spirit (a basic confusion is generally made between Spirit and Psyche).

It has not been the task of this book to spell out how to pursue that major change of dimension: the great religious traditions provide the safest means, but the ways are many that lead there. All one can do here is point out a general principle that, although Gaia may be one role model for a priestess, another is Aphrodite Urania, Goddess of Heaven. The physical analogue of her high standing is that as Sky she is beyond even the signs of the zodiac (Spiritual or Angelic principles) which she contains. Against the signs in turn move the energies of the planetary powers (the Gods of the Psyche, called the Underworld in relation to the illuminations of the zodiac). The world of the mind is a pivot with upper and lower sections that connect Spirit and Psyche: Athena, born from Zeus's head, represents Intellect, hence her helmet and penetrating spear.

Earlier we showed how water, or a mirror, symbolized this sublime Goddess – the unchangeable which holds the changeable. If we are concerned to serve and reflect her, mirrors and water in our rituals will be reminders. Priestesses who connect with Aphrodite Urania become a thousand times more operative through their connection with her by prayer,

meditation, use of Pythagorean music, colour or geometry. Bringing the Angels down to Earth to resuscitate the world is their work. Those who serve Gaia are contemplating the operations of the physical world at the end of the line of manifestations which, if cut off from an understanding of cosmic order, becomes meaningless. Ideally the priestess should be trying to serve both Goddesses.

In Classical philosophy this dual understanding of the Goddess was explained in Lucretius' *De Rerum Naturae*, which speaks of Aphrodite as both heavenly (*natura naturans*) and earthly (*natura naturata*) – in other words the Great Goddess (who encompasses lesser Goddesses) is one Being whose 'feet' are Gaia and who 'head' is Heaven: the body between these two extreme fills varied and specific realms of reality, either symbolized by the person of a woman, or by symbols such as the Kabbalistic Tree or a growing tree. During the Florentine Renaissance Botticelli, having read Lucretius, illustrated the extremes of the Goddess in his beautiful painting *La Primavera*, which shows the Goddess as Mary with her blue (heavenly) and red (earthly) lined robe, presiding over the creation of flowers at spring as an outward-going process, and the dance back to heavenly principle as the return process, aided by Mercury, Eros and the Three Graces. Constantly to have flowers on the altar, in one's hair or pinned to the breast, can be a reminder of the dual Goddess and all that is involved with her. Flower power is never out of date.

I have always found I need images of the Goddess in words or pictures to lead me to the Lake of Memory that Petilia mentions. I have over my altar (the mantelpiece in my front room) an enormous framed photograph of Kybele of Ephesos, Goddess of the Universe, to which I connect in any way I need in order to focus my thoughts and meditations. You may want to have a sculpture or painting of your favourite Goddess through which to address your thanks and your requests. Others may prefer an aniconic symbol such as a five-pointed star, a small baetyl, or whatever serves to remind you of some key aspect of her nature that 'turns you on'.

If there is a partner in your life you might want to have the God represented too, or worship them jointly as the holy Androgyne, Athtar (the role type for the sacred marriage). If you don't yet

have a partner, be sure your other half is somewhere waiting to join you in wholeness, and that he will appear when you have done the work you need to do on your own first. No one is meant to be self-sufficient, a sole creature. The confusion has been with some people to seek androgyny in physical manifestation, but it is a heavenly principle.

Exercise (perhaps together), not only physically, which is starting at Gaia, but also mentally and spiritually, so that your higher bodies are kept fit too. This is a lifetime's work, so start practising. As actors and actresses rehearse over and over again with an ultimate performance in mind, so the pioneer priestesses need to rediscover and continually practise their craft. Possibly material from individual chapters in this book can be used as workshop material for small or large groups to discuss and work on.

One day, sooner or later, you will be on stage, required to act in a specific situation with the knowledge you have stored up. It will always be a situation connected with your everyday life - not at all glamorous, but needing a solution which *you* can bring. Events erupt in the strangest way, in a supermarket, at the office, at a bus-stop. Your presence of mind, or simply your presence, can turn events to end on a high note rather than a decrescendo. From these small beginnings, and discussion about them with your local network, bigger events will arise.

The Universe has a way of giving you one situation to deal with before giving you something similar, but harder. I often think of the Qur'anic line (translated somewhat colloquially): 'God does not place a burden on the shoulders of a person which is more than they can handle.' The starting-point of your life is your circle of friends, your family, your work-mates. You are a spiritual revolutionary conducting subtle guerrilla warfare against lapses from cosmic law which lead to human degradation! There are chinks that will let you through the seemingly impenetrable armour that has been built up to keep Spirit out.

I have tried to keep my advice universal in this book, but bear in mind it has been written by someone with a Sun in Virgo, sextile to a Moon in Scorpio on the ascendant, whose natural interest, therefore, lies in improving people, and goading them to take the journey into the Underworld with its related realms of sex, love and death. There will be as many different priestesses as there are horoscopes, and I hope each will find the way to channel Heaven to Earth that is natural for them. Again, in time, workshops will arise so that priestesses of different temperament and gifts can exchange ideas and go out into the world reinspired with the will to turn Gaia and her people round, and fit her back into the larger scheme of the cosmos.

GREAT MOTHER, SACRED QUEEN SEATED ON THE LION THRONE OF TIME, GUARD AND GUIDE US.

BIBLIOGRAPHY

Abbot, N., 'Pre-Islamic Arab Queens' in *American Journal of Semitic Languages* LVIII, 1941, pp.1-22.

Akurgal, E., *The Birth of Greek Art: the Mediterranean and the Near East* (London, 1968).

Alföldi, A., *A Festival of Isis in Rome under the Christian Emperors of the 4C BC* (Budapest, 1937).

Aly, W., *Der Kretische Apollonkult* (Leipzig, 1908).

Amiet, P., *La Glyptique Mésopotamienne Archaique* (revised edn., Paris, 1980).

Andrae, W., *Die Jüngeren Ischtar-Tempel in Assur* (Leipzig, 1935).

Asher-Grève, J. M., *Frauen in altsumerischer Zeit* (Malibu, 1985).

Bachofen, J. J., *Myth, Religion and Mother Right* (Princeton, 1973).

Bammer, A., *Das Heiligtum der Artemis von Ephesos* (Graz, 1984).

Barnett, R. D., 'Ancient Oriental Influences on Archaic Greece' in S. Weinberg (ed.), *The Aegean and the Near East* (New York, 1956).

Bäthgen, F., *Beiträge zur Semitische Religionsgeschichte: Der Gott Israels und die Götter der Heiden* (Berlin, 1888).

Bengston, H., *The Greeks and Persians: from the Sixth to the Fourth Centuries* (New York, 1968/9).

Bérard, V., *De L'Origine des Cultes Arcadiens* (Paris, 1894).

Bernal, M., *Black Athena: the Afroasiatic Roots of Classical Civilization* (4 vols planned: Vols I and II published London, 1987 and 1991).

Best, J. and de Vries, N. (eds), *Thracians and Mycenaeans* (Leiden, 1989).

Bevan, E. R., *Sibyls and Seers* (London, 1928).

Blochet, E., *Le Culte d'Aphrodite-Anahita chez les Arabes du Paganisme* (Paris, 1902).

Bloom, H. et al., *The Book of J* (London, 1991).

Bottéro, J., 'Mésopotamie et Israel' in *Grimal 1954*, pp.154-223.

Boyce, M., *A History of Zoroastrianism* (Vol II, Leiden, 1982).

Breasted, J., *Ancient Records of Egypt* (Vol IV, repr. London 1988).

Broneer, O., 'The Thesmophorion in Athens' and 'Decree in Honour of the Priestess Satyra' in *Hesperia* XI, 1942, pp.250-74.

Brothers, J., *What Every Woman should Know about Men* (London 1985).

Buren, E. D. van, 'The Sacred Marriage in Early Times in Mesopotamia' in *Orientalia* XIII, 1944, pp.1-72.

Burrows, E., 'Some Cosmological Patterns in Ancient Near Eastern Religion' in S. H. Hooke (ed.), *The Labyrinth* (London, 1935).

Cameron, A., et al., *Images of Women in Antiquity* (Beckenham, 1983).

Christopoulos, G. A. (ed.), *Prehistory and Protohistory* (London, 1970).

Clermont-Ganneau, C., *L'Imagerie Phénicienne et la Mythologie Iconologique chez les Grecs* (Paris, 1880).

Collon, D., *First Impressions* (London, 1987).

Crawford, H., *Sumer and the Sumerians* (Cambridge, 1991).

Culican, W., 'Phoenicia and Phoenician Colonisation' in *Cambridge Ancient History* III, 2 (Cambridge, 1992).

Dayton, J., 'Geology, Archaeology and Trade' in *Best et al.* 1980, pp.153-67.

Delatte, A., 'Le Cycéon, Breuvage Rituel des Mystères d'Eleusis' in *Académie Royale de Belgique: Bulletin de la Classe des Lettres*, fasc.12, 1954.

Delougaz, P., *The Temple Oval at Khafaje* (Chicago, 1940).

Diodorus Siculus, (12 vols), Loeb, London, continually reprinted.

Dupont-Sommer, A., et al. *La Déesse de Hierapolis Castabala* (Paris, 1964).

Durdin-Robertson, L., *Communion with the Goddess: Priestesses* (Enniscorthy, 1978, reprinted 1986).

——, *The Year of the Goddess* (London, 1990).

Dussaud, R., *Les Civilisations Préhelléniques* (Paris, 1914).

——, *Les Origines Cananéennes du Sacrifice*

Israelite (Paris, 1921).

Elayi, J., 'Le Rôle de l'Oracle de Delphes dans le Conflit Gréco-Perse d'après *Les Histoires* d'Herodote' in *Iranica Antiqua* XIII/XIV, pp.93-118/67-152.

Ellis, N. (trsl.), *Awakening Osiris: The Egyptian Book of the Dead* (Grand Rapids, 1988).

Evans, A., *The Palace of Minos at Knossos* (4 vols, London, 1921-35).

Farber-Flugge, G., *Der Mythos 'Innana und Enki' unter besondere Berücksichtigung der Liste der Me* (Rome, 1973).

Farnell, L., *Cults of the Greek States* (3 vols, Oxford, 1896).

—, *Greece and Babylon* (Edinburgh, 1911).

Foucart, M. P., *Les Mystères d'Eleusis* (Paris, 1914).

Gese, H. (ed.), *Die Religionen Altsyriens, Altarabiens und der Mandäer* (Stuttgart, 1970).

Gibson, J., *Canaanite Myths and Legends* (Edinburgh, 1978).

Giveon, R., *The Impact of Egypt on Canaan* (Freiburg, 1978).

Goodison, L., *Moving Heaven and Earth: Sexuality, Spirituality and Social Change* (London, 1990).

Goossens, G., *Hierapolis de Syrie* (Louvain, 1943).

Graindor, P., 'Parthénon et Corès' in *Revue Archéologique*, XI, 1938, pp.193-211.

Gray, J., *Near Eastern Mythology* (Feltham, 1982).

Grimal (ed.), *Histoire Mondiale de la Femme* (2 vols, Paris, 1954).

Halévi, Z. b.S., *Kabbalah, Tradition of Hidden Knowledge* (London, 1979) (see also under W. Kenton).

Hallo, W. W., 'Women of Sumer' in D. Schmandt-Besserat (ed.), *The Legacy of Sumer* (Malibu, 1976).

— and van Dijk, J. J. A., *The Exaltation of Inanna* (New Haven and London, 1968).

Harrison, R. J., *Spain at the Dawn of History: Iberians, Phoenicians and Greeks* (London, 1988).

Hauvette-Besnault, A. M., 'Fouilles de Délos - Temples des Dieux Etrangers' in *Bulletin de Correspondance Hellénique* VI, 1882.

Hawkes, J., *Dawn of the Gods* (London, 1968).

Haynes, S., *The Augur's Daughter: A Story of Etruscan Life* (London, 1987).

Herodotos of Halicarnassus, trsl. H. Carter, *The Histories* (London, 1962).

Honeyman, A., 'The Phoenician Title "Mithra-Ashtarte" ' in *Revue de l'Histoire des Religions* CXXI, 1940.

Hönn, K., *Artemis: Gestaltwandel einer Göttin* (Zurich, 1946).

Hood, S., *The Minoans: Crete in the Bronze Age* (London, 1971).

—, *The Arts in Prehistoric Greece* (Harmondsworth, 1978).

Hooke, S. H., *Myth and Ritual* (Oxford, 1933).

—, *Babylonian and Assyrian Religion* (Oxford, 1962).

Jacobsen, T., *Treasures of Darkness* (New Haven and London, 1976).

—, *The Harps that Once: Sumerian Poetry in Translation* (New Haven and London, 1987).

James, E. O., *Myth and Ritual in the Ancient Near East* (London, 1958).

Jeanmaire, H., *La Sibylle et le Retour de l'Âge d'Or* (Paris, 1939).

Kenton, W., *Adam and the Kabbalistic Tree* (London, 1974) (see also under Z. b.S. Halevi).

King, H., 'Bound to Bleed: Artemis and Greek Women' in Cameron et al., 1983.

King, P., *American Archaeology in the Mideast* (Philadelphia, 1983).

Klein, J., *The Royal Hymns of Shulgi, King of Ur* (Philadelphia, 1981).

König, F. W., *Mutterrecht und Thronfolge im alten Elam* (Vienna, 1926).

Kramer, S. N., *The Sumerians* (Chicago, 1963).

—, *The Sacred Marriage Rite* (Indiana, 1969).

—, *Sumerian Mythology* (3rd edn, Philadelphia, 1972).

Leisegang, H., 'Die Schlange' in *Eranos Jahrbuch* 1939.

Lenormant, C., *Etude de la Religion Phrygienne de Cybèle* (Paris, 1846).

Levi, M. A., *Political Power in the Ancient World* (London, 1965).

Levy, G. R., *The Gate of Horn* (London, n.d.).

Lewy, H., 'Nitocris-Naqi'a' in *Journal of Near Eastern Studies* XI, 1952, pp.264-86.

Lewy, J., 'The Late Assyro-Babylonian Cult of the Moon and its Culmination at the Time of Nabonidus' in *Hebrew Union College Annual* XIX, 1945-6, pp.405-89.

Lloyd, S., *The Archaeology of Mesopotamia* (revised edn, London, 1984).

Lucian, *De Dea Syria* (ed. H W Attridge et al.), (Missoula, Montana, 1976).

Mallowan, M., *The Nimrud Ivories* (London, 1978).

Marglin, F. A., *Wives of the God-King: the Rituals of the Devadasis of Puri* (London, 1985).

Marshack, A., *The Roots of Civilisation* (London, 1972).

Maury, L-F. A., *Histoire des Religions de la Grèce Antique* (2 vols, Paris, 1857).

Mellinck, M., 'The Native Kingdoms of Anatolia' in *Cambridge Ancient History* (Vol.III,2, Cambridge, 1992).

Mitchell, T. C., 'Israel and Judah' and 'Judah until the Fall of Jerusalem (c.700-586 BC)' in *Cambridge Ancient History* III, 2, Cambridge, 1991, pp.322-409.

Musaios, *The Lion Path* (2nd edition, Berkeley, 1987).

Musès, C., 'The Politics of Psi: Acculturation and Hypnosis' in Joseph K. Long (ed.), *Extrasensory Ecology* (Metuchen, NJ, 1977).

—, *The Sacred Plant of Ancient Egypt* (Miramonte, n.d.).

Mylonas, G., *Eleusis and the Eleusinian Mysteries* (Princeton, 1962).

Nilsson, M. P., *The Minoan-Mycenaean Religion and its Survival in Greek Religion* (Lund, 1950).

—, *The Mycenaean Origin of Greek Mythology* (Berkeley, Los Angeles and London, 1972).

Oates, J., *Babylon* (revised edition, London, 1986).

Oppenheim, A. L., 'The Interpretation

of Dreams in the Ancient Near East' in *Transactions of the American Philosophical Society* XLVI, 3, Philadelphia, 1956, pp.179-373.

Pallis, S., *The Babylonian Akītu Festival* (Copenhagen, 1926).

Parke, H. W., *A History of the Delphic Oracle* (Oxford, 1939).

Parrot, A., *Mari I: Le Temple d'Ishtar* (Paris, 1956).

Peissel, M., *The Ants of Gold* (London, 1984).

Persson, A., *The Religion of Greece in Prehistoric Times* (Berkeley and Los Angeles, 1942).

Philby, H. St J. B., *Sheba's Daughters* (London, 1939).

Picard, C., *Ephèse et Claros* (Paris, 1922).

—, *Les Religions Pré-Helléniques: Crète et Mycène* (Paris, 1948).

Pirenne, V., 'Aspects Orientaux du Culte d'Aphrodite à Athènes' in *Studia Phoenicia* V (Leiden, 1987).

Plutarch, *Parallel Lives* (ii vols, Loeb, London).

Pollard, J., 'On the Baal and Ashtoreth Altar Discovered at Kanawat in Syria' in *Proceedings of the Society of Biblical Archaeology* XIII, 1891.

Popov, D., 'Artemis Brauro' in J. G. P. Best et al. (eds), *Interaction and Acculturation in the Mediterranean* (Amsterdam 1980).

Prout, J. A. (trs.), *Iphigenaia in Tauris*.

Radet, G., *La Lydie et le Monde grec au Temps des Mermnades* (Paris, 1892).

Raubitschek, A. E., 'The Priestess of Pandrosus' in *American Journal of Archaeology* XLIX, 1945, pp.434-5.

Redford, D., 'The Temple of Osiris,

Karnak' in *Journal of Egyptian Archaeology* LIX, 1973.

Roaf, M., *A Cultural Atlas of Mesopotamia and the Ancient Near East* (Oxford, 1990).

Robins, G., 'The God's Wife of Amun in the 18th Dynasty in Egypt' in Cameron et al., 1983.

Root, M. C., 'The Parthenon Frieze and the Apadana Reliefs at Persepolis' in *American Journal of Archaeology* LXXXIX, 1985.

Ryckmans, G., 'Rites et Croyances préislamiques en Arabie méridionale' in *Comptes Rendus de l'Académie des Inscriptions*, 1942, pp.232-5.

Sack, R. H., 'Some Remarks on Jewelry Inventories from Sixth Century BC Erech' in *Zeitschrift für Assyriologie* LXIX, pp.41-6.

Samson, J., *Nefertiti and Cleopatra* (London, 1985).

Sandars, N., *The Sea Peoples* (London, 1978).

Schmandt-Besserat, D. (ed.), *The Legacy of Sumer* (Malibu, 1976).

Schultes, R. E. and Hofman, A., *Botany and Chemistry of Hallucinogens* (Springfield, Illinois, 1980).

Schwenn, F., *Die Menschenopfer bei den Griechen und Romern* (1915).

Seibert, I., *Woman in the Ancient Near East* (English edn., London, 1974).

Sherwin-White, S. M., *Ancient Cos* (Göttingen, 1978).

Shulgin, A. T. et al., ed. G. Barnett, *Quasar Research Monographs* no.22 (Washington DC, 1978).

Sladek, W. R., *Inanna's Descent to the Netherworld* (PhD thesis, Johns

Hopkins University, 1974).

Stakenborg-Hoogeveen, J., 'Mycenaean Thrace from the Fifth till the Third Century BC', in Best and de Vries, 1989.

Stevenson Smith, W., *The Art and Architecture of Ancient Egypt* (Harmondsworth and New York, 1981).

Stone, Merlin, *The Paradise Papers* (London, 1976).

Strong, H. A., et al., *The Syrian Goddess* (London, 1913).

Sulimirski, T. et al., 'The Scythians' in *Cambridge Ancient History* III, 2, Cambridge, 1991, pp.547-608.

Teissier, B., 'Egyptian Iconography on Syro-Palestinian Cylinder Seals of the Middle Bronze Age' (unpubl. PhD thesis, Oxford, 1989).

Troy, L., *Patterns of Queenship in Ancient Egyptian Myth and History* (Uppsala, 1986).

Ward, W. P., *Essays on Feminine Titles of the Middle Kingdom and Related Subjects* (Beirut, 1986).

Wasson, G., Hofmann A., et al. *The Road to Eleusis* (New York, 1978).

Watterson, B., *Women in Ancient Egypt* (New York, 1991).

Weber, O., *Arabien vor dem Islam* (Leipzig, 1901).

Wiseman, D. J., 'Babylonia 605-539 BC' in *Cambridge Ancient History* III, 2, Cambridge, 1991, pp.229-51.

Wolkstein, D. and Kramer, S. N., *Inanna, Queen of Heaven and Earth* (London and New York, 1983).

Woolley, C. L., *Ur Excavations: II, The Royal Cemetery* (2 vols, London and Philadelphia, 1934).

INDEX